AFTER EATING THE APRICOT

Nearly all the material which follows has seen the light of day in the chapel or the lecture room of St John's College, Nottingham. It has also been used in Bible expositions or seminars at the Greenbelt Festival, the Anglican Evangelical Assembly, the annual houseparty of the Church's Ministry Among the Jews, the Tyndale Fellowship Old Testament Study Group, the Universities of Essex, Reading, and Kent; Downing College, Cambridge; Worcester College, Oxford; and in Nottingham at Christ Church, Chilwell; All Souls Church, Radford; and Cornerstone Church. I am grateful to all these groups for giving me the excuse to expound the scriptures.

I dedicate it, though, to Diane, Jeanette, Jonathan, Judith, Mark, Martin, Phil, Scilla, Sue, and Sue, with love, appreciation, and thanksgiving for what they have been for me in 1995.

In earlier recensions the material in chapter one first appeared as part of a Grove Ethics Booklet entitled *God At Work* (1994), and that in chapter eleven in *Anvil* 12 (1995) 21–33.

For an explanation of the title, see page 45.

AFTER EATING THE APRICOT

By

John Goldingay

solway

First published 1996

02 01 00 99 98 97 96   7 6 5 4 3 2 1

Solway is an imprint of Paternoster Publishing,
P.O. Box 300, Carlisle, Cumbria CA3 0QS U.K.

British Library Cataloguing in Publication Data

Goldingay, John
    After Eating the Apricot. – (Inside Out Meditation Series;
    v. 1)
    1.Bible. O.T.
    I.Title
    221

ISBN 1–900507–02–1

Typeset by Photoprint, Torquay, Devon
and Printed in Great Britain by
Guernsey Press Ltd.

Contents

Introduction:
Scripture and our Life with God

The chapters which follow offer examples of the way
Old Testament stories may illumine our lives with God.
In this introduction I aim to set that study in the broader
context of the way scripture relates to those lives before
God. There seem to me to be two complementary aspects
to that. Essentially, there are times when scripture determines the agenda and we respond, and other times
when we set the agenda and scripture responds. I want
to consider both of these, but to come at each one
obliquely, starting from an issue and a story.

Scripture and our worldly drivenness

First the issue. With my wife Ann, who is disabled, I
once spent a weekend at the L'Arche community north
of Paris. L'Arche is a fellowship of mentally handicapped people and their companions, living together.
After we came back I read a book called *The Road to
Daybreak* by Henri Nouwen, the journal of a year he
spent at L'Arche. One of the most interesting aspects of

1

it was Nouwen's account of the contrast and the tension between the life he had spent as a theologian and lecturer on life in the Spirit in a divinity school in the United States, the life he then lived at L'Arche, and what he subsequently found when he returned to the United States. It was interesting because it rang bells with our own experience in the church in Britain, not least in the theological college where I work. Nouwen talks about the competitiveness of the life of his divinity school and of his own sense of being forever busy but never sure whether he was really on the right path. Of course he found that the mere move from divinity school to community for the handicapped made absolutely no difference in itself, because the competitiveness and the compulsive busyness were internalized. They were part of our culture which Nouwen knew were therefore part of him.

People sometimes suggest that one of the faults of a theological college or divinity school is that it is too cut off from the real world. The truth may be the opposite. It is a microcosm of the world, very like the world, haunted as the world is. Not surprisingly, perhaps, this can also be true of people in ministry. A colleague once told me about research which suggested that one major reason why people were not offering themselves for the ministry was that they were not attracted by the frantic, harassed, under the cat-o'-nine-tails nature of the way clergy live. Ordinands come out of a world – that is a church – which is compulsively busy and harassed, are on their way back into such a world, and while they are at college behave in the same way. And the world looks the other way for inspiration because all it sees in us is the mirror image of itself.

After nine months at L'Arche, Henri Nouwen went back to North America and found himself talking with people from the Senate and from business. He discovered two things. One was the importance of taking Jesus into this world of busyness so that a person himself was not sucked into its way of being. The other was that what people wanted to talk about was Jesus, partly because they themselves did not like their way of being.

How might we separate ourselves from that drivenness that characterizes the world and the church? This question raises managerial issues, but also personal issues. Because the world and the church are likely to stay haunted we need to develop the ability for ourselves to stay separate from it. God is likely not to be calling us into the desert as a witness against the world and the church in its drivenness. God is likely to be calling us to the tougher task of staying in the city, in the church, in the world, but dwelling in our own place of stillness there. To put it another way, the world, the church, the theological college, have all the temptations of the desert. They make us face the demons inside ourselves, and we had better learn to live with these temptations, with our own demons, precisely because what we find outside ourselves in the world and the church is what we also find inside ourselves.

Living with scripture is a potential key to being able to do that. Anthony Bloom tells a wonderful story about a woman who after breakfast each morning would go to her room and put her armchair in a position that would enable her to ignore all other things that might worry her, so that she could sit in quiet and peacefulness and stillness. There she would knit before the face of God for 15 minutes, until the room was suffused with God's presence. There, says Bloom, she would experience how 'at the heart of the silence' there was the One 'who is all stillness, all peace, all poise' (*School For Prayer*, p. 61). In the evangelical tradition the place of knitting is played by the Bible. (I hasten to reassure evangelical knitters that you can of course simultaneously belong to the knitting tradition and the evangelical tradition and the catholic tradition and so on.) You go into your little room as that woman did, you light your candle if you find that helpful, and you open the Bible and submerge yourself in it. You believe that it is the story or script of an alternative world,

a world different from the world's world and the world's
church, a world (for instance) not characterized by
compulsive busyness and competitiveness designed to
reassure you that you actually do exist. You want not to
be conformed to this world but to be conformed to the
image of Jesus, to be transformed by the renewing of your
mind, and you know that the Bible is of key importance to
that end.

If you are a theological student, you know that
studying the Bible in the lecture room and for the writing
of essays can play a significant part in this. But you know
that this study is also part of a system which easily gets
allied with competitiveness and busyness, and you know
that you need to be distanced from that. An important
role is played by sitting on your own with the Bible and
your candle and/or your knitting and/or your cup of coffee
(but it is inadvisable to try to hold onto all of these at once:
it conjures up a picture like that suggested by a wonderful
story in Judges which I do not consider later in this book,
when Gideon and his army run down a hill into the
Midianite camp, each man holding a torch under a bucket
and simultaneously blowing a trumpet, a feat which by
my reckoning requires at least four hands). You sit not on
your own but with God and with the book God gave us to
be the means of conforming our mind to that alternative
world, so that we can live in the everyday world in the
light of the nature of this real alternative world of God's.

Being transformed by the renewing of your mind
involves recognizing that your whole framework of
thinking and attitude tends to be adrift, and being given
a whole new framework. It is for this reason that
reading the Bible systematically is so important. It is for
this reason that a system of Bible reading such as that
published by Scripture Union is so valuable, because it
refuses to let us off with reading only favourite parts of
scripture, or reading scripture to find the answers to
questions we already have. It is for this reason that the
weekday lectionary of a church such as the Church of
England is so valuable, because it is much less affected

by the selectivity which inevitably characterizes the
Sunday lectionary.

Scripture: story, way of life, vision, testimony

What is it about scripture that enables it to rework our
frame of thinking in this way? Its most prominent
characterictic is the one on which we will focus in most
of this book. Scripture is distinctively a story in which
we locate our own story.

In our age we are a very existential people. Only the
present counts, only what I have experienced counts.
The really important thing is telling *my* story. Yet in
reality we are what we are because of the story in the
midst of which we are. We are who we are because we
belong to our particular century, because we live in our
particular decade, because we live where we live. When
people studying church history in two hundred years'
time write essays on the church in the twentieth and
twenty-first centuries they will think we were very odd.
Living where and when we do has many advantages,
but it also involves limitations, ways in which our
perspective is skewed. Scripture sets us in the context of
a different story, a story which extends from a
Beginning to an End, a story which has Jesus at its
crucial point. It sets us in the context of a story in which
things happen which we have not experienced (yet). It
does not thereby take away from our importance; it
enables us to see our story more clearly by seeing it in
context. Reading part of scripture's story can therefore
do amazing things to us.

Such reading needs to take us right inside the story,
so that we relive it. We need to allow ourselves to be
sucked into it. When my mother-in-law watched soap
operas on television, she did not merely watch them.
She took part. Marshall McLuhan once taught us that
television was cool communication – it does not involve
us and our imagination, as radio does. Ann's mother

had not read McLuhan. When someone was about to do
something unwise, as they often do in soaps, she would
tell them not to (unfortunately they took no notice,
rather like us reading the Bible). Our college staff once
had an outing to see *The Taming of the Shrew*. The
performance was in the round, to encourage the
audience to feel part of it, and when there was a
rhetorical question addressed to the audience, one of
my colleagues (who did not feel as bound by the rules
as the rest of the audience) answered the question out
loud; the cast never relaxed again. That is the way to
read the Bible, taking its stories as told for us.

   In the studies of the Old Testament in this book we
will be focusing on stories, but in the broader context
there are other ways in which scripture shapes us.
Scripture is, second, a set of commands, values and
principles to live by; sometimes its stories illustrate and
inculcate these (or their opposites). Someone in my
family who does not go to church once commented on
the difference between Christians and Jewish people.
For Jewish people their faith was something that
shaped their everyday lives, for Christians it was more a
matter of what they did on Sundays. That is the
impression the outsider gets. If you ask Asians about
the nature of their religion, they will tell you about what
they do, if you ask Westerners about their religion they
will tell you about what they believe. See what we have
done to our Asian religion!

   Parts of the Old Testament lay great emphasis on
observances governing 'cleanness' and 'stain', observances which distinguished the people of God from
other people and which were then terminated within
New Testament faith. Christians have often wanted to
re-establish such observances, to make themselves look
and behave differently so as to provide protective
boundaries around their community. My own generation was thus brought up with an alternative sub-
culture: Christians did not go to the pub or the cinema
and did not shop on Sunday. The contemporary

younger generation tends to have an opposite attitude. Christians are now entirely at home in the pub. We have moved from having a silly kind of distinctive Christian lifestyle to not having one at all. Scripture's nature is, among other things, to give us a set of priorities that is different from the world's, at points where it needs to be. For instance, in the world the family is often idolized; Jesus says turn your back on your family. Scripture is a set of commands and values and principles to live by, so we look to it to transform our priorities in life.

Third, scripture is a nightmare and a dream of the future. The calling of the prophets is to share God's nightmares and to dream God's dreams, and then to pass them on to the people of God. These nightmares and visions are not bound inevitably to take place. They are disasters that hang over the people or blessings that God wants to give them, but whether they come true depends on the response people give to God. Scripture thus holds before us possible scenarios and invites our response.

Fourth, scripture is people's testimony to how experience with God has worked for them, testimony to shape our experience. It is often assumed that the way we experience things comes from inside us: it is part of us, a given, expressing who we really are. That is a fallacy. We experience things the way we do because of the way we have been shaped, the way we have been taught. The process thus involves a mixing of what is inside us and what has come to us. Liturgy, for instance, is designed to shape us, or rather it does inevitably shape us, whatever its own nature is. It is for that reason important that the liturgy itself is of the kind that we would want to shape people. That is why it is important that liturgy is commonly stiff with scripture; it is in this way that scripture trains us in the way we experience life. If scripture reflects the truth about God, it appropriately shapes us so that we truly experience God.

In the same way scripture is designed to be a key shaping factor with regard to the way we pray. The Psalms thus offer us a clear model of how life with God is, of what prayer is like and how it works. The Epistles in the New Testament do the same. As far as I can see, how we actually pray reflects very little of the way scripture prays. We pray in the way of our tradition. Scripture is designed to provide a pattern for our prayer.

We belong, then, to a driven society, a driven church, a driven ministry, and scripture is a resource into which we escape to give it opportunity to conform our story to God's, our way of life to God's, our visions and night-mares to God's, our experience to the one God offers. Scripture sets the agenda.

Scripture in response to our agenda

It is also possible and important to come at the question of scripture and our lives with God from the other end, from when we set the agenda.

A few years ago I went through an experience of particular personal loss. The ultimate in loss is literal bereavement, but we all go through other sorts of losses in life, losses which are little bereavements. Changing jobs can be like that, especially if it involves moving house and changing churches; it can take quite a while to get used to life after those little deaths. We all experience losses like these when our children leave home, or when a key relationship in our life comes to an end, or when our church gets amalgamated with another one, or when we are made redundant. I myself went through something a little like one of those, something which indeed felt a fearsome bereavement. For months on end I lived much of the time with a deep hole inside me, a pain that really seemed physical, a heart that ached inconsolably. I would get up in the early hours and cry out to God from my armchair, sitting in the early morning sun which shines through our patio windows in the winter and which that year belied the way I felt (it was a lovely sunny winter). I would cry out 'Will it be all right?' And I knew God always said 'Yes', and I knew that it would be all right in due course. I had read books on real bereavement and watched people go through it, and that did help me to believe that the tunnel would come to an end, but of course you do also have to live with the darkness in the meantime.

There were one or two things that helped to sustain me. One was students and colleagues who I knew I could ask to pray with me and whose prayers were always a blessing. But another, and the most astonishing, was the Bible. It was the most astonishing, not because of the mere fact that it proved capable of being an encouragement, a resource, a well, a rock, through that experience of hopelessness, emptiness, desert and drowning. I would have taken for granted that the Bible could be *a* help from time to time. What was astonishing was the extraordinary consistency with which it did that.

One of the keys was this: If you are an ordinand and you are finding it impossible to cope with life, one of the natural things to do is to give up coming to chapel. If you are the principal, however, and you have a reasonably average superego telling you what to do, you cannot do that. You have to go to chapel anyway. So each morning I would join with other people there, join them with that deep gaping hole inside me, that hurt in my heart that I knew would heal one day but which was not healed then. I would join them, with all that inside me, and listen to the scriptures being read and join in the reading of the Psalms, and *every single day* there was something in those scriptures that directly addressed me, consoled me, challenged me or made a promise to me.

I wonder now whether I am exaggerating, painting an experience of scripture other than it was, but that *is* how I remember it. Perhaps it was not really every day and I have misremembered it in that way. Perhaps it

was only four days out of five – though as Meatloaf once
said, even two out of three ain't bad. What I do know is
that if the cloud outside was overwhelming me and the
hole inside was consuming me at 7.55 a.m., one way or
another through the scriptures and/or someone's ministry
and/or just sitting with God, by 8.55 a.m. the hurt had
not been healed, because it had to take its time, but
balm had been applied to it, and I could face another
day. And in that process in which God did not fail
me, the scriptures played a key role. They were the
indispensable and the most consistently soothing anoint-
ing.

Fortunately I can demonstrate to myself that I am not
making it all up because I kept a kind of diary in an old
school notebook. I cannot remember why I started
doing that, though I do know that it became important
because when I was being overwhelmed by the gaping
hole at 4.00 a.m. and I was hesitant to wake some
hapless student or colleague to ask them to pray with
me (though I know they would not have minded) it
became my resource book, or perhaps more my comfort
blanket. I would carry it round with me in case I needed
a fix from time to time. I would be fearful of being
separated from it, because it was the evidence that God
still existed and cared about me, because God was
speaking to me through the scriptures. When at those
moments I could not remember anything about what I
believed and what might be the grounds for hope, it
contained all these golden pages with things that God
had said to me, that the scriptures had said to me.

Recently I again wondered what sort of things these
were, and I worked through my red notebook to see if I
could categorize them. Now the schema I have just
used for articulating the kind of thing scripture is (story,
imperative, vision, testimony) is deeply engrained in
me and it is probably inevitable that it partly also shapes
the way I categorize my experience of scripture. But not
entirely, so perhaps I am not fudging the evidence too
much. Further, I found that I could trace an interesting

order in the prominence of the different functions of
scripture as I went through that healing process.

Early on, not surprisingly the most common thing I
found scripture did for me was provide me with means
of articulating my feelings to God. But what I found as I
read back in my book was that it hardly ever *just* did
that. What it did was set a conversation going, something like the conversation in Psalm 42, where the
psalmist asks 'Why are you so downcast, Trust in God!'
The psalm makes clear that talking to yourself in prayer
is important.

One day, for instance, we apparently read Psalm 107
in chapel. I noticed and noted that this psalm is all
about people being in distress, darkness, and affliction,
but that it keeps moving onto 'But God took them out of
their trouble'. The next day we of course read Psalm
108, which starts 'My heart is fixed, O God, my heart is
fixed', and I noted 'It didn't feel very fixed last night'
when I had felt depressed and oppressed, but then that
'it's God's mercy and God's glory that are decisive – I
mustn't think it depends on me' and on my capacity to
stay fixed. The next week we had reached Psalm 119
and I noted verse 57: 'Yahweh, you are my portion'.
'My portion': my means of support and life, something
and someone specially for me. The same day, I am
amused and embarrassed to report, I received a special
blessing from a lesson from the book of Baruch in the
Apocrypha, a lesson which acknowledged to God that
'it is the living who mourn their fall from greatness,
who walk the earth bent and enfeebled, with eyes
dimmed and with failing appetite – it is they, Lord, who
will sing your praise and applaud your justice'. There
was a promise there to lay hold of. The next week it was
2 Timothy, where Paul is made to say that his life is
already being poured out on the altar, that he has run
the great race and finished the course, that there now
awaits him the garland of righteousness; and I wrote
'I do not want a garland of righteousness. I want to
be loved, to be talked to, to be appreciated, to be

understood. But I am willing to be poured out. I will run. I will finish the course'.

As I hinted, what strikes me now as I read the way people's testimony to their experience in scripture was interacting with my experience is that scripture was indeed giving me means of articulating my experience, but all the time it was not confined to doing that. It was moving me on, not just mirroring where I stood. Here were people who had been where I was and therefore had authority to say things to draw me on, which is what one might expect, on reflection.

When I did this analysis of my notebook, I expected the way scripture gives its testimony and shares its prayers to be prominent. I was surprised at the second function I found running through what I'd written, which was scripture directly being confrontational, demanding.

'The person who wants to come after me must deny self and take up their cross and follow me', we read one day early on. My loss was not my cross in the strict sense, but there is something a little like taking up the cross in what you do with painful experiences – rather than giving in to self-pity. 'Reckon others better than yourselves; look to each other's interests', we read in Philippians 2. There are times when you have to give way to someone else. I have rights but I do not have the right to claim them, we read in 1 Corinthians. My rights lie in the gospel, not in anything else I am entitled to claim. There was an element of confrontation in the way scriptural testimony sought to draw me on, but there is a more explicit element of confrontation here. In our situations of need God does not simply say 'There, there', does not merely exercise accurate empathy. God challenges us about moral issues, about the stance we take to these situations. In a strange way that is part of the good news. 'God's judgments are in all the earth; he confirmed it to Jacob as a statute', I noted in Psalm 105. In relation to our destiny, what we call God's 'law' is good news, it is promise. Israel never saw the law as a burden. It was a delight, it was a wonderful gift of God's.

Less surprising was the third role I found scripture fulfilling. It was telling me stories with an implicit promise. That was not surprising as I have already noted that the most prominent feature in scripture is story. Much of this material in my diary comes from October and November, the weeks leading up to Advent and Christmas. Then, at the beginning of the church year, we read the Abraham and Sarah narrative, which we will consider in chapter five, and that is the kind of story which is in scripture to offer implicit promise to us. Genesis 15 is where God affirms the promise that there will be a future, and I wrote: 'There *will* be unpredictable grace for me in fulfilment of God's promise and I have to trust. If it was predictable [if I could see how it could work out], it wouldn't be un-predictable [it wouldn't have the characteristic nature of promise of being something that surprises you when it comes true]. I can't see how the future can work out happily – [but] that's why there has to be trust [the kind of trust Abraham had to show, which led God to approve of him]'. I still find this paradox difficult but important. I cannot see how the future can work out in a way that honours what had come before, but if I could, it would cease to have to be a matter of trust.

A fortnight later we reached Genesis 22, Abraham's offering of Isaac, and I wrote about 'holding the most precious thing[s] on an open hand before God. God doesn't take them away without restoring them in some way'. But I still do not know what that means. Later those stories became linked in my mind with Jesus's silly remark about the girl who was not dead, just asleep what looks like the end may not be the end.

Of course there is an ambiguity about our relation-ship to stories about the past. When we got into Advent itself the lectionary moved on to Isaiah 40–66 and I noted the verse which Von Rad puts at the front of the second volume of his Old Testament Theology: 'Stop brooding over days gone by: I am going to do something new'. In the new year when we read John 2 one Sunday after Epiphany, I noticed that marvellous comment about Jesus keeping the best wine till the end. Scriptural stories contain implicit promises for the future.

There were two other ways in which I found scripture ministered to me. The fourth was scripture as a way of looking at what goes on, as something which gave me new perspectives. At the end of the old church year we read Ecclesiastes, and I made a note of the passage about there being a time for this and a time for that, about accepting changes of the time, about accepting what is possible. Alongside Ecclesiastes the same morning we read Paul declaring that as far as he was concerned life *was* Christ, and that if he was to go on living in the body there was fruitful work for him to do. So, I noted, there was no reason to balk at actual loss or the prospect of loss, because there would still be fruitful work to do. Passages like that were another way of God being confrontational, but they were doing so by inviting me to look at the whole situation in different ways, giving me new perspectives.

And fifthly scripture often reminded me of facts about God. I wrote out much of Psalm 46 one morning, about God being a refuge and strength, and accessible help, and about there being a river whose streams make glad. I also wrote down Matthew 10:29, I suspect when Professor David Ford memorably preached on it after his wife had had a stillborn child. It tells how no sparrow falls to the ground 'without your Father': not so much that your Father wills it, causes it, or plans it, but that your Father knows it, and determines to get a grip on it, to do something creative with it and with its consequences, and somehow to bring new life out of death.

In due course I stopped writing verses down in my notebook. The process of inner healing that God built into our minds and bodies was taking place and the

pain of loss came to be mostly memory. Indeed, when a
fracture heals the join is actually stronger than the bone
around it, so that if you break that limb again it will be
at a different place. I know that in several senses the
place of that healing is one that is less vulnerable than
it was before, when I did not even know it was
vulnerable. I would still say that the pain of loss is
'*mostly* memory', because when you touch a scar you
mostly still feel something there. Jacob always limped
after someone insisted on wrestling with him. Indeed,
one would not want the loss completely to have gone
from memory, because that would be to forget the thing
one lost and to stop valuing it. But the pain is nearly all
gone, and of course the irony is that the pain therefore
no longer drives you to God. It stopped driving me to
scripture, desperate to hear God speak to me through it.
The stimulus that drove me in my helplessness to
scripture was no longer there.

But having realized all that in connection with doing
this analysis of my little red book, once or twice I have
again come to scripture with expectancy and openness,
despite the fact that I am not feeling especially
bereaved, and I have found it had the same power to
speak. So I invite my readers to two forms of openness
to scripture. On a regular basis let it set the agenda as
you listen to its story, its priorities, its nightmare and
vision, and its testimony; let it shape you. And also, as
you need to, come to it as who you are, with your
agenda, and let it respond to you with its testimony, its
confrontation, its stories with implicit promises, its new
perspectives on your agenda items, its reminders of the
facts about God.

In particular, let these stories from Genesis to 1 Samuel
do that.

ONE

God, and Men and Women Before God

When I was young my wife used to accuse me of preaching most of my sermons on texts from Genesis. I did not deny this but declared in self-defence that if it was good enough for St Paul it was good enough for me. Over the years I have tried to broaden out a little and in these studies have ventured as far as Judges and Ruth, and even over the page into 1 Samuel. The stories these books tell relate how God is at work in people's lives and in world events, and is working out a purpose in dialogue with the constraints of people and events. The story with which the whole story begins relates how God does a week's work, a week which comes to one of its climaxes when God makes human beings as creatures designed to reflect God's own being in the world. They are made to represent God, to be people through whom (or in practice often despite whom) God can be at work in the world. Human beings are made in God's image, and God's image is the image of someone at work.

In Western culture work is generally something people do for other people in exchange for money; work implies employment. One of the things we will expect to happen when we come to scripture is to find that it broadens our understanding of things, and this process begins immediately. The very first chapter of scripture is about work, and it subverts our understanding of the matter. Work is not essentially a commodity which ordinary people sell to human bosses. That way of looking at work is a means of people being oppressed, whether they are people who have some of this commodity to sell or whether they are not. If we can see something of what work means for God, even though God is self-employed (as vicars have traditionally been), we may be able to see something of what it might mean for us.

God the first worker: artist, whirlwind, spoken word

'In the beginning God created the heavens and the earth.' There are already some hints of the significance of this week's work in those opening words. God's work goes back to the very beginning. That is less striking than it might have seemed to Israel at first hearing; it is now a very familiar point. The moment when God started working was not when Joshua and company were given the land, or when Moses and company were given their freedom, or even when Abraham and company were given hope for the future. Scripture *can* see all those as the beginning of God's work. But Genesis invites its hearers to a truly wide-ranging view of the work of God. This work goes back to the beginning. Labour and paid work may have been invented only after sin came in, but human beings had real work to do in the Garden of Eden, because they were made in the image of God the worker.

God's work goes back to the beginning, and it is a programme that is quite all-encompassing. It embraces the heavens and the earth, which leaves room for little else. In other words, before we are told any of the detail

of God's work, each of its individual aspects is already
set in the context of a whole. What God does each day
could otherwise be seen as a discrete whole – indeed it
is a discrete whole – but it is also part of a greater whole
to which each individual part eventually contributes.
And for our understanding of our individual work, it is
important to see it as part of some whole. No one wants
to be a mere cog in a machine which they cannot
appreciate or envisage as a whole.

Perhaps we are to infer that God operates according
to the rules of management by objectives; there are a
number of indications in scripture that this is so. Here,
for instance, at the beginning God stands back from the
project of creating a totality called the heavens and the
earth, puts a day off into the heavenly diary, then in the
light of that divides what needs to be done into six bite-
sized chunks, allocates one day to each, and works
through them systematically.

Perhaps this is so. Or perhaps God is more charis-
matic than that. The older I get the more I like flying by
the seat of my pants, playing things off the cuff,
trusting my hunches, and much of the scriptural story
indicates that God also does that. God tries something
and works out subsequently how it fits into a pattern.
Sometimes God works like an old-fashioned band who
went into the studio with all their songs rehearsed so
that they could record it straight over two days, but
sometimes God works like the opulent rock-star who
spends months in the studio jamming and discovering
what comes out. God tries creating light and sky and
land and sea and then stands back from them and says,
'O, that's nice, I'll keep that'. God creates, works, with a
combination of purpose and playfulness, spontaneity
and system.

God 'creates'. People make much of that word, and
rightly. It is used in scripture only with God as subject.
Now admittedly that may be misleading; if Israelites
wanted to speak of human creativity, I imagine 'create'
would be the word they used, as is the case today. Our

talk about God regularly involves using language for human activity and stretching it to apply to God. We can do that precisely because we as human beings are made in God's image, so language which applies to the image can be used for the original, and presumably that is true about the language of creativity. Human beings create, and it is one of the most extraordinary things they do, so the language is also naturally used of God, in the conviction that our creativity reflects God's.

What creativity suggests is the mysterious, joyful, magical, powerful moment when a person makes something come into being out of nothing. There was nothing there, and then there was something amazing – a painting or a pot, a bridge or a car. Beforehand there were admittedly some raw materials, but they seem hardly worth mentioning, such is the gulf between them and what was created from them. There is a power and authoritativeness about creativity.

God's work, too, was creative. There was nothing, there was a formless, shapeless, dark waste, and God in power and imagination set to work, and then there was a created wonder.

What makes the difference? Part of the answer is that the spirit of God was hovering over the face of the waters, though that is an enigmatic observation, almost a self-contradiction. After all, the spirit of God is the tumultuous, gusting, divine whirlwind which lifts Elijah or Ezekiel and wafts them from one place to another, the supernatural invisible but irresistible gale of God which whips up seas and flattens trees without anyone being able to see whence it comes or whither it goes, but which can be the agent of new creativity. Elijah, Ezekiel, John the Baptist, Jesus – something inexplicable, tumultuous, unpredictable, creative is here. In the light of that, what does it mean to talk about the spirit-wind of God 'hovering'? It is an odd way to speak. The word 'hover' is used only once more in scripture, of the vulture hovering over its young in Deuteronomy 32, and perhaps that tells us something, because there again is a being of soaring and dangerous power, but one capable of exercising its power for positive, even gentle ends. When God does a week's work, tumultuous resources are harnessed to divine creativity (as we harness nuclear power to human ends).

Clearly God's work needs to be described by means of some forceful images. There is the image of the creativity of the artist, and the image of the energy of the whirlwind. Then there is the image of the spoken word. God's first act was to speak. 'Can't we have some light around here?' said God: and there was light. Why?

In a sense there is a certain inevitability about it. As long as God was one step away from this inchoate world there could be darkness here, but once God started getting personally concerned with it, started looking at it, started talking about it, darkness was bound to be replaced by light. Once God is there, there cannot but be light. But God also consciously wills it. 'Let's have some light here', says God. And there is, by the mysterious, magical power of words.

Words are indeed mysteriously, magically powerful. Admittedly, this is not true of all words. Not everyone's words are powerful. But when the person is powerful for one reason or another, the words are. So when someone you love says 'I love you', or when someone you have wronged says 'That's OK', or when a minister says 'I baptize you', or when the admissions tutor says 'Yes, you can come to this college', or when Jesus says 'Your sins are forgiven' or 'Little girl, get up', their words are fantastically effective. Their words have the power to do things. They are like magic. We talk about magic when something happens and we cannot see how it could have been made to happen, we cannot see the links. The magician does something, there is a puff of smoke, and something amazing has happened. So it is when God is at work. God says something and light replaces darkness, healing replaces sickness, forgiveness replaces guilt. All God does is speak. Speech is of the essence of work, it is how God works. It is another way to describe God working magic, alongside God's being creative and alongside the idea of God's spirit being let loose in the world. The question then is how we encourage work to involve speech, how we encourage workers to work by speaking.

God's work: the whole, the parts, and the goal

So God sets about this week's work, bringing into being light and sky, land and seas, vegetation and fruit, sun and moon and stars. One aspect of the way God went about this work is that it was what I might call both a wholistic and an analytic process. The way the story is told, I've suggested, there was a whole in mind from the beginning; the parts are on the way to being a whole. At the same time, the parts are brought into being one by one; God keeps separating one thing from another. There is an intuitive, wholistic aspect to God's work, and an analytic, rational aspect. These two aspects of work go together; they are complementary, not rivals.

And now what more shall I say? Space fails me to tell of the swarms of living creatures, the birds flying across the firmament of heaven, the animals of the wild, the cattle, and the creeping things, the beings who came into existence because God thought things out and had moments of inspiration, set to work and exercised creativity, and brought something good into being – though perhaps we should reflect on the significance of the fact that this was the concern of God's work, that this work had as its aim the bringing into being of a world of living beings, a world characterized by order and beauty, by diversity and ecology. Perhaps that provides us with a criterion for evaluating our own work. It is easy to make cheap points about the way development and industrialization have spoilt the creation and imperilled the planet and that is a trap to be avoided, but at least let us note the general point that

the result of God's week of work was to bring into being
a created world characterized by beauty, order, diversity,
and mutuality. That was the result, and also the implicit
goal. It had to be that way because the work reflected
the nature of the worker, and God is characterized –
among other things – by beauty and order, diversity
and mutuality. Those features of God's aims and achievements suggest criteria for our evaluation of our own work
as financiers or homemakers or ministers or manu-
facturers or theologians or smallholders or social workers
or whatever: to bring into being a world characterized
by beauty, order, diversity, and mutuality.

Yet all those creatures, though well-attested by their
place of intrinsic significance in God's purpose, were
not the climax of God's project, since God had foreseen
something better for us, that apart from us they should
not be made perfect. The magician saves the most
mind-blowing trick, the *piéce de resistance*, for the climax
of the programme. Having brought into being all the
manifold species of the animal world, God says 'Now
let's create a being on earth who is the mirror image of
us in heaven'.

'Let us create'. It is a nice question who the 'us' is. Of
course we now know that the God who was making the
world was Father, Son, and Holy Spirit, and Luther
therefore assumed that this 'us' reflected the fact that
the members of the Trinity were talking to each other,
but Calvin recognized that in Genesis this is anachronistic. God knew about being the Trinity, but Genesis and
its original audience did not, so the question is what did
the God who inspired scripture expect them to infer
from this 'us'?

What is most significant is simply the fact that this
moment when human beings are about to be created is
marked as a moment of special reflection. God stands
back from work halfway through the day (in the way
that executives are supposed to if they are to think
creatively and have new ideas, if they are not to be
bound by the parameters of what they have been doing

already and be sucked into mere maintenance rather than creativity). Up go God's feet onto the desk for ten minutes after lunch and there on a Friday afternoon when everyone else is preoccupied with getting away a bit early for the weekend, God has this amazing idea. 'How about including among the population of this planet some people who are actually just like God?'

This will indeed be an amazing trick if God can pull it off. In theology it is often assumed that God becoming a human being and God raising Jesus from the dead are really amazing ideas, really difficult to believe. I do not find them so difficult at all, once I have granted the other ideas that lie behind them. If human beings were created in God's image, that means they are exactly the kind of creatures that God would be if God were a human being; and if God has already brought a species like that into being, persons who are like God, there is no problem at all about God becoming one. There is no logical or metaphysical problem, at least. There is admittedly a sort of moral problem, or a moral challenge, because God has to pay a price for becoming a creature. There is a self-lowering involved. Incarnation is difficult in that sense, but it does not involve a philosophical difficulty. Philosophically incarnation is simple. What is really amazing is not God becoming a human being, but that person then dying.

For some Christian groups in the early centuries it was the death of the Son of God that was difficult to believe in, so they thought that perhaps it was just a pretence of some kind – like a magician's trick, in fact. You could not see how he did it but there must be some rational explanation other than the unthinkable idea that the Son of God died. But when you have accepted that he actually did die, believing that God then raised him from the dead is no problem at all. After all, if this is the Son of God whom God has allowed to die, it is not very likely that God will allow him to stay dead. It is easy to believe in the incarnation if you know about creation in God's image, and it is easy to believe in the resurrection of God's Son once you know it was God's Son who died – as I think Barth emphasized. It all fits together. And it all starts with humanity being created in God's image. It all starts with God's feet on the desk and God's eyes shut and after ten minutes' nap God has this brilliant idea. 'How about making a creature who's the mirror image of God, and letting them be in control of all the other creatures?'

Why? Why do it? Well, why create the world at all, anyway? The story does not give any direct answers, but maybe it contains some implicit ones. A fuss was caused a hundred years ago when people discovered a Babylonian creation story and declared that the Genesis version had been taken from it. It was always a silly idea because the stories are so different. But what one can sometimes see is the Genesis story confronting what the Babylonians believed, or even making fun of it. It is a familiar fact that some of the events in Genesis 1 come in a surprising order. It is surprising that the sun, the moon, and the stars are not created until day four. Israel knew as well as we do that the sequence of darkness and light on day one presupposes the movement of sun, moon, and stars. So what is going on? Why is there no sun until day four? The Israelites also knew that the Babylonians believed that the sun, the moon, and the stars actually decided the destiny of the world. They took the sun, the moon, and the stars too seriously. So in God's week's work the sun, the moon, and the stars are demoted so that they do not even appear until over half way through, to show how insignificant they actually are. Light and time are the gifts of God. God may choose to put lampposts in the sky to be the means of our receiving light and time, but they are significantly subordinate entities. They are not to be taken too seriously. It is not that the Genesis story learned anything much from the Babylonian one, except that it learned what were some of the strange or foolish ideas of the Babylonians which needed confronting, and which the people of God needed to be wary of.

What the Babylonian story says about the gods' reasons for creating human beings also illustrates the point. In that story there has been a major fight among the gods and they are rather tired. One of them has the bright idea of creating creatures called 'human beings' who 'will be charged with the service of the gods that they might be at ease'. So they make a 'plan for the relief of the gods', which involves recycling some bits of the god who led the losing side in the battle: and 'out of his blood they fashioned humanity'. The chief of the gods 'imposed the service and let free the gods', says the story (*Ancient Near Eastern Texts*, ed. J. B. Pritchard, p. 68).

We can see an irony in saying that human beings were created as God's mirror image. The Babylonians also believed that. They knew from their own experience how human life was characterized by violence, frustration, and disenchantment, and by rivalry and conflict between the sexes, and when they told stories about the life of heaven, they assumed it was the same. The gods were involved in violence, frustration, disenchantment, rivalry, and sexual conflict. And when they created human beings, they created them out of bits of one of the more violent of these gods. That is where we came from, on the Babylonian theory. It is a depressing vision. It is not at all surprising that our human life is characterized by instincts towards violence and all those other things, given the kind of raw material we were made from. We are created in the divine image, we are a mirror image of that kind of god. Chaos on earth reflects chaos in heaven. It is built into the structure of reality. That is what Babylonian religion told its people.

Along comes Genesis 1 with a gospel, a gospel that says 'Yes, we were indeed created as a mirror image of God, but God is a very different being from what the Babylonians thought'. The Babylonian gods have absolute power over the world, but at the same time they are powerless because they are so at odds with each other.

The real God, the God whom Israel knows, is one who is in real control, because there are no rivals to this God's power. The one who in cool and orderly fashion took a week over bringing into being this whole universe and any other universes that exist, this God has real power, real authority, real control of the situation.

Potentially that is really frightening. One of my local football teams, Nottingham Forest, used to have a manager called Brian Clough who had real power, real authority, real control, unlike that exercised by any other football manager, and he scared people stiff. The same has been true about many political dictators. It has been true about a few ministers, as well as a few popes. Absolute power is frightening, and that could include absolute power exercised by God. But this is a different kind of God. For power is a little like wealth. We do not have to feel guilty about finding ourselves in possession of it, as long as we use it to give it away, use it for other people's benefit. It is a commonplace today to say that there is nothing wrong with power as long as it is used to empower other people. We can see this as a feature of the way God goes about work. What God does is use power to empower other workers. God gives power away to them.

Something like that was a feature built into God's creation project from day one. I think this is a point I owe to Jürgen Moltmann's book *God in Creation*. When things started, or rather before things started, God was all there was. God was everything. When God set about creating the world, the first thing God had to do was accept a degree of self-limitation. God had to withdraw from being everything in order to make room for something else to be. The self-emptying that came to a climax with the cross began not with the incarnation but with creation, with the creation of anything.

To put it another way, creation was an act of love. That week's work on God's part was an expression of the love of God sharing the life of God with a new world. Creation is not just an expression of power but an expression of love. 'In created things,' I believe Luther said, 'lies the forgiveness of sins'. That is, in creation you see the footprints of the God whom you know as the God of grace, mercy, and forgiveness. God's week's work was an act of costly love.

This self-emptying is extended when God creates human beings with a certain degree of independence, more like grown-up children than little children, and shares power in the world with them. God does not just use the workforce. God empowers it. 'How about making human beings as mirror images of God, and letting them have authority over the fish and the birds and the cattle and the reptiles – well, over all the world really, might as well go the whole hog', says God. How wonderfully risky and irresponsible! After all, when a boss gives power to the workers, he or she takes a chance on it all going horribly wrong. Indeed, God has the resources to run a computer projection and know that, odds on, it will go horribly wrong. One of the theories about who is being addressed when God says 'Let us make humanity in our image' is that God is consulting the angels and one can imagine their response to God's idea. 'Give these human beings authority and power in this world that you haven't even finished creating yet? Are you off your chariot? I mean, look at what happened with that Lucifer character. And you're thinking of giving power to this lot?' But God does it anyway. That is how committed God is to worker participation. The process is as important to God as the end product. The people and their involvement is as important as what gets produced. God will sacrifice production levels for the sake of collaborative working.

So the idea that human beings were created to serve God is there in Genesis as it is in the Babylonian story, but the atmosphere is quite different. When human beings are created to rule the world on God's behalf, God is not just using them. God gives power to them.

Furthermore, God recognizes that this future work-force is a collection of people who are of similar nature to their boss. God does not look down from the office across the factory floor and see the workforce as a collection of units or things or aliens or enemies. God sees them as people of the same nature. They are not just things that God has created. They are people.

The 'they' are both men and women, and the world of work for which they are created embraces both what we think of as the world of work out there, and the world of the home, the domestic world. Here is another point at which Genesis subverts our sinful understanding of work as equivalent to employment by someone for monetary payment. It is men and women together who are created as God's mirror image to share jointly in God's work project, in the world of the home and the world out there. It is only when we have men and women together that we have God's own nature reflected, in the work that goes on in the big wide world, in the home, in the community, and in the church. It is men and women together, standing and working side by side, who have authority and power in God's world.

That interest of God's in process as well as production may again be significant here. In our culture, at least, women tend to be better at process, and arguably therefore one reason why the world of work is in a mess is that it is so shaped by men's values. When human beings came to let sin loose in the world, one of the ways in which the world of work was deeply affected was by the taking of women out of it. The world of work was redefined so that it is mostly a world that works in men's ways even when it does leave space for women to take part. It needs men and women working together at this point as at every other if God's image is to be reflected and mirrored in the world of work.

We reflect God's image in the way we control the world on God's behalf. Genesis says human beings are given power and authority over the world. Well, of course, it would, wouldn't it? After all, it was written by human beings. The Babylonian story ends up with God establishing kingship in the world: surprise, surprise, after all the Babylonian story was sponsored by the palace. It is a warrant for the power and authority of the king. The king can do what he likes because God put him there, like the vicar or the bishop. Now Israel has no kings at the time this story is written. Indeed, at its best Israel does not believe in having kings, just as the New Testament does not allow for bishops and vicars. It believes everybody is created in God's image. It does not believe in a king who especially reflects the power of the divine king or a bishop or priest who especially represents Jesus. So Israel's creation story ends with God giving power and authority in the world to humanity as a whole.

Surprise, surprise, however, for if the camels had written the story, it would presumably have ended up with camels made in God's image. This looks like a typical example of religion being used to buttress people in power. The Babylonian king used his story ideologically to justify his power; we use this story ideologically to justify our power. We can do what we deem fit to the world because God gave us authority in it, because we are made in God's image.

But there lies the snag. There lies the way the story subverts our ideological use of it. We are made in the divine image, made to reflect God's way of working in the world. And God, we have seen, exercises power and authority, but exercises it in such a way as to give people and things space, give people and things their own authority. God uses power to empower. Genesis's picture of God at work subverts our ideological use of it to do what we like with the world in our work. The criterion it challenges us to apply is, in our work at home, in business, and in manufacturing, in the church and in the city, are we mirroring the God whose work was designed to give space, authority, and power?

Work, rest, and play

There is one more point to be made. I said God's week's
work comes to one climax on Friday with the creation
of humanity. It then comes to a second climax on
Saturday, when God's week's work has come to an end.
The chapter divisions in the Bible obscure this point.
We have to remember that the Bible is inspired but that
the chapter divisions are not. They were added to the
text when universities were invented and people
started giving theology lectures in which they needed
an easy way of telling students how to look things up in
the Bible. Chapters were invented in Paris in the
fourteenth century to meet this need. Sometimes they
were put in at sensible points in the text, but quite often
not. The very first is extremely uninspired, because it
obscures the fact that the story of God's week's work in
Genesis 1 comes to an end not on Friday but on
Saturday. 'On the seventh day God finished his work
which he had done' and had a rest. 'So God blessed the
sabbath day and hallowed it, because on the seventh
day God rested from all his work which he had done in
creation.'

Of course it is a picture, and we cannot press it. When
people complain because Jesus is working on Saturday,
in healing someone, he snorts 'My father is still at work
even though it is Saturday, so don't complain if I am'
(Jn. 5:17). On the first Saturday the sun still shone, the
rain still fell, and the vegetables still grew. They do not
do that automatically; they do it because God makes
them. God continues working on Saturday, doing what
has to be done. It cannot all be left until Sunday. God is
not a legalist.

So what is the point of the picture? In its context,
there was originally another bit of gospel here for
Israelites troubled by the Babylonians. The Babylonians
did not treat Saturday as a holy day, and perhaps
laughed at Jews for doing so. For Jewish people their

Babylonian context would raise sharp questions about themselves and their own faith. Why do we stop everything on Friday night and light the sabbath candles and try to make the next 24 hours different? Is it just a peculiarity of our religion – the Babylonians have theirs, and the Canaanites have theirs, and we have ours? Israelites lived all their lives in a multi-faith context, like us, and faced parallel questions.

Genesis 1 gives them an answer. No, keeping Saturday special is not just your peculiarity, any more than the kosher laws and circumcision. They really were God's gifts to you, signs of God's love. They were designed to show something forth to the world. There was a pattern about the way God set about the work of creating the world; there was a beginning, a middle and an end to it. Each day God sat back at the end of the day, looked over what had been achieved, and said, 'Well, that's not bad, is it, I rather like that'; and there was a moment when all the basic creative work had been completed and God sat back for a whole day and made Saturday special. So that is why you yourselves keep Saturday special, the story said to Israel in exile. It is not just your religious peculiarity. It reflects something about God's pattern of work.

It is not that God is tired at the end of the week. That is not the reason for the sabbath. God did not find that first week's work was horrendously taxing. It was not laborious. On the sabbath you do not rest because you are tired. You rest because you have completed a job and it is time to sit back and enjoy it. Sometimes when we go on holiday it takes a week to unwind and we only start actually enjoying relaxation in week two. That is when work has become a tyranny. 'God does not spend the seventh day in exhaustion but in serenity and peace', Walter Brueggemann comments. And for Israel the celebration of a day of rest was 'the announcement of trust in this God who is confident enough to rest. It was then and is now an assertion that life does not depend upon our feverish activity of self-securing, but that there can be a pause in which life is given to us simply as a gift'.

The sabbath confronted the culture. It still does. I have hinted in the introduction how our gentile world, including our gentile Christian world, often seems to know very little about a pattern of work and repose of the kind that Genesis pictures. It knows very little of a rhythm of activity and reflection, of creativity and sitting back looking over what you have done and enjoying it, admiring it and letting it be there, and being there yourself. In some way we owe it to ourselves and to God to refuse to be in bondage to the world of work. It is part of being human, and it is part of being human because it is part of being divine, part of being made in God's image, because God did not work a seven-day week. God worked Sunday to Friday and then had Saturday off. And the pattern of God's story says something to us as workers, and says something to us as people who influence patterns of work for other people.

God was the first worker. God's work was a whole. God worked both purposefully and playfully. God worked creatively. God worked with the unpredictable energy of the whirlwind. God worked magically, just by speaking. God worked for beauty, order, diversity, and mutuality. God worked in order to give space to other people and to give power to them. God worked out of costly love and with costly love. God worked in a way that cared for both process and production. God worked in a way that involved both women and men. God worked, but God also sat back and rested. This is the God before whom we live and work.

TWO

Adam and Eve

The more I try to think about it, the more puzzling it becomes, and the older I get the harder it is to remember what happened. Some of what I recall seems so implausible that I think I must have misremembered it. I wonder if the snake has carried on beguiling me.

Did God say?

Adam told me how God had formed him as a human being, and had planted a garden to provide work, food, and beauty – something to look at, to eat, and to do. So far so good, but it was not very far, because the garden included two special trees, a life-tree and a good-and-bad-knowledge tree. God encouraged him to eat the fruit of the garden's trees, the life-tree apparently being implicitly included. The good-and-bad-knowledge tree was proscribed, and with a solemn warning: 'in the day you eat from it you will die'.

I am still puzzling about this and wondering if Adam heard right, but he always insisted on it. It is so odd, because knowledge of good and bad is such a wholly

33

and unequivocally good thing, and something I have
discovered God will want for people. Priests will need
to be able to classify the gifts people offer as good or bad
(Lev. 27:12,14). Israelite spies will have to determine
whether the land is good or bad (Num. 13:19). Adults in
general will be defined as people who know good and
bad as children do not (Deut. 1:39, Isa. 7:15–16). The
covenantal community will be called to perceive the
difference between life and what is good, and death and
what is bad, so that it can choose the former (Deut.
30:15; cf. Amos 5:14–15). David will have the capacity of
the angel of God to discern good and bad (2 Sam. 14:17).
Solomon will pray for the same discernment, and
Yahweh will be pleased and will grant it, though I am
tempted to suspect an irony there (1 Ki. 3:9).

The Bible's every reference to the capacity to know
good and bad will make the obvious assumption that
this capacity is a good thing willed by God. If Adam had
told me that God had placed a good-and-bad-knowledge
tree in the garden and encouraged us to eat from it, and
a malicious fellow-creature had beguiled us into failing
to do so, I would have found it entirely easy to believe
him. The story he told me and everyone else in the
family, the story we became over-familiar with, has a
quite different cast. God indeed placed there such a tree
which looks as if it was designed to give humanity a key
survival skill which will in due course be affirmed by the
rest of the scriptures, and God then forbade access to it.
A friendly, particularly knowledgeable fellow-creature
spilled the beans and told the truth about the tree: we
would not die if we ate from it. He assumed, as those
other passages of scripture will, that on the contrary it
would give us a skill that would contribute to our living
adult lives. Indeed, as the creature itself put it to me, it
would make us like God. And I know it was God's own
intention for us to be like God, to be in God's image and
likeness. Indeed God also in due course granted the
truth of the snake's words – eating from the tree meant
that we would become like God.

There were further puzzles. 'Of the good-and-bad-knowledge tree you are not to eat, for in the day that you eat of it you will die', Adam reported God to have said. Yet we ate of it and we did not die. 'Well,' you say, 'you lost your fulness of life, you lost real life, you died inside'. Perhaps so, but that is not what Adam said God said would happen. There is little ground for understanding the straightforward Hebrew word for 'die' to have this subtle meaning here.

'Well, you will literally die in due course', you go on. Yes, but Adam said 'in the day . . . .' Some people think God just meant '*When* you eat . . . .' But we did not in any sense die when we ate of it. Adam is 900 next week. And anyway, God made a point of not attributing our mortality to our having eaten of the good-and-bad-knowledge tree. God had to take further action to ensure that we did not live for ever, namely by barring our access to the life-tree, a much more plausible means to that end. Though I confess that it all worried me because of the sad resentment it almost sounded as if it implied in God: 'O dear, they've become as clever as us, we'd better take action to stop them becoming as eternal as us'. So God briskly expels us from the garden.

Why did God say?

Anyway you can see why Adam's version of what God said to him has always seemed a bit implausible, which has had me worrying at it over the centuries, wondering why Adam said it or why God said it, especially with it being about the first thing God ever said. It would be easy to imagine why it might have been invented by someone who wanted to subvert belief in the kind of blessing God whom Adam and I knew. But if God said that, or was willing for Adam to keep telling us that God said it, what was going on?

I wondered if it was a test. It was the kind of action that fitted the nature of the God who will give Abraham

and Sarah a son and then tell Abraham to kill him, the
God who will allow another enigmatic character to have
Job's family killed to see how Job will react. Israel will
discover that God tests it by taking away or threatening
to take away what is most precious to it, to find out
what happens; so such other stories will say.

One of their strong features, I presume, is that they
resonate with an important feature of life and of God.
Many people experience moments of impossible demand,
unbearable loss, or senseless accident (or, in some ways
worse, its moments of devastating and irretrievable
mistake). Yet their lives are lived (we affirm) within a
world in which God is sovereign. Our scriptures will
commonly take that sovereignty with utter seriousness
and therefore assume that the tough, unbearable
experiences of life are God's responsibility. When Saul
will turn from victorious charisma to manic rage, the
latter must be attributed to a spirit from Yahweh if the
former is to be so attributed. Neither we nor God can
have it both ways, or rather both we and God must
have it both ways.

All that may be uncomfortable with regard to life east
of Eden (or it may not: I find it encouraging that our
scriptures will look such terrors in the face, and would
rather have its God who does strange things but is
clearly in control than Christianity's God who will be
very nice but not very efficient). If it is uncomfortable
with regard to life east of Eden, however, perhaps
Adam's account of the way things began makes matters
worse by declaring that this is how things were within
the garden itself. Not only was there work there to spoil
paradise; there were theological enigmas. There was a
God who made prohibitions that were not ultimately
intended, threats that were not to be kept, and
economies with the truth regarding where disobedience
would lead. It may seem uncontroversial to assume that
God's words to us about the consequences of our taking
the fruit, about how life would be henceforth (the
uneasy relationship between us and the animal world,

the pain between mothers and children, the hierarchical relationship between husbands and wives, the domination of men by their work), that all these indicate reflection on the nature of human experience in God's world east of Eden. Perhaps God's words and actions at the beginning already involve that. Perhaps they were not merely an inspired introduction to life as God originally intended it, made by extrapolating an opposite to what people experience. God's dark side as people experience it provokes dark thoughts about God within Eden, and God's being willing for Adam to tell the story this way means God was saying, 'Yes, do think these dark thoughts about me'.

To put all that a slightly different way, I wondered whether God might have been saying things that we were expected not to accept. After all, teachers succeed not by giving their pupils all the answers on a plate (or a fruit tree) but by making them think things out for themselves. Teachers ask questions, wonder out loud, tell jokes, exaggerate, speak ironically (saying things they know are not true which they hope their hearers will recognize not to be true, though they sometimes come unstuck because people do not see their invisible 'Joke' label). They use these very serious forms of speech to seek to be provocative and to encourage people to think, for instance. They assume that they may be most effective when they are not merely providing answers but stimulating questions. I wondered whether God used those forms of speech. Does God tell stories, seek to provoke, say things that are only half-meant, speak ironically, rejoice to be a little paradoxical and not obviously coherent because people learn better if they figure things out for themselves, provide people with variegated, even contradictory, resources and free them to get on with discerning the truth?

So might God's words to Adam have been designed for Adam to question, designed to jolt us into thinking out what God is really like, because God is clearly not like this? God is not the sort of person who prohibits access to a key resource, who wants to keep us like children rather than like adults, who asks for obedience without thought to commands without reason, or who keeps special gifts such as good-and-bad-knowledge for people such as kings and denies them to ordinary people. God is not the sort of person who has to try out patently unworkable ideas before arriving at a sensible one, who says one thing and does another, or who regards scrumping as mortal sin. So God speaks as if inclined to behave in all those ways, to jolt us into seeing that. To put it positively, turned upside down God's words (and our experience of God) suggests that God planned the world as a place for people to grow to adulthood and responsibility, and provided every opportunity for them to do that, but people prefer childhood and dependence. God designed humanity from the beginning as male and female, so that only when the world has both does it have humanity complete and God imaged, this being all part of a carefully-thought-out creative project. When human beings fail to behave like adults, God does not then intervene with a bolt of lightning. God continues to treat us as adults, leaving us with the consequences of our decisions. God is really rather relaxed about humanity's un-wisdom, as long as we do not start hurting each other. God is a person in whom word and deed are one; there is no inconsistency between the two. All that is the opposite to the surface meaning of God's words to Adam, and of how things turned out.

Somebody suggested to me that our fall was a fall upwards. This is an implausible surface reading of what went on, but it is a possible reading if you assume that you are sometimes expected to read between the lines of a story, to question whether you are really meant to accept everything at face value. Was Adam having me on (for some positive reason)? Was God having Adam on? Am I having you on? Or did Adam mean it, but is he a bit like Forrest Gump (we saw some films in Eden, too) – honest, but limited in what he saw? Was the experience of an apparent fall downwards designed to make us believe in a fall upwards? There was surely a sense in which Adam and I were not in an ideal state in the garden. We needed to grow up.

One of the factors that made me wonder all that was when God told us the broader story of the creation of the world as a whole – of the week's work it took to bring everything into being. You see, that story seemed to give a very different picture from the one Adam gave me, and the one that unfolded in my own experience. It offered a picture of a God who is very organized, with whom word and deed are one. Its humanity is designed to image God and to rule the world for God, and men and women are created together to do this standing side by side. The picture ends with a job well done, God enjoying a sabbath's relaxation, and everyone living happily ever after.

Our experience seemed to say 'Just a minute. When I look at creation and at the way things work out in the world and at men and women, it seems much more random than that, much more serendipitous. When I look at the things God says and at what happens, it's much less neat. There are things God says and then has a change of mind about and doesn't do, and there are things God does without announcement. And talk about humanity being like God surely needs nuancing. It could imply we have got above our station. There is considerable evidence that there are whole realms that God keeps reserved, vast files that God does not allow us to access. There are so many issues on which it would be wonderful to have some divine insight, but we are forbidden it. And insofar as people indeed become like God, is this not a reflection of a proud desire for moral and metaphysical autonomy, expressed despite God's will and not merely by God's will? It seems to be through disobedience that people become

like God, become aware of themselves and begin to take
initiatives and learn survival skills. Further, it is
possible to be hopelessly romantic about the relationship between men and women. Even at its best, it is a
relationship born in blood and mystery, and (worse) a
relationship based on the need of one party for the
other, a relationship which issued in jealousy and one
in which the needy party is the physically stronger
party, and that is a recipe for trouble. These two
creatures who are so different from each other are
drawn into a relationship that has built into it the
inevitability of misunderstanding'. And our experience
with the snake and with God afterwards certainly
seems to deconstruct the idea that sabbath rest brings
the story to a neat end.

   Not that I think that that had really got much to do
with the 'fall' and the invention of sin. It was those two
first sons of ours, whose mothering brought such grief
and pain to me, as God said they would, who first heard
the words 'fall' and 'sin'. Indeed, their story about sin
and God's story about creation form significant brackets
around our story about Eden. They offer contexts of
interpretation for it. You mustn't read our story in
isolation from those – or read them in isolation from
ours. Each of the three puts questions to the other two
and puts questions to the way people are inclined to
hear the other two. And it is Cain and Abel's story (I
grieve again every time I utter their names) that offers a
more straightforward account of the nature of Yahweh,
the God who wants people to understand not to remain
in ignorance, challenges them to take responsibility for
their destiny, and is concerned about matters such as
violence rather than scrumping. It is when worship
leads to resentment, assault and death (cf. 1 Cor. 11)
that we are in the realms of sin and fall, but that is too
uncomfortable, so as readers people evade it. Whereas
God wanted people to learn from all three stories –
especially where they are in tension with each other.

Man, woman, and snake

Why did God create me that way? I don't just mean why
create me by building up a new body from one of
Adam's ribs – that was rather a nice touch, it makes us
feel really one, especially as we stand or lie side by side
and equal. But why was I created after Adam? When
Adam and I have an argument (we have less since we
were 700 or so) he is inclined to remind me that I was
anyway only God's afterthought. As such I am inferior
to him, only of secondary importance to God, the
world, and history. I am inclined to retort that on the
contrary, I was the Mark II version (never buy the Mark
I version of a chariot or the 3.0 version of a program
– wait for the Mark II, the 3.01, with the wrinkles ironed
out). Privately I remind myself that this is another bit of
the story of our origins that I have to rely on Adam for,
and I wonder whether I came second because this is a
man's story and that is the way he would tell it, just as is
the case when Ecclesiastes glumly records he could not
find one good woman among a thousand. For all the
egalitarian implications of Adam's story, it is told from a
man's angle. After all, it was the man who recognized
his other half in the woman created from him. Whether
or not that is an indication of his authority over me, as
some people think, it is an indication that the point of
view is male. 'That is why a man leaves his father and
mother . . . .' What I thought when I saw him, or what
my origins imply regarding the significance for me of
this cleaving, is simply not within the purview of this
male perspective (still less is what I think about being a
substitute mother and father for this rather pathetic
creature).

Not that I mind the story being the way it is. After all,
in our culture it's mostly men who read the Bible, and
this story gives them something in which they can see
themselves mirrored, so that they can then be self-
critical. It seems to us women that biblical stories about
women often mirror men's fear of women's sexuality,

for instance, so perhaps what God wants to issue from them is that they help men to recognize this fear within themselves, to come to own it, and to do something about it. There is admittedly another worrying feature of Adam's story. He did not look at me, see me in my distinctiveness, and as a result discover himself. He looked at me and saw himself, his own bones and flesh. He hardly saw me in my differentness. Is God really happy for men to use women as mirrors for their own identity (let alone as a substitute mother and father)? Is that maturity? On the other hand, there is a vision there. There are societies in which the men seem to prefer to relate to the men, and in which the women seem to prefer to relate to the women – I don't mean merely sexually, I mean they find their main friendships with people of the same sex. And that's natural enough. If you're a woman, you find it's another woman who immediately understands you, and I guess it's the same with men. It's much more complicated relating across the sex divide. But it must be worth it, because God made us to image God together. Just relating to people of the same sex is too simple. But I'm not sure Adam has understood much of the dynamics of that.

So one day, when they let women write, I am going to write my own version. By its nature Adam's version was a male account of how the creation of men and women looks to a man. And the God who sponsored his story is one in whom as creator and redeemer there is neither male nor female. So I wonder if God handed over his story to us as an unfinished project, in the way that God handed over the world itself to us, handed it over as an invitation to women to tell a women's story which will provide the other half of the tale? To put it another way, perhaps God inspires texts such as this in ironical mode, to inspire us to generate fuller ones, perhaps because that has the potential to achieve what is the text's own concern, the realization of a complementary relationship between men and women. Such a project could not be realized by telling women and men the answer, only by inspiring us to create it. Only in the telling of the story is the reality of which it speaks realizable.

When my women friends and I gather over a Turkish coffee (Huh! Chance would be a fine thing) we find ourselves making jokes about Adam's unselfconscious admission that men are more primitive creatures than women, one stage behind the animals (more hair, too, as if they are more closely related to the animals), and making jibes about the fact that they don't actually seem to relate to each other in the instinctively close and supportive way that we women do. And I suppose what we are doing is warning ourselves about the danger of some forms of entanglement with these alien creatures who can beguile us but will lead us astray and let us down. The concern is Adam's concern in the way he tells the Eden story, and Ecclesiastes' concern, in reverse. Adam offers man-to-man warnings about women (which are men's warnings about themselves to themselves) but these are set in the context of the assumption that men and women are truly on a level in their humanity. He implicitly invites women to complete the story that he begins and to complement the wisdom that Ecclesiastes expresses, to articulate our own wisdom and tell our own story.

It's not all Adam's fault. It's as much the way people have heard his story. I mean, that business of us being ashamed of being naked. I don't remember that being much to do with sex for either of us, but people have read sex into the story. When we became aware of being naked, it was that we became aware of being exposed and vulnerable. We were such a contrast with the snake who then appeared – we were '*arum* (naked), you see, and he was '*arom* (clever).

I've kept asking Adam why he thought it was a snake, and every time I ask him he gives me a different answer. His most recent theory is that the snake is a symbol for human sexuality, or at least for male sexuality. It is sex which is humanity's downfall; there is

nothing like sex for getting people into a mess. Or it is
the combination of sex and womanhood which will be
manhood's downfall; the image is a reminder of the
threat that women's sexuality is to men. There is
nothing like a sexy woman for getting a man into
trouble. This is of course again a comment on maleness
not on femaleness.

His previous answer was that the snake is a significant
religious symbol in Middle Eastern cultures like ours.
He told me about a bronze snake which will be a
sacramental means of curing snake bite and will then
become an object of worship in Judah and have to be
destroyed. The Hebrew word for divination sounds like
the word for a snake, if it is not actually etymologically
related. Later the snake will become a figure for
supernatural evil in Christianity, and this will be read
back into Genesis. So the snake stands for false religion
and its capacity to lead astray.

The story about the making of the bronze snake
draws our attention to a more obvious characteristic of
snakes. They are dangerous. They bite. They can kill
you. That association is entirely in place in a story about
life and death.

But the snake can be a symbol of wisdom. Here,
indeed, Adam made a point of telling me that the snake
was the cleverest of the animals. Perhaps it is its
cleverness which enables the snake to act on behalf of
the animals and achieve what they all want. The way of
a snake on a rock is one of the incomprehensible
wonders listed in Proverbs 30: 18–19, along with the
way of a man with a young woman – a significant
collocation in the present connection. The animals want
revenge for their being replaced by me when God made
me to fill the role they were created for. When a man's
work beguiles him away from his love, the snake has
triumphed again.

There's another thing about Adam's readers, though
it also reflects on Adam himself. People have often
talked as if I was so much more guilty than him for

taking the fruit – and obviously in one sense I was, I mean I was the one who took it. But when I was having my tutorial with the snake and partaking of some refreshment, what was Adam doing? Why wasn't he protecting me? He was there all the time, as you will see if you read the story, but he says nothing, and in his version of the story he doesn't tell you what he was doing. I will now tell you. He was asleep. You know what men are like afterwards. But a woman wants to talk. And I was thirsty. So I just fancied an apricot or two.

'Apricot?', you ask. Well, there were no apples about in the Middle East then. Nor were there any jaffas in Jaffa yet. Botanists call two common species of banana *musa sapientum* and *musa paradisiaca*, apparently on the assumption that it is the banana which is the 'fruit to make one wise' (and on the assumption that Moses – Musa – wrote Genesis), but bananas haven't reached us yet, either. The favourite fruit of lovers is in Hebrew *tappuach* (Song of Songs 2:3,5; 7:8 [9]; 8:5). People long thought this was the apple, and I guess that was how they came to introduce the apple tree into the Garden of Eden. But *tappuchim* were most likely apricots, a much more refreshing fruit, gold-'n'-gay (see Prov. 25:11). So that's one reason why I was a pushover for the snake after Adam had lapsed into unconsciousness. I had to talk to somebody, and my throat was as dry as a bone.

Well, you may or not believe all that. You may decide that I am an unreliable narrator. As I said, there are lots of ways in which the more I think about what happened, and what I myself remember of it, and what I had to rely on Adam for – the more I puzzle over it, the more puzzled I get. The story is rather ambiguous at lots of points, but it does not seem to be a disaster if I do not solve all these problems. I am helped by thinking about them even when I do not reach definitive answers. The story still functions to shape me as some-one who belongs to God, even (especially) when it is ambiguous or puzzling.

THREE

Cain and Abel

So Adam and Eve have been expelled from God's garden and mysterious guardians and a flaming flashing sword bar the way to their return. Outside of Eden Adam makes love to his wife and Eve bears her first child. Sex and parenthood, love and family life, have been from the beginning two of the ways men and women have tried to escape from the facts about their loneliness in the world. In our culture, of course, we would resist any suggestion that only the man enjoyed the sexual relationship and only the woman enjoyed the baby. We are past that sexist stage: we are the new man and the new woman. But we are not past the stage of subconsciously hoping that our relationship with the one we love and our life as a family together might be the things that give some meaning to our life east of Eden.

Smith and Vanity

'With the help of Yahweh I have brought a man into being,' says Eve (Gen. 4:1). It seems a strange way to put it. Admittedly there is a pun on Cain's name here,

and Eve has to speak in a slightly strange way to make
the pun work. But that does not explain *how* strangely
she speaks. 'I have got a man with God.' There is a
pride in the fact, a pride in achievement, in creativity. It
is pride with religious nobs on, of course, as our own
pride is likely to be. Not that Eve did not mean what she
said; she really was grateful to God for the gift of a
child. But her language nevertheless gives her away.
The same pride appears with a meaning of its own in
Cain's actual name. Cain is the Hebrew word for a
craftsman, a smith, a creative person. Cain's story
begins with human beings attempting to make sense of
life east of Eden, attempting to achieve, and it should be
frightening us already.

Then 'afterwards Eve had another child, Abel' (4:2).
That is a throw-away line compared with the account of
Cain's origin. Perhaps people do remember their first
baby more than their second, though I confess as a
father I remember the way our second son almost
emerged when my wife was still in the corridor of the
maternity hospital in Nottingham, as vividly as I
remember the way I drove through red lights in North
London in the early hours lest I missed my first son
being born in a maternity hospital there. After Cain
there is Abel, with no explanation of the name. It does
have a meaning, as the hearers of this story would
know well enough. In scripture they have heard it most
often in Ecclesiastes. 'Vanity of vanities, says the
Preacher. Everything is vanity' (Eccl. 1:2). 'Abel' is an
ordinary Hebrew word for vanity, emptiness, nothingness. Literally it means a mere breath, a puff of wind. It
comes in Job and the Psalms, too, when they want to
say that human beings and human life are as insubstantial
as mere breath. Vanity, nothingness, a mere breath of
wind is the name of Adam and Eve's second baby. A
frail, vulnerable person he will turn out to be. It will
only take a breath of wind to blow him over. The two
characters in this story are an achiever and a breath of
wind. Yes, a frightening story it is being trailered to be.

So two sons grow up, with their destiny implicit in their names. There is Smith, the achiever, the man who bears the burden of his parents' longing for meaning in their life east of Eden, the one who takes up the commission his father had received from God and begins the task of tilling the earth on behalf of the great master craftworker. And there is Vanity, the younger, the mere nothing, who keeps sheep.

The hearers of the story can guess in general terms how things will turn out. They know the attitude God takes to people who look as if they have everything going for them. Not that this means there is anything morally wrong with such people; it was not Smith's fault that he was the elder and that everything in life should work in his favour. They just happen to be people whose lives cannot help giving the wrong impression about God, about what it means to be human, and about what counts. The hearers also know the attitude God takes to younger brothers and other people who look as if they do not count. Jacob and Esau, Joseph and his brothers, David and his brothers: there was little to commend Jacob, Joseph, and David to anyone (a swindler, a gasbag, and a murderer), but God takes and uses each one, partly in order to turn human opinions and evaluations upside down. The hearers know those stories. They know that a person such as Vanity whose very name says he is a nothing is likely to end up God's favourite.

The terrible truth emerges from worship. Smith, the man whose name testifies to the way God was involved in his birth, the man whose work involves tilling the soil as his father had been told to do by God, naturally brings some of his produce to God, just the way Israelites later on did. Vanity limps behind as usual, but he does the equivalent out of his own work. He, too, brings the kind of offering an Israelite would, fat portions from some of the firstborn of his flock. And 'Yahweh received Vanity and his gift with favour; but Smith and his gift he did not receive' (Gen. 4:4–5).

Why? And how did they know? And what gave them the idea of making an offering, anyway? The story refuses to answer those questions. People have reckoned that we should infer something from the fact that Vanity offered fat portions of a sheep; but that might only imply that he was trying to outdo Cain, who was the person who took the original initiative in the matter of offering things to God. Leviticus in any case makes it clear that exactly the kind of offering Cain brings is one which does please Yahweh. The story does not make explicit why God accepted one offering and not the other. We can use it to illustrate the fact that what counts in our relationship with God is faith; the New Testament does so. But the story itself makes no point of that kind – at least, not yet. It might even give the impression that things worked out the way they did simply because Abel was the younger son.

Neither does the story tell us how they knew that God accepted one and not the other. Did Smith's sacrifice simply refuse to burn? Did Vanity's flocks flourish more afterwards and Smith's crops fail? Was it just that there was a beatific smile on Vanity's face during the service, while Smith felt nothing, had no sense of God's presence as they worshipped? All that we know is that they knew it was the case. God had been there, ignoring Smith, pleased with Vanity.

The fall and the first sin

Now we wait with bated breath. This is where the drama in the story starts. How will Cain react? 'Cain was very angry and his face fell. Then the Lord said to Cain, Why are you so angry and cast down? If you do well, you are accepted; if not, sin is a demon crouching at the door. It shall be eager for you, and you will be mastered by it' (Gen. 4:5–7).

So says the New English Bible, which is the translation used for this story in the Church of England's *Alternative*

Service Book. Now in a church to which I once belonged they had the NEB as the pew Bible, and certain preachers used regularly to play a game called 'Let's rubbish the NEB' in which we pointed out how odd it was at this point or that. The authorities tried to ban this game, but eventually gave in and bought New International Versions instead. At this point the Cain and Abel story has two good examples of NEB oddness. But the general point is clear. It is that God's accepting Abel in a way that does not extend to Cain is what brings to the surface questions about right and wrong in Cain's attitude. But they are questions about the attitude he now takes, not the attitude he took before.

That is why it is so important not to get bogged down in the question why God accepted Abel and not Cain. To do so is to miss the point in the story, which is the issues that are raised for Cain when God accepts only Abel. It raises problems between Cain and God, and problems between Cain and his brother. For all we know from what we have been told in the story so far, Cain comes to worship in all love, gratitude, and dependence on God, the way we all hope to on a good day, and God spurns him. God blesses Abel and not him.

It is an experience we are familiar with ourselves, so that the questions God addresses to Cain are ones we also have to handle. Why does God bless her and not me? Why has he got the gift of an evangelist and I have not? Why has she got such a superb job in God's service? Why has he got a job at all when I have not? Why is he such a success in Christian work? Why don't I get chances like the ones she has? Why is their church growing in a way that ours is not? Why is she married and I am not? Why have they got children and we have not? Why does he look as if he is caught up into the third heaven in worship and I do not? Why does she get pictures and words from the Lord and I do not?

The moment when we start asking those questions is the moment when sin is crouching at the door like a demon lusting after us, threatening to master us. The language is the language of the Adam and Eve story again. There the marriage relationship gets turned into one where two people lust after each other and try to dominate each other (Gen. 3:16). That provides a picture of what the demon sin can start doing to us when we start asking 'Why has God blessed him or her the way God has not blessed me?'

And in the way Genesis actually speaks, astonishingly this is the moment when sin is about to break out in the world. Theologically, of course, the Garden of Eden story was about the origin of sin in the world. Yet that is not the way God actually speaks. Indeed, at one level all that happened there was that some people stole God's apples or ate from the wrong menu. Even though it was the terrible moment when humanity first asserted its autonomy from God and settled the world's awful destiny, the word 'sin' was not used to describe what Adam and Eve did. Genesis 3 is in one sense not a story about 'sin'. Something of a different order is now poking its head round the door. According to the Cain and Abel story, when 'sin' comes in, it is in connection with what we human beings do to each other. Because once we start asking the question 'Why has she got what I have not got, why has God gifted him the way God has not gifted me?' the demon resentment threatens to destroy other people through us. We might have made a better job than Adam and Eve of living with God; Adam and Eve were a bit pathetic, we may think. But living with other people . . . .

In a parallel way, theologically Genesis 3 is the story of the 'fall', but in the Bible's own way of speaking the 'fall' comes in Genesis 4, which is the story of the fall of a face and the fall of a person.

This is also the moment when a human being is challenged to make a choice, to exercise his human freedom. People often talk as if God gave human beings freedom in Genesis 2 in telling them to keep away from the orchard. That is not really so. In a sense God denies them freedom there, tells them what not to do and dares them to disobey – and of course they do. Here in Genesis 4 is when we get the challenge to a human being to exercise his freedom. While he is the victim of birth into a sinful and fallen world, he is not treated as a mere hapless victim of original sin, but is challenged to accept responsibility for his reactions, for his resentment, and for his destiny. And of course he will not.

When our sons were small they would periodically complain in some situation, 'It's not fair', and their father would respond, 'Nothing's fair'. Did God ever say that life would be fair? Cain complains at how unfair life is. His unfair experience and his complaint at it gives the demon sin access to his life and threatens to separate him from God. A great danger lies in the way a human being handles anger and resentment. It is a danger to other people and a danger to ourselves: it may destroy us, too.

God's fundamental expectation of us is love – love for God and love for other people. What is the cutting edge of love will vary in different situations. In the gospels, there are some interesting differences over what love and community mean. In Luke, for instance, the emphasis lies on sharing our possessions. In Matthew the emphasis lies on forgiveness and mercy; it is these that count, as opposed to resentment and grudge. For Cain the one thing that brought out whether he was a person of love or of hate was the fact that his brother got on with God better than he did.

The Cain and Abel story suggests how Matthew's emphasis and Luke's emphasis are related. A famous meditation by Paul on Jesus's incarnation and death takes these events as a stimulus to our being willing to let someone else take what we have, even if it belongs to us and we treasure it, and even to rejoice that our loss is their gain. It involves an end of grasping and a beginning of emptying (see Phil. 2). Often one thing, something which is especially precious to us, will be the test whether we are willing to live by that principle.

God asks just one thing. The trouble is that it is the most important thing, it is everything. How much energy do we use bottling up anger, Walter Brueggemann asks, because we cannot face Philippians 2?

God urges Cain to take responsibility for his grudging. He must take responsibility for where he stands, otherwise there will be a fall. This fall will be essentially then a matter of relationships between human beings, relationships in the family, relationships in society. This fall has come about when a man is asked where his brother is and when he responds by declaring that it is not his business. The family that prays together slays together. I believe the statistics indicate that most murder is committed by people who know and are close to their victims. Is it not the people you are closest to that you have most opportunity and stimulus to come to hate? The story keeps rubbing in the fact that Cain and Abel are brothers; seven times in 11 verses the word comes.

Abel had done nothing to deserve Cain's hatred except have God love him. God did not accept Cain's offering, so Cain killed Abel. Cain takes Abel out into the open country where no one can see, out to where he can kill Abel and disguise it all as an accident in the way Joseph's brothers in due course would. Except that there is no country open enough to escape God's awareness. Where can Cain go from God's spirit, where can he flee from God's presence? God knew all about him from the beginning, knit him together in his mother's womb as God and Eve cooperated in the shaping of Cain. God knows all about him, knows the terrible temptation that his rejection brought to Cain, knows how Cain might react, hears Abel's terrible cry as God hears every cry of the oppressed. 'Before him no creature is hidden, but all are open and laid bare to the eyes of him with whom we have to do' (Heb. 4:13).

'Why are you so angry and downcast?' The failures and the rejections of life seem like the end of some story, but actually they are the beginning of a different story, the story of how we will live with rejection and failure, with God blessing other people the way we are not blessed. Will we let that experience twist us and turn us bitter in relation to God and smouldering in resentment towards other people?

'Sin is a demon crouching at the door. It shall be eager for you and you will be mastered by it.' That NEB translation actually involves emending the text, and every other translation and commentator agrees that the NEB is mistaken. God's words are actually a challenge or an invitation or a promise to Cain. 'It will be eager for you but you must master it', or 'you can master it'. The words are designed to bring Cain up short and open him up to the possibility of victory by God's grace over the demon of resentment which imperils his relationship with God and with other people. That is what they are for us as modern readers of his story. But even if we fail, as Cain did, we have a promise in Hebrews to turn to. Even at the point which for poor Cain did mean defeat, indeed especially at that point, 'we have a high priest who in every respect has been tempted as we are, yet without sinning. Let us then with confidence draw near to the throne of grace that we may receive mercy and find grace to help in time of need' (Heb. 4:15–16).

FOUR

Noah and God

In Los Angeles, I understand, it is often difficult to see the sky. Indeed, writing in the London newspaper *The Independent* a few years ago William Leith described the sky there as looking as if it was ill, diseased. You gaze at it and wonder if it will get better. 'This is a place where you can taste the pollution. It tastes metallic, mineral – actually it tastes of trichloroethane, methylene chloride and benzene.' Apparently the University of Southern California performed autopsies on a hundred young people who had died in car accidents and the like – i.e. they did not die because they had some illness. Eighty of the hundred had 'notable abnormalities in lung tissue', twenty-seven had 'severe lesions'. A pathologist said that these young people were 'running out of lung'. Leith found that people in Los Angeles talked about pollution the way people in San Francisco talked about Aids and people in New York about mugging. They asked how it got there, and what can be done, and whether we have gone too far. 'This is a place with more cars per capita than anywhere else in the world. This is a place where, every day, barbecue briquettes *alone* produce four tons of air pollutants.'

If the history of the world continues until, say, the

year 2200, from that vantage point the key fact about our own age may seem to be that it was the first time that humanity put itself into the position where it had found a way to destroy itself and destroy its world. Indeed, it found not just one way but two. We did it in inventing the bomb, as Jonathan Schell has pointed out in *The Fate of the Earth*; and we did it again by means of the broader development of technology and industry that has generated the ecological crisis. During the second decade of the twentieth century, in the midst of the First World War, and again during its fourth decade, in the midst of the Second World War, there seemed to be a real possibility of evil winning a temporary victory over good. Since then in these two different ways we have put ourselves into a world where we could effect a permanent victory of death over life. In the 1980s people watched open-mouthed as the Berlin Wall came down and the nuclear threat seemed to fade from view, almost like the floodwaters receding. Then Saddam Hussein rolled into Kuwait, and the waters returned as Iraq, Israel, and who knows who else began to prime their nuclear missiles.

Professor James Barr has tartly suggested that when the average churchgoer is solemnly assured that they are in exactly the same position as Moses in the Old Testament or Cornelius in the New, they really ought to burst out laughing (see *The Bible in the Modern World*, p. 47). There is something in that. Yet one of the unnerving things about the Bible is its capacity to keep generating new insights, often out of old and apparently irrelevant texts. Who would have thought that the quaint old tale of Noah and the flood had anything to say on the eve of the third millennium? Yet these three pages from the Bible turn out to address something very like the situation in which the contemporary world finds itself. The situation is not identical, because in Genesis the world is imperilled directly by an act of God rather than by human acts. But the situation is sufficiently like ours to provide nourishing food for thought. One of the most widely regarded novels of the early 1990s was Julian Barnes's *History of the World in 10 1/2 Chapters*, and it was essentially a secular retelling of the story of the flood. Perhaps we should have been forewarned by that that this was a suggestive story.

You may wonder what we can say about whether Noah and the flood happened. I think it unlikely that it is a story made up from scratch; I doubt whether stories in the ancient world were often like that. But I also think it unlikely that it relates a flood which actually affected the entire globe; apart from the logistical difficulties, the story's horizon is a local one, the country we now call Iraq, Saddam Hussein's own territory. I imagine that there was some event which we cannot now trace, that a story was told about it, and that this tradition then provided an author with raw material for formulating a piece of far-reaching narrative theology, a theological statement in story form. But we need also to see that this story is but one episode in a longer narrative, an epic which stretches from creation to the apparent end of Israel's life back in the Iraq from which it originally came. When the story talks about events such as the creation and the exodus, David and the exile, I take it that it is talking about events on an actual time line, and in some sense this must also be true about the flood. But in what sense?

Part of the answer to that may emerge from considering a feature of the story which is often missed as people wonder about whether it is historical fact. Humanly speaking the flood is, of course, Noah's story. But it is also God's story. When the Bible talks about our human lives it does not picture them as we often do, as essentially happening to us on our own down here, with God perhaps watching them up there somewhere but not actually being part of the action. For the Bible, God is part of the action down here, and in the story of the flood God is the subject of many of the key verbs. God determined that the flood should happen, and announced it; it was not one of those against-all-the-

odds accidental hurricanes unpredicted by the weather
forecasters. God made it rain, says Genesis. God (a nice
touch this) shut the door of the ark so Noah and
company would all be safe and sound. Later on, God
made a wind blow the water away. God told Noah
when to emerge from the ark. God is *in* the story, not
outside it. The flood is a story from the life of God. That
human tradition to which I referred is the means of
articulating something going on between God and the
world, an aspect of the purpose God has been pursuing
from the beginning of history. I do not know what a
video security system would have caught if it had been
switched on in Mesopotamia through pre-historic
times, and I doubt whether it would help us a great deal
in understanding this story. It is one that lets us into the
life of God in history.

We may focus on three of the most remarkable things
that are said about God, three of the most striking verbs
predicated of God, words which take us into the mind
of God.

God grieved

This is a story of which God is part, and also a story for
which God provided the plot. At least, so God thought.
God dreamed up the idea of creating a world in which
there could be other people of quite a similar nature,
people who could share God's experience of beauty and
creativity, of achievement and world-creating and
shared happiness. God had the bright idea for the story,
and started it off, but then it all went wrong. God was
rather like one of those experimental novelists or
dramatists who appear in their own plays – and not just
in cameos like Hitchcock. God has a *central* place in this
story. The trouble is that God finds that the other
characters also do not keep to the conventions by
playing the parts assigned to them. In the Woody Allen
film *Purple Rose of Cairo* the romantic lead in a film walks

off the screen to start a romance with a girl in the audience. This is very frustrating for the film director. It imperils his entire world.

So it is for God. The characters God dreamed up first take no notice of what they were told about their diet. That might not seem too troubling, but it is a hint of much, much worse to come. Soon their children are killing each other. Then *their* children are indeed entirely throwing off the constraints of the story-line and getting involved with characters from a different story altogether (Gen. 6:1–4). In the end all that God can see is a spoiled world, a fairy tale gone wrong, comedy become tragedy. It is a world filled with violence – a world like ours. And it grieved God to the heart (6:6).

When Adam and Eve took the forbidden fruit, God warned them about the awful consequences that were bound to follow, once they had set themselves on writing their own script for world history, and one of the things God said to Eve was that she would find motherhood became an experience of pain and hurt. I do not believe the words merely mean that giving birth would be painful. They mean that *parenthood* would be painful. We have considered the next episode in the drama which in fact involved Eve watching her first son kill her second son. That is the pain of parenthood, for her. God similarly tells Adam that there will be pain and hurt for him in the realm of work. All that he does will be subject to frustration. It will always be threatening to dissolve in his hands. What is the point, he will ask, as he struggles to achieve anything worthwhile in a spoiled world and experiences pain and hurt in the realm of work. Adam and Eve will grieve at their pain.

It is the same word that is now used about God himself. Adam and Eve know the pain of a spoiled life, the pain of parenthood and the pain of the struggle to achieve anything worthwhile before it turns to dust in their mouths. God knows those same pains. God is the grieved mother who has watched helpless as her children have determined to give themselves to killing each other, the way that children can. God is the grieved artist whose actors have torn up the script of the play, demolished the set, and threatened to burn down the theatre. But God determines to have the last word. If anyone is going to destroy the theatre it is the playwright. Or at least God will close down the company and leave the theatre empty against the day when it might again be possible to dare to risk dreaming another plot. God grieved.

There has been much Christian talk about whether God is green and about the greening of theology. It feels a bit pathetic the way the church has to jump on the bandwagons that often the world has to set rolling, but there it is. What difference does it make when we look at ecological questions with a Christian eye rather than with an agnostic eye? Here is one difference that ought to count. We know that when God looks at a spoiled and violent world, God is grieved the way a mother is grieved when her child goes wrong, grieved the way an artist is grieved when a painting gets defaced, grieved the way a trainer is grieved when a much loved horse breaks its leg and is shot. The grief of God ought to make us care about God's world. It can also make us rejoice that our concern to care for the world goes with the grain of God's own concerns. The odds are with us, not against us.

God remembered

The second time when we are taken into the mind of God is when we are told that God remembered. God remembered Noah and all the wild animals and all the domestic animals that were with him in the ark.

What happened was that when God closed down the company, as they slouched out of the theatre there was one person whom God called back. Noah turns out to be the only actor who is at all prepared to work with God's script, though it is not absolutely clear whether he has already proved that, or whether God can see his potential, or whether Noah was just the slowest out of the stage door, the last person to collect his cards. You often cannot tell about human motivation and desert in Bible stories, and when you cannot it is often a sign that human motivation and desert are not the really important factors in the story. The significant factor is that God decides to make an exception. When God destroys the set and dismisses the company, one person is kept on the books. For all that grief God is not actually finished with this drama.

So when the waters that had been restrained at creation are let loose in this great act of de-creation, uncreation, when all the fountains of the great deep have been allowed to burst forth and the windows in the sky have been opened wide, when all the land has been covered and all that lives has been drowned except that that stupid ungainly floating box full of smelly animals and one smelly human family is tottering about precariously with nowhere to land, God remembers Noah and the wild animals and the domestic animals.

God remembered. It is actually wonderful that God has control of memory. It is an embarrassment about middle age that you start forgetting things. I ask my secretary to do something and she not only tells me that we discussed that last week but that when we did I told her to do the opposite. Worse, you forget people's names. I meet some former student and have to stall for ages when all I am getting from my internal computer is that message that says 'Searching, please wait'. The wretched thing seems to get more sluggish every year. Worse still is the fact that the things you wish you *could* forget you cannot. There have been things that I should not have done that I wish I could forget, and things that have hurt me that I wish I could forget, and I cannot, or at least not at will. My memory is not under my control.

God's memory is. God can forget things at will, cast them out of mind so that they are no longer there, can forgive and forget. Thus when looking at me God does not see the wrong things I have done, because those have been cast out of mind, thrown into the depths of the ocean (see Mic. 7:19). They have been cast into the depths of space, we might say. God can forget at will. And God remembers. When God wants to keep things in mind, they do not escape. God remembered Noah.

Of course there is another sense in which our memories *are* under our control. Freud identified a human experience that people have always had, that we remember the things we want to remember. If I were to forget my wife's birthday, it would tell her something about how important she was to me. I forget to do the things I do not want to do. In a subconscious sense, our memories are under our control. We keep in mind the things we want to keep in mind. It is an act for which we are responsible.

God remembered Noah, kept him in mind, remembered the reason for retaining Noah when all the other actors got the sack. It was not fundamentally something about Noah but something about God's own purpose. God was not actually giving up on this theatre project. The show was to go on. God had promised Noah that he would emerge from the ark. God remembered Noah.

God keeps the world in mind. That is the world's most fundamental security.

God made a commitment

There is one more time that we are taken into God's mind. God made a commitment. That is a modern way to put it, but it is the gist of what went on. The God who had told Noah and family to go into the ark, in due course told them it was safe to come out, and gave them a commission which amounted to getting the original drama on the road again. Once more humanity is told to fill the earth and take control of it on God's behalf.

Of course we know that the second edition of the script was no more successful a project than the first.

Indeed it goes wrong more speedily and perhaps more comprehensively. But this time the divine dramatist will not be taken by surprise. God is less naive now. You might have thought that experience would have made God cynical or disillusioned, but somehow it has not. The dramatist looks in the eye the actors' uncooperativeness and recalcitrance and determines to put on the play anyway. God will give everything to make it work. God does give everything, in the end.

In the meantime, there follows one of the most remarkable statements in the entire Bible. Here is the nature of God's commitment. 'I will never again curse the ground because of humanity, for the inclination of the human heart is evil from youth. Nor will I ever again destroy every living creature as I have done. As long as the earth endures, seedtime and harvest, cold and heat, summer and winter, day and night shall not cease' (Gen. 8:21–22).

There is a splendid illogic in that. 'I will never again curse the ground, *because* the inclination of the human heart is evil from youth.' Some of the modern translations spot the illogic so they rewrite the text and make God say that he will not curse the ground *although* human beings are inclined to evil. But Genesis does not say 'although'. It uses the ordinary everyday word for 'because', and it makes a deeply profound point. The dramatist has discovered how adventurous this cast is, knows that they insist on rewriting the script, and therefore now recognizes that there is no point closing down the production and destroying the set. God just has to make a commitment to staging the play successfully anyway.

Here there is a further element in our security when we are overwhelmed by the insecurity of a fragile world. If natural forces should threaten to destroy, we are secure. God has made a commitment to the world.

But what of that point with which we started? What about when it is not *natural* forces that are our insecurity, but the power we have acquired for our own

hands, *our* power to destroy the earth? What God says
here gives us no basis for saying that it could never
happen. God has allowed us to acquire that power and
we could use it. The good news at that point is twofold.
It is first, that even if the cast should itself destroy the
set and commit suicide, that is not the end of the play.
The play will go on, because the dramatist is committed
to it.

The good news is also that, second, when we seek to
work for the play to go on rather than to be abandoned,
we are working *with* the dramatist. The play in which
we take part is not one in which we are on our own, a
play whose ending is undevised until we devise it. We
know how the play is designed to go. Once again we
are working with the grain, and in seeking to make it go
towards that end we work with the dramatist. And this
is a dramatist who is not helplessly outside the play but
vulnerably yet actively involved in it. God is still getting
hurt, but is still remembering, and is still committed.
The show will go on.

God was grieved in heart. God remembered. God
said inside, 'I will never again curse the ground because
of humanity, for the inclination of the human heart is
evil from youth. Nor will I ever again destroy every
living creature as I have done. As long as the earth
endures, seedtime and harvest, cold and heat, summer
and winter, day and night shall not cease'.

FIVE

Abraham and Sarah

When Paul comes to the end of his initial systematic exposition of his gospel in the most systematic of his epistles, the question he immediately has to answer is 'How does all this fit in with the story of Abraham?' (Rom. 4:1). Paul knows that his understanding of how relationships with God work has to pass the test of being compared with what the Bible says, and he knows that *the* scriptural model of how relationships with God work is the story of Abraham. That was a commonplace of Jewish thinking in his day, and a commonplace assumption in keeping with the dynamic of the Old Testament itself. Isaiah 51 encourages Jews in exile to look back to Abraham and Sarah if they want to see how God's dealings with them may be expected to work out. Indeed, the first people in the Bible whose relationship with God comes into detailed focus are Abraham and Sarah. Their story dominates the heart of the Book of Genesis, and for all future generations of Israelites it sets out what it means to live with the God of Israel. The motif which dominates it is that of the promise of God as the key to God's dealings with us.

Living by God's promise

To all appearances, there had been nothing special
about Sarai and Abram (as they were originally called).
They had been born in the country we now call Iraq, in
a century we cannot specify. They had grown up and
married. Abram's younger brother had died relatively
young, while their father Terah was still alive. Terah
had set the extended family on the move from their city
life in Old Babylon toward the furthest western parts of
Asia, until they stopped and settled two-thirds of the
way round the Fertile Crescent at Haran, in Syria. That,
perhaps, was simply part of the migratory activity that
was going on in Western Asia at the time. Nothing on
the surface of the story makes Abram and Sarai stand
out, for them or for other people. God was not overtly
involved – though he was there behind the surface of
the story.

Unknowingly Abram and Sarai are people who live
by God's promise. The purpose of Yahweh the God of
Israel who is the God of all the world took them from Ur
to Haran. That God was Lord of all the events of their
lives from before the moment when the promise was
announced to them – having been the God of that
promise from long before the time when they were
born. That meant also being Lord of the painful features
of their story: Sarai's inability to have children (Gen.
11:30) and Abram's loss of his brother (11:28) which in
due course makes Abram responsible for his nephew
Lot. These facts will have a significant place in the story
of Sarai and Abram living by God's promise, reflecting
the fact that God most of the time works out a purpose
in people's lives by working behind the scenes, through
the ordinary processes of human decision-making
and the 'chance' privileges and sufferings of human
experience.

But then God speaks to Abram (12:1 the NIV translates
'The LORD *had* said to Abram', but there is no indication
in the text that this happened before the incidents at the

end of chapter 11). I have never heard God speak in the 'out loud' way that some people in the Bible evidently did (see especially the comic story of Samuel and Eli in 1 Sam. 3), but I do not regard as cranks *all* those who say they have. But if it *was* that kind of experience which set Abram and Sarai back on the road, south from Haran, this was not the way God regularly related to them. That was true of them before Yahweh spoke on this occasion, and it was true subsequently, most of the time. On about six occasions God spoke to them, but most of the time even after that first revelation from God they lived their lives the same way as we do, living by the words God has spoken in the past and the deeds God has done in the past, words and deeds that continue to stimulate and challenge and encourage in the present. They live by God's promise.

'Go from your own country, your own people, and your own family . . . .' The words are words of command: God expects Abram to commit himself in a direction which suggests sacrifice and loss to add to the pain and hurt that Abram and Sarai have already known. But before the sentence of command is over, it is hinting at a built-in promise: '. . . to a country I am going to show you'. The content of God's own commitment to Abram is expounded in the under-takings that follow: 'I am going to make you into a great nation, I am going to bless you and make you famous. You are going to be a blessing for people. I intend to bless people who bless you; anyone who despises you I will despise. And all the families of the world will pray to be blessed as you are blessed' (12:1–3). God's one command has a whole series of promises attached to it, though they can be summed up as a promise of blessing, which will mean Abram will possess a land and become a people. At creation God had given people this blessing, encouraging them to fill the land and subdue it (in 1:28 the word for 'earth' there and that for 'land' here is the same). The story so far (Gen. 1–11) has been one where humanity's rebellion against God has

led to the curse wrestling with the blessing for victory in
the world; now Yahweh's blessing of Abram reasserts
God's purpose that humanity should increase and
possess the land. The promise is that Abram should
become famous as the spearhead of God's purpose and
that his blessing will become the standard by which
people will 'bless themselves' (RSV): they will 'pray to be
blessed as he is blessed' (NEB). In the Prayer Book
marriage service the minister prays for God's blessing to
be sent on bride and groom as it was on Abraham and
Sarah, and each time people pray that prayer God's
promise to Abram is once again fulfilled.

So God says 'Go'; and Abram and Sarai go, as God
said. That is what living by the promise involves (cf.
17:23; 21:4). People who do as the God of the promise
says then find that the commitment expressed in God's
promise is reaffirmed and by the same act begins to be
implemented. Abram arrives at Shechem and there
Yahweh appears to him, promising once again to give
this country to his descendants. Precisely by appearing
here Yahweh acts as the Lord of *this* country, not
someone confined to the territory where Abram has
experienced God speaking to him before. Abram in turn
builds an altar in Yahweh's honour there at Shechem in
the north of the country. Subsequently they continue a
preliminary tour of the land of promise, building
another altar in the midlands between Bethel and Ai,
and eventually another in the south in the area of
Hebron where they make their home (12:7,8; 13:18). So
living by God's promise involves not only obedience but
worship, not only going to the land but dedicating it to
Yahweh by naming that name in it and over it. It
involves letting the mini-experiences of God fulfilling
promises be the confirmation of complete fulfilment. It
involves the response of praise in such contexts, praise
that the promise is being fulfilled.

It is a while, however, before Abram and Sarai
complete their tour of the country, their symbolic
entering into possession of it. In the meantime, some

odd notes are struck. The picture of people receiving
God's command and beginning to live by God's promise
is an idyllic one, but there are complications to it. There
are obstacles to the fulfilling of the promise. 'I will give
this country to your descendants', God had said. But it
is occupied by someone else (12:6–7), so how can they
have it, and Sarai cannot have children, so anyway how
can they have descendants? Living by God's promise
regularly means living by a word that seems more than
somewhat unlikely to be fulfilled.

Before they complete that symbolic tour of the
country, further threats to the promise emerge. God has
promised that Abram is to live in the land of Canaan
and to become a great nation and a blessing to others.
But as a result of an entirely human response to a real
crisis each element in this promise receives a kind of
anti-fulfilment. A famine leads Abram to leave the
country of Canaan, he watches the potential mother of
his descendants join the Pharaoh's harem, and he
causes Yahweh to bring affliction instead of blessing on
the Pharaoh and his household, in response to which
the Pharaoh understandably withdraws his visa and
deports him (12:10–13:2). All ends well (very well, in
fact – Abraham profits in terms of flocks, retinue, and
other possessions), but the story is a sombre one. The
idyll of living by God's promise is easily shattered. And
the point of the story is not to warn us to avoid reacting
to crises as Abram did, but rather to acknowledge the
fact that the bearers of God's promise do get themselves
into messes as Abram did. Fortunately the God of the
promise does not then simply abandon them to the
mess, but rescues them from it.

So Abram returns to the altar he had built near Bethel
(13:3–4). He returns to the place where he had been
before things began to go wrong, to the place and the
occasion where God had begun to fulfil those promises
and where he had been living by them, to pick up the
threads again. No doubt the later readers of the story
are encouraged both to return to the occasions of that

kind in their own lives and to return to the occasions like this in scripture on which our faith depends, occasions when God met those whose story our faith depends on.

Then there is another surprise and disappointment. Strife breaks out within Abram's own wider family, arising out of the presence of other peoples in the country which is destined to belong to Abram. There is not enough room for Abram's family in the land promised to them. Abram finds a generous solution, but it involves hazarding the best part of the land, letting Lot have it, and contenting himself with the harder hill-country (13:5–13). Yahweh responds to Abram's generosity and peaceableness by reaffirming the promise yet again (13:14–17); and it is now that Abram makes his home in Hebron and builds his third altar there, completing the symbolic entering into his inheritance that was interrupted by those puzzling incidents, the famine and the quarrel.

The key features of Abram and Sarai's life with God emerge from these opening incidents in their story. They bear God's promise and live by it, they see some measure of fulfilment of it, but it is ever threatened by circumstantial and human factors which obstruct the path to its complete realization.

Living by a promise which we see fulfilled, but only in part, is a constitutive feature of life with God. For us the Messiah has come, the Spirit has been given, but the work of the Messiah is not completed, the Spirit is the foretaste of a new age which is still future. We still live by the promise that the messianic age will come. Holiness, maturity, healing, a close personal awareness of God, are partial realities in our experience, but only partial realities. All the promises of God find their 'Yes' in Christ (2 Cor. 1:20): but that does not mean that in him they have all been fulfilled – manifestly they have not. Rather it means that in him they have all been confirmed. He is the guarantee that they will be fulfilled. He makes living by the promise newly possible.

Believing in God's promise

After that initial symbolic taking possession of the land, and then a military escapade that reveals another more activist side to the personality of Abram (Gen. 14), Yahweh speaks to Abram again in a vision. 'Don't be afraid, Abram. I am your deliverer' (15:1) – after all, have I not delivered your enemies into your power (14:20)? 'Your reward will be very great' (15:1). So it should be, Abram might have thought, given the wealth I have sacrificed to show that I am a man who lives by God's promise (14:22–23). When Abram does take up the question of what God will give him, however, he speaks not of material possessions but of that family of their own that he and Sarai have long been promised but even longer been denied. When is Abram going to have a son and heir? 'Then the word of Yahweh came to him, "Your own son will be your heir" ', and God took him outside and invited him to survey the myriads of stars that flash through the clearness of the Middle Eastern sky. 'Count the stars, if you can. That is how numerous your descendants will be.'

'O yes?' says Abram, 'Promises, promises'? It would have been forgivable if he had responded in skeptical fashion at nothing more than a reaffirmation of the old words in more vivid technicolour but accompanied by no more concrete evidence of fulfilment. Yet that is not Abram's reaction. On the contrary, 'he believed Yahweh, and he counted it to him as righteousness' (15:6). Calvin observes that Abram was not justified because he laid hold of a particular word, the promise about offspring, but because in responding to this word he embraced God as Father; and sometimes there will be a particular issue between us and God, a situation or need or decision or desire, which becomes an index of whether we are living on the basis of trust in this Father or not.

Something more fundamental also emerges from

Genesis 15. So far in Genesis there has actually been a
certain ambiguity about the portrait of Abram. We have
been told a number of things that Abram did and said,
but nothing at all about what he felt or thought, about
his attitude or motivation. He did what God said and
went where God directed, but why? I have assumed
that it was out of an attitude of trust and commitment,
not resentment and resignation, but this has not been
stated. Here for the first time we are taken inside
Abram, and what we are told is that he trusted God.

And 'God counted it to him as righteousness'. It is
one of the most earth-shaking, epoch-creating statements in scripture. Statements of this kind come
elsewhere in the Old Testament both in the Torah (the
first five books) and in the Prophets. When a priest
accepts a person who brings an offering, he 'counts'
their sacrifice (e.g. Lev. 7:18). In a broader sphere,
including ethical behaviour, if people live sexually pure
lives, give bread to the hungry, and concern themselves
with justice between other human beings, God regards
them as 'righteous' and declares that they will live
(Ezek. 18:5–9). The epoch-making innovation of the
Abram story is that this declaration that a person is
counted as righteous is made not on the basis of keeping
religious observances or living by ethical demands but
on the basis of – doing nothing, only trusting God to
fulfil promises Abram had received long ago and had no
grounds for trusting except the grounds that lie simply
in God. It is revolutionary. Not that this implies that
before this Abram had been justified by works, or that
before Genesis 15 was written people thought they had
been justified by works. Genesis comes before Leviticus
and Ezekiel; grace comes before law. It is revolutionary
because human beings – especially religious people –
find it difficult to believe in or live by.

The seal is set on this gracious relationship between
God and Abram when it is turned into a 'covenant'
(Gen. 17), the kind of relationship that involves a

solemn commitment of one party to another or of two parties to each other. The stress in the covenant between God and Abraham (as he now becomes – the name could suggest 'father of a multitude') is on God's commitment to Abraham: all Abraham has to do is accept the covenant sign of circumcision. The covenant embodies God's grace, to which Abraham responds in faith. That is Paul's point in Romans 4, and it is the point which makes Old Testament spirituality fundamentally one with New Testament spirituality (or rather, the point which makes the gospel biblical).

It is, indeed, the very foundation of spirituality. If we go wrong here, everything we build will be destined to fall.

When I find that my prayer-life has gone dead, a place to which I often return in order to seek a new beginning is the book on *Prayer* by Otto Hallesby, which begins with a quotation from Revelation: 'Behold, I stand at the door, and knock: if anyone hears my voice, and opens the door, I will come in to them and eat with them and they with me' (Rev. 3:20). This invitation has often been used to picture what happens when people first open their lives to Christ, when they first come to repentance and faith. But Revelation is written to people who are already believers, and Hallesby suggests that no verse of scripture throws more light on prayer than this one. 'To pray is to let Jesus come into our hearts' (p. 7). It is giving him access to our needs. Studying spirituality is not looking for ways of screwing ourselves up in order to find God. It is learning to recognize the ways in which our gracious, promising God is knocking on the door of our lives (and to recognize the ways in which we avoid hearing that knock). The foundation of Christian spirituality is the priority of the seeking, knocking, gracious God, the God of Romans 4, who is the promising God of Abraham, and before whom the key response is bare trust.

Interceding on the basis of God's promise

One of those rare occasions when God spoke to Abraham led Abraham into prayer (Gen. 18). Three 'men' – as they seemed – 'happen' to pass Abraham and Sarah's encampment and are offered that hospitality which is a moral obligation in the open country (lacking in wayside restaurants). Being apparently on the way to act in judgment on Sodom, Yahweh decides first to tell Abraham of his intention. The reason relates to that promise under which Abraham lives: it is because Abraham is to become a great and mighty nation and all the nations are destined to pray to be blessed as Abraham is blessed (18:19). Further, the implication is that although God has made a decision regarding Sodom, that decision is not irrevocable. It is an open question whether God will act in judgment. All depends on investigations still to be completed (18:21). The other two 'men' leave to undertake them, while Yahweh remains standing before Abraham (18:22, cf. the margins of the modern translations) – as if to say, 'Well, is there anything you want to say to me by way of response to that announcement of Sodom's doom?'

So Abraham prayed for Sodom, because God drew him into prayer. He had no alternative but to pray: God kept getting in his way. He carried on praying, through the extraordinary conversation which follows, because God encouraged him to do so by continuing to agree to what he said. And then he stopped praying, when God 'finished speaking to Abraham' and left (18:33). So it turns out that this intercessory conversation between Abraham and God is actually a conversation between God and Abraham, initiated by God and terminated by God. Abraham prayed because God drew him into prayer. He discovered for himself that intercession is not twisting things from an unwilling God (God wants to give them) nor is it a meaningless ritual (as if God would grant these things anyway). It is our accepting an involvement in the way God does things in the world. God wants Abraham as friend, partner, and collaborator, not just as creature. In his book *People in Prayer* (p. 15), John White observes about this story, 'Whatever else prayer may be, it is intended to be a sharing and a taking counsel with God on matters of importance to him. God has called you to attend a celestial board meeting to deliberate with him on matters of destiny . . . . [Prayer] is not intended primarily to be centered in my petty needs and woes . . . . [God] moves onto a matter which lies beyond the scope of Abraham's personal concerns.'

Abraham's particular prayer involved love, courage, and humility. He cared about the people of Sodom. He had already had contact with them, of course: his nephew Lot had gone to live there, and the king of Sodom was one of the figures involved in the military escapade related in Genesis 14. Indeed, from the Judean mountains where Yahweh met Abraham you could see the Sodom area on the floor of the Rift Valley. The people of Sodom were real people to Abraham. Further, those for whom he is speaking in prayer are people he has already taken action on behalf of: action and prayer go together. But there was more to his caring than that. We have noted that the reason why God accosted him was that Abraham was destined to be a means whereby blessing came to all peoples, which would include Sodom. His prayer invites contrast with Jonah's sulking at Nineveh, resentful of Yahweh's letting the Ninevites off from the punishment Jonah is looking forward to witnessing. He prayed the way he did because he cared about the people of Sodom as people he knew who were on their way to judgment when they were the kind of people he was destined to be a blessing to.

Abraham's prayer is a stimulus to prayer for the world. Sodom was a city renowned for its wickedness (13:13), which cried out to God for justice (18:20–21), as Abel's blood had cried out to God, and as the Israelites' later affliction would (Gen. 4:10; Exod. 2:23). Sodom's fundamental sin is not the grievous sexual disorder which Genesis 19 describes, but its oppression, presumably that practised on the people who live around it in the Jordan Valley, who cry out as the oppressed do, and are heard by God. Sodom as a whole is guilty. But perhaps there are 'innocent' people there? That is the basis of Abraham's prayer.

There was a courage about his prayer. While it involved Yahweh's standing there tacitly inviting him to pray, it also involved Abraham's actually 'drawing near' this suspiciously ambiguous figure (it is not clear precisely when Abraham realizes that there is more to these 'men' than meets the eye, but the prayer presupposes that the penny is dropping). While it involved Yahweh's mercy in continuing to agree to what Abraham said, it also involved Abraham's sticking his neck out further and further: 'Would you let Sodom off if there were 50 just people there? Otherwise it wouldn't be fair, would it? OK, what if there were only 45 . . .? 40 . . .? 30 . . .? 20 . . .? 10 . . .? (that is perhaps as far as it is meaningful to go, because 10 would imply just one family). We sometimes qualify our prayers with 'If it be your will', but that can reflect a failure of courage. Prayer is in part about telling God *our* will, declaring before God how things look to us.

Yet in this extraordinary barter, Abraham is not actually haggling with God. He is more seeking to understand God. 'Forgive me for speaking like this . . . . I know it's your world . . . . I know I'm a mere human being . . . .' The keynote of Jesus's prayer for himself, 'not what I want but what you want' (Mk. 14:36) is already a keynote in this intercessory prayer of Abraham. Some people who pray for healing have to be wary of the failure of courage involved in not asking for that healing which we covet for someone; others need to be wary of an arrogance that fails to let God be God. Abraham thus illustrates another characteristic feature of true prayer, a combining of courage with submission, a willingness ultimately to bow down to the will of God.

And he experiences an answer, though not the one he asked for. This too is true of Jesus, who was 'heard' even though it looks as if he was not (Heb. 5:7). Sodom does not escape, but Lot and his family do – because God was mindful of Abraham (Gen. 19:29). It is not what he asked for, but it is apparently something he would not have received had he not prayed the way he did.

Sodom stands for any nation and Abraham's prayer is a stimulus to prayer for our own nation and for other nations. The God to whom we pray is concerned for justice, for the oppressed and for the oppressor, and part of our being a blessing to the world is to pray for God's justice to be at work. Even the oppressors need that prayer, because it may be that they will be preserved for the sake of the just in their midst (so the justice and the mercy of God are not opposed). A city can be preserved if there are only ten righteous people there. We will not resent that, like foolish Jonah: we know that life on earth only continues at all because of the mercy of God which keeps hesitating to bring final judgment on a world which deserves it (a judgment which as sinners none of us would have grounds for escaping).

Surrendering God's promise?

In due course Sarah has the baby God said she would, and she laughs a more joyful laugh than the one she had let out at Mamre, and calls her son after the two experiences: 'Isaac' means 'he laughs'.

And then the time came when God put Abraham to the test with regard to this laughter. Why? After all, God could surely have run computer projections to discover what a person like Abraham would do in different situations. But the God of the Bible does not believe in simulation exercises, only in trying things out. It is perhaps tied up with taking us seriously as people. God lets us decide things for ourselves, make our own mistakes, foul up heaven's plans. God always hopes we will fulfil heaven's longings and disprove heaven's fears, but gives us the chance to do so. It has been so from the beginning, according to Genesis. As the flood story shows, God learns to live with our mistakes. God takes risks and is prepared to live with the consequences.

'Abraham.' 'Yes?' 'You know your son, Isaac?' 'Yes.' 'Your only son.' 'Yes.' 'You love him, don't you?' 'Yes.' 'I want you to take him north from here, through the mountains to the land of Moriah.' 'Yes.' 'And kill him as a sacrifice to me there.'

The way that God speaks indicates an awareness of the horror of what is asked of Abraham – 'your son, your only son, the one you love, Isaac'. God knows the knife that twists into Abraham's own insides when he somehow senses that God is laying this terrible burden upon him. Perhaps it was not an utter surprise; it was not as unbelievable as it would be for us. The first of the fruit of the ground, and the first of the fruit of the womb, were reckoned especially to belong to God. People in Canaan sometimes did actually sacrifice their children to their god. It was not a regular practice, but in a crisis, when they needed to prove their devotion to their god, that was a way they might do it. Abraham, and the readers of the Abraham stories, knew that. Offering your child to God in that way was not something beyond imagining.

There is something more to it. 'Your son, your only son, the one you love, Isaac.' It was only in the previous chapter that we read about the birth of this son (though that does not mean that Isaac is only a child when all this happens; Genesis calls him a 'young man', the same word it uses to describe the servants Abraham takes with him). He was born after years of longing and hoping and trying, years of disappointment and frustration and pain. It is not just the disappointment and pain that any couple might feel, but the hurt of people to whom God has specifically promised that they are going to have a son, and that he will be of key importance for the blessing of all peoples. They never do, and then when all hope is as dead as Sarah's womb, she conceives. Thus God's promise becomes not just words but reality, and Sarah laughs like somebody who has found that the world of her dreams has become the world of reality. Now God says 'give him back to me'. She always knew love and grace were illusory, that life was inexorably cruel, that reality is pain and disappointment and hurt and that joy is illusion. 'You know your son, your only son, the one you love, Isaac? I want him back.'

What happened to Abraham was unique to him. It belonged to a once for all moment in the story of how God came to fulfil promises to Abraham. Yet we may have our Isaacs, some gift from God that embodies God's promise, God's faithfulness, God's generosity, God's incalculable love. 'You know your son, your only son, the one you love, Isaac? I want him back.'

So Abraham arose early in the morning, to set out. 'Early in the morning': the way you do when you have something important to do, something you are committed to doing. Yet apart from that phrase, we get not the slightest hint of what went through Abraham's mind as he set in motion the chain of events that were to lead to his son's death, any more than we get hints of what went through Sarah's mind (I have had to imagine that), let alone Isaac's. Abraham gets up and saddles his donkey, and chooses two of his men, and collects Isaac himself, and splits wood for the fire on which he will burn the body so that the smell of roasting flesh rises for God to savour. And we are told nothing of Abraham's thoughts or feelings. As we noted above, that is often the case in Old Testament stories. And one of the results is that these stories affect us by making us analyze the feelings we would have, the questions that would be in our minds. The disbelief ('this can't be happening'). The guilt ('how can I be about to do this?'). The panic. The anger.

They travel for a whole day. They find somewhere to sleep. They dream about the past and the future. They travel another day and sleep and dream. They set off once more, and in due course Abraham's keen eyes spot the place he has been looking for. 'You two stay here with the donkey. We're going to go over there to worship. Then we'll come back.' What's going on? Why is he leaving them behind? So that they can't stop him? And what does he mean – 'we'll come back'? Does he know what he means? Or is it one of those things that you sometimes say without having thought about it, and you aren't quite sure what you mean?

He loads the firewood onto Isaac's back (is there no end to the horror of this: the sacrificial victim carries the means of his own burning?). Abraham himself carries the flint to light the fire, and the knife to kill the victim. Father and son walk together. Now for the only time in the story Isaac emerges from the shadow. 'Father.' 'Yes, son?' 'We've got the flint and the wood, but where's the actual sacrifice?' What do you say? 'God will give us one, son.' Again, what does he mean? Does he know what he means? Or is it another of those things that you sometimes say without having worked out the words ahead of time, and without quite knowing what you mean?

Once more father and son walk on together. They come to the place God had told Abraham about (like lots of aspects of the story, we do not know how he knew this was the right place). He builds an altar with stones. He builds a fire on it ready to light. He ties Isaac up and puts him on the top and reaches for his knife . . . . And now the imagination quite fails: is Isaac not fighting and screaming, are the two men not rushing to restrain the madman? But no, they are all apparently frozen. The story long ago left behind the kind of logic we are used to. Like a nightmare, it is all of a piece with our worlds, yet it is also quite outside it in a world of its own.

And it is out of another world that a voice comes to break the nightmare. 'Abraham, Abraham!' 'Yes?' 'Put the knife down. Don't touch the boy. You've done enough to prove that God comes first for you. You would even give me your son, your only son.' For the question was, how important to Abraham had the fulfilled promise become? Had it perhaps become even more important than God? Did Abraham still need God now that he had Isaac? But the destiny of the people of God does not rest on Isaac alone, but on every word that proceeds from the mouth of God. If God does not say the word, all the Isaacs in the world will not mean that God's purpose comes true. If God does say the word, that purpose can be fulfilled whatever happens to Isaac. To prove it imagine Isaac taken away . . . .

Perhaps that is all the story itself does – dramatize the idea of Isaac being taken away. With these stories in Genesis, we often do not really know whether they actually happened or whether they are like parables. Either way, they invite us to name our Isaac to ourselves – that gift of God that embodies God's promise, God's faithfulness, God's generosity, God's incalculable love. They invite us to imagine that Isaac on our open hand, capable of being taken away by God. It is the way that God and we discover whether Isaac matters more than God to us.

You have to do it with your hand actually open, not with your fist clenched (I owe the image to Isobel Kuhn's *In the Arena*, p. 97, though I have applied it in a different way). You have to see what God will do, taking nothing for granted, not knowing how the story will end. We know how Abraham's story will end; even if we were not familiar with it the opening line of the chapter has told us what is going on. Abraham did not know how it would end. And when it is a matter of our own story, we have to live through it as Abraham did.

We can do that, because Abraham's God is not someone who takes things away just for the sake of it. Yahweh is the one who when we offer things on an open hand does give them back one way or another and deepens what they mean to us. Indeed, thereby what

God means to us and what we mean to God is also deepened. Eventually God proves it by being prepared personally to do what Abraham was asked to do: 'he did not spare his own Son, but gave him up for us all – will he not also, along with him, graciously give us all things?' (Rom. 8:32). But Abraham knew God as that kind of person, because he had a demonstration of the fact. The place where Abraham held Isaac on his open hand before God became the place where God gave. The God who threatened to be one who took was shown to be by nature one who provides. 'So Abraham called that place "Yahweh will Provide". And to this day it is said, "On the mountain of Yahweh it will be provided".'

SIX

Hagar and Ishmael

In telling the story of Abraham and Sarah we omitted
that of Hagar and Ishmael, as often happens (unless
they receive mention as problems). It is time to redress
the balance.

The patriarchy of the patriarch and his wife

Hagar is the multiple victim of patriarchy – not only at
Abram's hands it must be said, but at those of Sarai, of
Yahweh, and of Genesis itself. And that is so, of course,
because patriarchy is built into the society in which
Hagar, Sarai, and Abram live, and within which Yahweh
works. 'Sarai, Abram's wife, bore him no children'
(Gen. 16:1). The nature of patriarchy is already advertised in those words. Sarai's own identity comes from
belonging to Abram. It consists in being a particular
man's woman. And as a particular man's woman, her
specific task is to bear him children. Women are to be
barefoot, pregnant, and in the kitchen. Sarai is barefoot
(that is, unequipped for functioning in the big wide
world outside) in chapter 14, when Abram is off on
heroic exploits in Damascus. She is in the kitchen in

chapter 18 in that wonderful vignette where Abram behaves like the typical husband expecting her to organize dinner for four at no notice. She is pregnant here in chapter 16. Except that she is not. And if she fails here, she fails altogether. She is not really a woman.

That feeling is still about, and not just among women. When the Ethics Advisory Board of the Department of Health, Education, and Welfare in the United States was considering *in vitro* fertilization, the ethicist Stanley Hauerwas was asked to testify before it (his testimony is included in his book *Suffering Presence*). He asks what is the importance of having children, particularly children who are biologically our own. Why is it so important, that we should be willing to expend huge amounts of time and money to provide them? Is there not something as bizarre about this as there is (it will probably seem to us) about the alternative arrangements which obtained in Abram and Sarai's culture with which we become acquainted in this story? Is this procedure (Hauerwas asks) a mark of our sinful pretension to ensure immortality through biological continuity?

Sarai is the victim of patriarchy, yet she is also its agent. The hierarchical tree of patriarchy puts men above women, but that is not its only piece of prioritizing. In varying cultures it has further gradations such as free human being above slave, white above black, employer above employee, landowner above peasant. In relation to these, Sarai is privileged and Hagar is victim. The one is free, the other slave; the one Israelite (to be anachronistic: strictly, Israelites do not yet exist), the other Egyptian. Instead of sisters doing it for themselves, patriarchy perpetuates itself by dividing them from each other, putting them into a hierarchy of their own. At least we may note that Hagar has a name (for the storyteller and for God, though it is noteworthy that Abram and Sarai do not use her name – for them she is just their slave). This is not a privilege accorded to every oppressed woman in the Bible story. At least she exists as a person. The story will show that she insists on doing so, and that God insists on the point, too.

In the meantime let Hagar's body belong to Abram as well as to Sarai. If a woman's chief function is to be a walking womb, let Hagar do for Sarai what Sarai cannot. 'It may be that I shall obtain children by her', says Sarai, and thus that you, Abram, will, too. 'OK', says Abram. This exchange has put me on the track of the suspicion that Abram is rather a wimp. After all, he only left Ur in Babylon because his father took him (Gen. 11:30). When his father died in Haran it required a divine intervention to get Abram moving again (11:2; 12:1). Admittedly, when there are supermarket short-ages in Canaan he is out of the promised land into Egypt as quick as a participant in a Christian Aid lunch making a beeline for the sweetshop on the way home (12:10). But in general he is a man who is happiest responding to other people's initiatives. He only went to Damascus because someone more or less dragooned him (14:13). Here he 'hearkens to Sarai's voice': a worrying phrase, because the previous person in Genesis who hearkened to a voice like that was Adam (3:17).

Sarai and Abram's conversation is in general a chilling one because of the disparity between who speaks and who is spoken of. 'Yahweh has prevented me from having a child', says Sarai. 'Why don't you sleep with Hagar and see if she has one'. There is an unfilled gap between the piece of theological reflection and the taking of that initiative. They have been ten years in Canaan and Yahweh had promised family as well as land, but Yahweh has closed that door, closed a womb. Shall we therefore try another door/womb and see if that opens? Or is that to wrest the helm of the story from the divine storyteller? Either is a possibility; the chillingness of this aspect to the story is that Sarai and Abram do not ask the question. Sarai refers to Yahweh when she suggests what they should do, given that

Yahweh has closed a door, but she speaks of Yahweh without suggesting speaking *to* Yahweh. In this story it will take a Hagar to dare the thought that a mere woman can take the initiative in addressing God as well as in asking questions about God.

So Yahweh is one unspeaking referent in this story. But Yahweh is not the only one, for so is Hagar. All the way from predicament to plan to sex (I hesitate to say lovemaking) to pregnancy, Hagar is simultaneously central and marginal to the story. She features in almost every sentence, but she is never present, she never speaks, her views or words never surface. The conversation between Sarai and Abram marginalizes both Hagar and Yahweh in a way which will make life complicated and painful, perhaps for both.

Even her pregnancy thus gives Hagar no voice in the story, but it is evidently pregnancy with attitude. 'When she saw that she had conceived, she looked with contempt upon her mistress.' It is again the case that the psychological insight in these Old Testament stories is unmistakable but is explicit only sparingly, if at all. 'When she saw that she was pregnant, she looked with contempt upon her mistress.' Of course that is what would happen, you say after it has happened (but not before), as in the best films or novels. More literally what Genesis says is that Sarai 'was someone slight, trifling, insignificant, in the eyes of Hagar'. Sarai has taken an action that has unwittingly overturned the power relationship between them. Hagar, the Egyptian, the slave, has life in her womb. If we are operating with the assumptions of patriarchy, that defines true womanliness. So it is Hagar who now holds her head high as the complete woman in the house that she and Sarai and Abram share and over whose table they look at each other at breakfast each morning as Hagar's periods stop and her sickness starts and her belly swells. The Sarai who was not humiliated before an Egyptian king in chapter 12 is humiliated before an Egyptian slave in chapter 16. Sarai was someone significant, Hagar someone insignificant; now the positions are reversed. Sisterhood is spoiled in a second, reciprocal way.

There is more to the contrast with chapter 12 and more to this statement that Sarai was someone slight, trifling, insignificant. When Genesis talks about things or people being 'cursed', as it often does, this is one of the words it uses. They are belittled, treated with contempt, made nothing of. And in particular, back in that promise which impelled Abram and Sarai into the land at the beginning of chapter 12, one of the elements of the promise was that they would be people who would be blessed not cursed, and here is Sarai experiencing the opposite to what Yahweh promised, experiencing belittling because she felt she had to do something when Yahweh was not doing anything to fulfil other aspects of the promise. And you grieve for Sarai. And you fear for Hagar too, because the promise said that the people who do belittle, despise, Abram's family will themselves be cursed, and Hagar has put herself in that company. The interplay of divine purpose and promise with human need, instinct, dilemma, and hurt, are simultaneously wondrous, awesome, frightening, and comforting. The fact that God uses us is fearful, because no one likes to be used – though as long as God can be trusted, it means that being used can be faced.

Forms of patriarchal violence

The insight into the human experience continues. When Adam's listening to Eve rebounded on him, he was soon making sure that Eve and Yahweh knew it was her fault. When Abram's listening to Sarai rebounded on her, she was soon making sure that Abram and Yahweh knew it was his fault. Everything always has to be somebody's fault, does it not? If I can blame somebody other than me, in some sense that makes things OK. Sarai said to Abram, 'May the

violence done to me be on you! I gave my maid to your
embrace, and when she saw that she had conceived,
she looked on me with contempt. Yahweh must judge
between you and me'. Sarai has no doubt what the
judgment will be – but then we are always pretty
convinced that God will look at things the way we do,
are we not?

Like Hagar's contempt, Sarai's response seems inevitable once it has happened. It is again just what
would happen, you see afterwards. Hagar is the person
who rubs in the fact of Sarai's childlessness, in the very
act of being the one who can vicariously end it. Hagar is
the person who can give Sarai's husband the one thing
he most wants and the one thing Sarai longs to give
him. In the course of arranging for this, could one not
say that Sarai and Abram have done violence to Hagar?
And Sarai with wonderful Freudian slippage complains
about the violence that Hagar has done to her! The
word 'violence' is the word *hamas*, the word which
gives its name to the violent wing of the Palestinian
liberation struggle. It is used twice elsewhere in
Genesis. It first refers to the worldwide violence which
leads to Yahweh's decision to destroy the world (Gen.
6:11,13). It then refers to Simeon and Levi's massacre of
the men of Shechem (49:5). That is striking enough. But
so is the fact that in the Old Testament it is the word
Jeremiah uses when he wants to talk about rape (Jer.
13:22; 20:8). In our culture the way Hagar is treated
might indeed seem rather like rape. It is what Sarai and
Abram have done to Hagar, so it is what Sarai accuses
Hagar of.

Abram has held another woman in his arms, and it
was Sarai's idea, but she hates it, and she hates her, and
she hates him, and she hates their soon-to-be child, and
she hates herself, and she probably hates the God who
closed her own womb, though for the moment she will
hang onto that God because she can use God to beat
Abram over the head with, the way one does. 'Yahweh
judge between you and me', she says. Abram evidently

listens well; this is the Bible's first reference to God
being judge, and a couple of chapters later, in a story
we have already considered, Abram is making good
theological use of Sarai's idea in a conversation of his
own with God when she is in her place in the kitchen
and once again contemplating the possibility of her own
pregnancy (see Gen. 18:25). But then Abram copes
better with outrageous suggestions on God's part than
with outrageous suggestions of Sarai's. Pulling his
wimp's tee-shirt closer to his chest (as often, Abram is a
type of David, also a wimp with his family, and on the
vaster scale that befits an antitype) he assures Sarai that
she has his complete support in the way she manages
the domestic arrangements. After all, a capable wife is a
notable find (Prov. 31), one who can manage a home
and vary the menu and pitch a tent and keep an eye on
the winter clothing and keep the maids in order and
push out the ones who undertake unwelcome preg-
nancies. 'Do to her as you please', he says. 'Do what is
good in your eyes', more literally. 'What is good',
indeed. Throw the benighted woman out.

I remember when our first son was a year or eighteen
months and we began to think about the possibility of
another baby, and Ann suddenly became much more
interested in what time of the month it was when we
made love and that kind of thing. I remember starting
an argument because I felt she was not really interested
in making love with me. I was just a means of achieving
conception. I might as well have been a test tube, I felt.
Hagar was just a means of achieving conception, and
when she has done what was asked of her, too well, she
pays the price. Sarai deals harshly with her, oppresses
her, Genesis says. It uses another word for rape, in fact
the nearest Hebrew has to a technical term for rape, the
word used (for instance) of Absalom and Tamar (2 Sam.
13). But it is also the word which God has just used for
the way the Egyptians will in due course treat the
Israelites in Egypt (Gen. 15:13; cf. Exod. 1:11–12). It is
the kind of action that will be forbidden to Israel

because they know what it is like to be on the receiving
end (Exod. 22:21), but the kind of action that they know
how to be on the giving end of, too – the kind of action
that manipulates its victim into giving up, into running
away into the hopelessness of the desert where death is
the best end you can hope for, and where your death
can be blamed on you rather than on your manipu-
lators. After all, you chose to go. You did not have to.
You were not thrown out. You went of your own free
choice.

Or perhaps there is a positive way to read the point.
Hagar runs barefoot, pregnant, and into the desert. She
declines to play the role of victim, designated for her by
Sarai and colluded with by Abram. She takes her
destiny into her own hands. If she is on her own, she
declares 'I will survive'. If in due course Yahweh's aide
finds her by a spring in the desert, that is because she
had already found her own spring in the desert. The
trouble is, Yahweh will not let her take her destiny into
her own hands. The one who had prevented one
woman from becoming pregnant now pursues another
when she has.

In her study of some distressing biblical stories about
women, *Texts of Terror*, Phyllis Trible notes that Hagar
was oppressed on the grounds that she had done
violence, and she never opens her mouth in this story.
She illustrates what it means to be the suffering servant
who is oppressed though he has done no violence – the
words are the same – and who does not open his mouth
(Isa. 53:4,7,9). Professor Trible tells us how she could
not have faced these stories in scripture if she had not
first studied some more joyful texts in her *God and the
Rhetoric of Sexuality*. I am not sure I could have told
Hagar's story were it not for where it now leads.

Hagar has moved from the voiceless and loveless
inner margin of Sarai and Abram's family and society
(slave, foreigner, surrogate womb) to its voiceless and
rights-less outer margin (unwantedly pregnant and
'raped' by Sarai as she has been by Abram) to a margin

far beyond that, the margin between culture and nothingness, the wilderness where sheep survive only with the most expert of shepherding to find them the secret wells and cisterns and patches of green. There, for the first time in this story, God speaks – and that to Hagar. For the first time in this story, someone speaks to Hagar. For the first time, Hagar is addressed by name. For the first time, Hagar herself finds voice. The ultimately marginalized person is the one with whom God engages in conversation; Sarai and Abram are left on their own to speak with each other (though I cannot but believe that Hagar was the unmentioned focus of their every shamed conversation after she left – and I cannot but believe this because I love Abram and Sarai and I cannot believe that this couple of whom I am so privileged to be the spiritual descendant would have been able to sleep the sleep of the innocent).

Hagar's bold theology and tough grace

The main road from Hebron goes south and then west towards Egypt, and no one would have needed a BA (Detective Work) to know that this was the direction Hagar would go from Sarai and Abram's settlement. Shur is somewhere on this route, east of Egypt proper. Hagar was resting at a spring on this route when Yahweh's aide found her. The aide is usually described as Yahweh's 'angel', but that gives various forms of misleading impression. It tends to suggest characters with wings wearing albs. Someone who knows too much Greek may alternatively think that angels are messengers. Actually Yahweh's aides are characters who (like God) look like human beings when they appear on earth, so people usually do not immediately realize they have met one; presumably Hagar at first assumes this is just a man entering into conversation at the well. The job of Yahweh's aides is to represent Yahweh in whatever way is needed – speech, action, or whatever. So whenever we have been met by someone who looked human but who has done or said something suspiciously divine, we have probably been in touch with angels.

Like God, they ask questions to which you might have thought they knew the answers; the story again recalls Genesis 3, with its 'Where are you?' to Adam – and also that first story of violence and flight in Genesis 4 with its 'Where is your brother?' to Cain. 'Hagar, maid of Sarai, where have you come from and where are you going?' An aide who knew where to find Hagar and knew her name and her mistress's name presumably knew what she was doing there, and even we can work out what an Egyptian who has been abused is doing on the road to Egypt – which is as well, because she omits to answer this half of the question; she focuses on the reason for her flight. She is fleeing from Sarai.

The aide's response astonishes. 'Go back', Hagar is told, colluding with slavery as Paul does when he tells Onesimus to go back to Philemon. Is there no end to the burden loaded on this woman's back? Will Jacob be told to go back when he flees from Esau? Will his sons be told to go back when they go down this same road to find grain in Egypt (aided, ironically, by the descendants of the child Hagar will bear: see Gen. 37:25–28)? And for her Egypt is home. Why can she not return home?

Perhaps Israelites who read this story knew why. They had their own stories about wanting to go back to Egypt, wanting to return to the leeks, the garlic, and the onions (Israelis do not have great reputations as cooks, but anyone who recognizes that cuisine starts with garlic and onions can't be all bad), but knowing that the road from Egypt has no return carriageway. 'You are not to return that way.' It was a command, but one of those commands that masked a promise. When Yahweh has rescued you from Egypt, you do not return to bondage. Yahweh has begun to do something with you, and bars the return loop.

The return loop is barred to Hagar out of the same tough grace. However she came out of Egypt, she is not to return that way again. There is a terrible price to be paid for not returning, the price of submitting to a mistress from hell and her wimp and to a God who seems to go along with both, but it is a price less terrible than the one she would pay by returning home to Egypt. That would be to turn her back on the promise Yahweh makes to her as part of the Abrahamic people. Sarai was once protected from being absorbed into Egypt, for the sake of the promise to Abram. Hagar is protected from being re-absorbed into Egypt for the sake of her own promise. 'I will so greatly multiply your descendants that they cannot be numbered for multitude.'

Who speaks? Hagar thought she was in conversation with an imperfectly-briefed presidential aide, the kind who remembers your name but has forgotten the rest of your file. Suddenly it transpires that this is the president in person. It is Yahweh who speaks. And note what Yahweh says: 'I will so greatly multiply your descendants that they cannot be numbered for multitude'. It is the same promise that was given to Abram. Hagar is urged not to return to Egypt, because that is to forsake her place within Abram's promise. Indeed, the promise ceases to be merely Abram's. It becomes customized for her. The promise has never been given to Sarai as an individual, but as a result of Sarai's affliction of Hagar the promise is given to Hagar as an individual. Indeed, such a promise has not been given to any woman before Hagar, and I am not sure its equivalent will ever be given to a woman again until perhaps it is given to Mary, of whom Hagar is a type.

The way Yahweh's words go on confirm that hunch. 'You have a child in your womb, and you will bear a son and you will name him Ishmael.' Towards the end of the Bible's macro-story the angel of Yahweh will tell that other woman, 'You will conceive in your womb and bear a son and you will name him Jesus' (Lk. 1:31). The

words to Mary resemble the angel's word's to the
mother-to-be of Samson, and resemble Isaiah's words
about the mother-to-be of Immanuel, but they are
closest to Yahweh's words to Hagar, the mother-to-be
of Ishmael. 'You have a child in your womb and you
will bear a son and you will call him Ishmael.' Hagar is a
type of Mary, and Ishmael is a type of Christ.

I am tired of the cliché about God being biased to the
poor and am sometimes inclined to reckon that it is
rather obvious that God is not biased to the poor. But I
have been caused to reconsider the possibility that God
is indeed biased to the poor and afflicted by this story of
Hagar, the woman thrown out by the original bearers of
the promise, thrown out by the people of God, thrown
out by the church, and therefore pursued by God on the
basis of a bias to the poor. She is pursued by God not
merely so that God can encourage her to return to her
homeland and assure her that Yahweh can be with her
there. That is how I might have expected the story to
turn out, and I could have theologized on the basis of
such a story quite happily. Once again, the story's
genius is that it unfurls in a way which is self-evident
only afterwards. God is not satisfied with obvious plots
to stories, Hagar's or yours or mine. Hagar is forbidden
the comfort of returning home because Yahweh has in
mind something tougher in the short term but wondrous
in the long term. She is to be the mother of a multitude,
and the way God works with her announces a pattern
to be followed when the Son of God is born. Abraham's
offering of Isaac in the absence of Sarah will give one
clue to what God will do in Jesus. Before that, another
clue is already given in God's announcing of Ishmael in
the presence of Hagar.

'Ishmael'. The name means 'God listens, God hears,
God pays heed'. Ishmael is not merely a type of Christ,
but a type of Israel itself. In Hagar's homeland in due
course the Israelites will verbalize the cry that Hagar has
not verbalized (though that has not stopped Yahweh
hearing it), and Yahweh will hear their cry and see the
```
```

affliction with which Hagar's people reward Abram and
Sarai's descendants (Exod. 3:7). That Yahweh hears
Israel's voice and sees its affliction is of key significance
for the world's salvation. But the first affliction Yahweh
sees in scripture, the first voice Yahweh hears, is
Hagar's. The fact is thus memorably encapsulated in the
name of her son. And that, too, is of key significance for
the world's salvation, for it affirms that the God of
Abram, Isaac, Jacob, and Moses is also the God of Nahor,
Ishmael, Esau, and Jethro, not to say Milcah, Hagar,
Judith, and Zipporah. Yahweh hears and responds to
the affliction of people outside the physical line of Sarai
as well as people inside that line. Indeed this enslaved
gentile woman is the first person in scripture to have
God respond to her in this way.

The fact that Hagar's is the first affliction Yahweh sees
in scripture is in turn memorably encapsulated in her
own naming of Yahweh. It is reflected, indeed, in the
fact that Hagar names Yahweh at all. There has been
much naming in Genesis so far. Adam has named the
animals and has named Eve, Cain has named a city,
people have named their children. In Middle Eastern
culture to name was not merely to designate with a label
but to determine someone's place, their nature, or their
destiny. Everything lay in the name of Eve or Seth or
Noah (or Abram and Sarai when they became Abraham
and Sarah). Naming is thus among other things a sign
of authority and power. No one therefore names God.
Except Hagar. She decides on a name for God.

Hagar has been addressed four times by the divine
aide, overwhelmed by his words as women often are
when men are talking, unable to get a word in
edgeways. She stands there waiting for an opportunity
to speak. But she does then have the last word, and at
that point becomes the Bible's first theologian, the first
person to name God. Except that her naming is not
addressed to other people but to God. She is scripture's
first worshipper, in the sense that she is the first person
whose words of confession we hear. 'You are a God of

seeing', she says. God is not only a God who hears but a God who sees. The implications of the two verbs are similar. When God hears, God responds; when God sees, God cares. Both verbs describe Yahweh's awareness of Israel's affliction in Exodus 3:7, and the storyteller draws our attention to the fact that Hagar's 'God who sees' is indeed that Yahweh revealed to Israel in her own land as Israel's deliverer.

It is no chance that the most packed manual of theology in scripture is the Book of Psalms, the book that is addressed to God as no other is. The risky task of naming God is most safely ventured in address to God, when God has built-in opportunity to answer back. It is most safely ventured in response to what God has said to us and done for us. And it is most safely ventured when accompanied by incredulous questions – 'have I really seen God?' How Hagar's question continues is not clear and translations vary, but that perhaps underlines the hesitant or uncertain nature of the question.

Dorothy Sölle has declared that all feminist theology begins in pain, and Walter Brueggemann (in a lecture from which I derive her observation) has glossed that with the suggestion that all real theology begins in pain. If this is so, then it is not surprising that Hagar is scripture's first theologian. She theologizes and worships as a woman in pain and sets a pattern for us to follow as we wish. Pain (and specifically women's pain, and perhaps even more specifically the pain of women from the margins) is not an inhibition or an irrelevance to theology or worship. It is their seed.

So Hagar returns to Sarai and Abram. She returns to 'submit' to Sarai: the word implies that she returns to accept Sarai's affliction. How paradoxical is the hearing of God, which recognizes affliction and pays heed to it, yet then sends the afflicted back for more. But perhaps (as Gerald Janzen suggests) the phrase 'submit yourself' implies at least that she is taking control of her affliction, as may have been the case when she left. She is not in submission because she has no alternative but to be so, but because she so chooses. In that sense in her inner spirit she will remain free.

And she returns to Abram, and bears Abram a son. She is thus sucked back into the patriarchy of Abram as well as that of Sarai. The child is not hers but his. But the story's own point is more that the child is Abram's not Sarai's and that Hagar is the one who bears Abram a son. Sarai had been the one who was due to bear Abram a son; when she could not, Hagar had been due to bear Sarai a son, a child who would count as her mistress's. Perhaps the story implies that the way Sarai has treated Hagar has ruled out that expression of sisterhood. Hagar not Sarai is Abram's effective wife, and the child is Abram's not Sarai's real son. Abram names him with the name determined by Hagar's experience of Yahweh and Yahweh's own word, and for better or worse he will always be 'the son Hagar bore'.

Ishmael

He will be a son with attitude, the son of his mother, 'a wild ass of a man, with his hand against everyone and with everyone's hand against him; and he will live at odds with all his kin'. The Israelites who told this story and listened to it knew what they were talking about from their own experience. The descendants of Ishmael lived the life of the desert, the life of bedouin, and they were people who would facilitate the enslaving of Joseph and become one of the neighbours/cousins with whom Israel had a love-hate relationship (cf. Jdg. 8:24, Ps. 83:6). But Ishmael will need to be that kind of man, if he is to survive. It is just as well that he will turn out to be his mother's son, not his father's.

After the story of Ishmael's birth God reaffirms the promises to Abram himself (Gen. 17). God had done this just before Ishmael's birth (Gen. 15), but the new reprise has further connotations after that event. Three times God declares that Abram is to be ancestor not merely of one great nation (as in the promise in 12:2) but of many nations (cf. the promise to Hagar in 16:10, and the emphasis on Hagar's having borne her son to Abram in 16:15–16). It is as ancestor of Ishmael's descendants as well as Isaac's that Abram becomes Abraham. Etymologically the name's meaning ('exalted ancestor') is likely the same; the difference is simply one of spelling. But the second part of the new name is also reminiscent of a Hebrew word for a multitude, so that the new name has a new connotation. When God also now adds the sacrament of circumcision to the commitment of covenant which was made in chapter 15, it is explicit that the sacrament applies to slaves like Ishmael as well as free-born sons: indeed, Ishmael is the first to receive the sacrament. When God reaffirms the promise that Sarai (now similarly renamed Sarah) will have her own son, Abraham affirms the sonship of Ishmael. God has other ideas, but listens to Abraham as previously to Hagar (and as Abram had listened to Sarai) and promises to Ishmael blessing and fruitfulness.

Of course the birth of Ishmael is not the end of his story. Or perhaps it is, for the main story we are told of his life (in Gen. 21) repeats the plot of his birth. When in due course Sarah has had Isaac, she has another reason to resent Ishmael; and what follows the account of Isaac's birth actually receives more space than the account of the birth itself. Sarah had resented Ishmael before he was born because she did not have a son of her own, and she resents him later because she does have a son of her own. The birth of her own son turns out not to be the uncomplicated joy she might have long dreamed it would be, as the birth of her surrogate son was not (but then, most people's experience of marriage and parenthood is more ambiguous than their dreams). Sarah sees 'the son of Hagar – the Egyptian – whom she had borne to Abraham' (one recalls the pathos of God's words to Abraham, 'your son – your only son – Isaac – whom you love'). He was having a laugh. The comment is very allusive, and the translations seek to clarify it, usually by suggesting he was having a laugh (or rather playing a game) with Isaac. Perhaps it suggests that Ishmael was laughing at Isaac as Hagar had fatefully looked with disdain at Sarai (16:1). But the main point likely lies in the verb itself, because the name Isaac itself means 'he laughs'. Ishmael had come into being at Sarah's behest in order to take Isaac's place by anticipation, and he lives as a standing reminder of that, and every time he has a laugh he is 'isaacing' and threatening to replace Isaac again. He is playing Sarah, too, of course, because it was Sarah's laughter that generated her son's name. So Ishmael's laughter reminds Sarah of her own, and he is thus a double reminder of the tension between faith and unfaith in her – he reminds her of that by his existence in the ambiguity of her original suggestion to Abram, and he reminds her of the way her own laughter could be a sign of faith or a sign of unfaith.

Once again Sarah determines to squeeze Hagar and Ishmael out from the margin to the very outside of the family. Once again Abraham plays the part of wimp, though neither God nor Abraham is willing to discard the elder son (neither seems so worried about the fate of Hagar herself). Walter Brueggemann compares them to two men trying to work out what to do with a cantankerous woman. Once again Yahweh's reaction, telling Abraham not to worry too much about Hagar and Ishmael because it is Isaac who counts, makes one wonder what kind of God this is, until the ground for reassurance about its being OK to humour Sarah are repeated: Ishmael has a commitment from Yahweh of his own.

Once again Hagar has no voice as the exchanges between Sarah, Abraham, and Yahweh proceed. Once again Abraham rises early in the morning to do what a man has to do (once again in the order in which we have looked at these stories, but of course in Genesis's own order this act of commitment precedes the act of commitment involved in offering Isaac). Is the provision of bread and water a statement of hope and faith or a sop to conscience, like the condemned criminal's last breakfast before execution? Once again Hagar leaves, this time directly exiled.

A key feature of Hebrew poetry in books such as the Psalms and the prophets is parallelism, a phenomenon whereby the two halves of a line complement each other. The second half often 'parallels' the first, but hardly ever by merely repeating it. It varies it, usually by heightening it or sharpening it or clarifying it. Something similar is often true when stories repeat themselves. In the first story Hagar found a spring; she was not doing too badly when the divine aide found her. In the second story the water is gone and she has found no spring. She sits the exhausted child in the shade of a bush and herself sits quite a distance away, not wanting to watch the dying of her child, his promises, and her faith. I cannot imagine what kind of desolation this is, an aloneness hardly exceeded even by the awfulness of parents in our culture sitting by the bedside of a dying child. She lifts up her voice and weeps.

And God hears the *boy's* cry. That is odd, because he has uttered no cry. We are reminded of God's hearing the prayer Hagar had not prayed, but we are also reminded the more forcibly of the further link between Ishmael and Israel. God hears the cry of the one as God will hear the cry of the other. And God's aide calls from heaven – again, anticipating the call from heaven to prevent Abraham killing Isaac. The aide speaks to *her*. 'What is troubling you?' One might be forgiven for wondering again about the selection system for the divine civil service which produces people who need to ask such a damn-fool question, but there is of course an implicit reassurance if not rebuke about it. 'What about the promises? What about what happened before?' The fact that this time the question is a rhetorical one is evidenced by the fact that the aide waits for no answer and instead offers God's explicit reassurance: 'Don't be afraid'. It is another 'first' for Hagar. She is the first woman to be offered this encouragement, and is once again a type of Mary, to whom it will in due course be given. Then God opens her eyes and she sees a well of water. Once more she anticipates the experience of Israel itself (see Exod. 15:25,27). And this happens yet again when her child as he grows knows the reality of God being 'with him', like his father (Gen. 21:20,22).

Abraham and Sarah are our spiritual ancestors; their relationship with God contains promises for ours. But Hagar is our spiritual mother too, and so does hers.

SEVEN

Jacob and Esau

Some of the stories of Israel's ancestors in Genesis are introduced in a puzzling way. What we think of as the story of Jacob and Esau begins by announcing itself as the story of Isaac and his family (Gen. 25:19) and continues to view itself as that until we read of Isaac's death (35:29). That partly makes up for the fact that there are not many stories of Isaac himself. What we are now to read is the story of Isaac and Rebekah and their family, even though it is the story of their sons. In Genesis the story of parents is tied up with who their children are going to be and how they turn out. To some extent that is commonly so; it is the burden of children that their parents' own sense of being, identity, and achievement, their hopes, fears, and joys, are often tied up with their children. In these stories of Israel's ancestors there is the special factor that by God's own design the relationship between the ancestors and God is tied up with their children. Their spirituality is what we have called a spirituality of the promise, they live toward the future that God is promising them, and that future centrally relates to the gift of children through whom they will become a numerous people. In this sense the story of Isaac *is* the story of Esau and Jacob.

Jacob's family background

So a burden that Esau and Jacob carry is that they are so
important to their parents. It is a burden to both sides.
We watch Isaac and Rebekah watching their children
grow up and fight with each other. We watch Esau and
Jacob carrying the burden of mattering so much to their
parents, of their parents' hopes and fears being so tied
up with them.

We have seen that their father was the child born of
God's promise. Their mother was herself someone who
came from the wider family of their grandfather
Abraham. Isaac had known that there was to be no
marrying out among the Canaanites; he was to find a
wife from among the people of God, and having found
one, he had loved her. Rebekah and Isaac look an ideal
couple. They have everything going for them. Their
wedding ought to be the beginning of a marriage and
family story in which everyone lives happily ever after.
But that is not how it works out. Like her mother-
in-law, Rebekah cannot have children, and she carries
the same burden that Sarai carried, the burden of any
would-be mother or father and the particular burden of
someone who is supposed to bear that promise of God.

So Rebekah and Isaac do the same thing as any other
couple in the situation. You go to the doctor, she gives
you some pills, later she sends you to the hospital, they
do some tests, they tell you to do some exercises, they
offer you an operation, and if none of that works you
try *in vitro* fertilization or you borrow someone else's
womb. One way or another in modern 'developed'
countries there are often ways of making it possible for
an infertile couple to have a baby (though that may
make it harder for people for whom these techniques do
not work). In traditional societies these techniques are
of course unavailable. So what Isaac did was pray. It
was a bold act, because such prayers are sometimes
granted but sometimes not, and there is no hiding from
whether or not such prayers have indeed been granted.

Nor do you know, until you have prayed the prayer, which will be the case. My wife Ann has multiple sclerosis and we have prayed for her to be physically healed. She has not been. You pray some prayers and they are granted; you pray other prayers and they are not. Every time you pray for something that matters, you are taking a risk, putting your faith on the line. Isaac and Rebekah had to do that.

To be strictly accurate, Isaac did (Gen. 25:21). Now that may be because praying was the man's job (or did he wonder whether the problem might be his? – the Bible always refers to the woman being infertile or to Yahweh's having closed her womb, but of course in many cases the infertility will actually be the man's). Yet we have met women such as Hagar who prayed, and we will meet women such as Hannah who did, so perhaps there is another consideration at work. Perhaps that element of risk makes it harder for Rebekah to pray such a prayer than it was for Isaac. I find it easier to let other people pray for Ann's healing than to do so myself. That is one reason for the importance of intercessory prayer. Within the people of God we ask for each other the things that we might hesitate to ask for ourselves, the things in respect of which we cannot handle the risk. I admire Isaac's bravery in praying this prayer which was so important to him, too, and which might have received a negative answer (was it easier or harder because of the miracle of his own birth?).

In turn the fact that they themselves were born in answer to their parents' prayer was another privilege and burden that Esau and Jacob carry around with them. Every baby is God-given, but they were God-given in a special sense, almost as if they were called by God from the womb like a prophet such as Jeremiah. They were people with whom God was specially involved from the very beginning of their life, indeed from before the beginning of their life, people in whom God was working out a purpose before they were even conceived. That is also true of all of us, yet true of them in a special sense.

But there are two parents, and there are two sons. Once there are two children in a family it is easy for one parent to love one more than another. A father may well love an elder son because he is the elder, the senior, the one on whom the father's responsibility for the family will in due course fall. A mother may love a younger son because he is the baby of the family. Isaac indeed favoured Esau, who was good at catching the game that Esau liked, while Rebekah favoured Jacob. Thus Esau and Jacob also have to live with the burden of their parents' favouritism. Their story is characterized by a whole series of conflicts – between Esau and Jacob, between Jacob and Laban (over who he is to marry and in due course over whose sheep are which), between Jacob and his wives, between Jacob and God. If the actual origin of those conflicts hardly lay in their parents' attitudes to them, the conflicts were at least fed by them.

The point is illustrated by an event which took place when they were middle-aged men facing the eventual death of their father. Knowing that his end must come one day, Isaac calls for his eldest son, who has the right according to customary law to inherit the major part of his property. This might seem unfair, but it does go along with having particular responsibilities for the family. Esau, however, is also Isaac's favourite son. 'Esau.' 'Yes?' 'I am getting on. Who knows how long I have left? Now. Go down to town and get one of those superb pizzas, not just cheese and tomato but ham and chilli and red pepper and pineapple and mushroom – the full house. I want you and me to have a meal on our own together. And there I am going to pass on to you my blessing.' Blessing suggests fulness of life and prosperity, which God gives a father the authority to pass on in the way that he wishes. In our terms, Isaac wants to make his will, to make his key bequests before he dies.

Of course it is not only when they die that parents

pass on the blessing. They share with their children their genetic blessing, their environmental blessing (the kind of home in which they bring them up), and their financial blessing. Like other children, Esau and Jacob already live with the burden, the responsibility, and the privilege of being shaped and blessed by their parents. But now Isaac plans a formal blessing for Esau, and Rebekah hears him doing so. She says to her own favourite son Jacob, 'Look, your father has sent Esau for a pizza. Go and get one from the freezer. I've got some spare mushrooms and ham. It will take an hour for him to get to town and back. We'll pull a fast one on that no-good brother of yours'. Jacob is sharp enough to remember that there is a physical difference between him and his brother which goes back to their birth. Esau's arms and chest are covered in manly hair. Jacob is more effeminate. 'Don't worry', says Rebekah. 'Get some of those furry carpet tiles from the bedroom and put them around you. Then your father in his dotage will think you are just like Esau.' So he does, and Isaac fortunately ends up eating the pizza and feeling the tiling and not the other way round, and he blesses Jacob.

'The smell of my son is like the smell of a field which Yahweh has blessed. May God give you of heaven's dew and of earth's richness, an abundance of corn and new wine. May nations serve you, peoples bow down to you. May you be lord over your brothers, may your mother's sons bow to you. Cursed be everyone who curses you, blessed be everyone who blesses you!' God's blessing is being passed on from father to son, on a basis of intrigue and deception.

Esau is about to discover that life is not fair. It is not. No matter how hard I work at it I will never understand computers like my elder son or play the guitar like my younger son. No matter how hard you work, you may not get as good exam results as the next person (who works less). There are inequalities in the amount of money, beauty, and good fortune that we have. Esau

and Jacob have to live with the burden and the privilege
of the fact that the hand that life deals you is not
necessarily fair. It leads to Esau's holding a quite
reasonable grudge against Jacob and planning to kill
him. Rebekah hears of that and sends Jacob off into
exile until his brother's fury subsides and he can return,
and so that she does not lose both of them in one day,
as she puts it.

It is yet another extraordinary story to find in the
Bible. God appears little, and it makes little mention of
the things that we may think that God is about. But it
sets Esau and Jacob's whole story, often tawdry, within
the context of the purpose of God. It reassures us that
whatever is the shape of our equivalent burdens,
responsibilities, and privileges, these are all part of the
way that God deals with us – or rather are capable of
becoming part of the way God deals with us.

The person of Jacob

But who was the man Jacob himself? The personality
began to emerge before he was born. When Rebekah
became pregnant, it transpired that she was going to
have twins – twin boys, but not identical. The first to be
actually born was swarthy in colour with lots of hair,
and that links with two alternative names he receives in
the story, Edom ('red') and Esau (which apparently
meant 'hairy', see Gen. 25:25). When in turn his brother
was born just after him, he seemed to be reaching after
Esau, trying to grab his heel. And that links with his
own name and personality. He was called Jacob, which
means 'he grasps the heel' or 'he supplants' or 'he
deceives'.

In financial and in other respects, Jacob is always
going to be number two. It would be hard to see so
much extra wealth and prestige going to your big
brother, just because he was older than you – ten
minutes older than you, in Jacob's case. Ten minutes

shaped Jacob's destiny and personality. He was always number two, and always wanted to be number one. People could see it in him from when he was a baby, from that moment when he slipped out of Rebekah's womb, already trying to catch up with Esau before he had cried his first cry or sucked his first mouthful of milk.

As Red and Grabber grew up together, Red became an accomplished hunter, a man of the open country, self-sufficient, capable, active, interesting, though easy-going. As we have seen, he was a young man who fulfilled his father's ambitions. Grabber was a quieter sort of person, more a stay-at-home, more the cook than the hunter, more his mother's boy. But he grew up as what his name suggested. That in part explains why his story is so dominated by conflict. The conflict emerges from the kind of personality he had, the kind which assumes that one makes it in life by grabbing, by reaching for things. That way Jacob finds blessings (he gains much) but also conflict.

One day when the two young men are teenagers or young adults, not yet married, Grabber is cooking a politically-correct lentil casserole. Red comes in from the open country. 'I'm starving', he says. 'Give me some of that red stew' ('red' comes in again). 'OK', says Grabber: 'Give me your birthright in return for it' – give me the rights that belong to you as the firstborn son in the family. 'All right', Esau yawns. 'Come on, I'm dying of hunger. Who cares about the birthright?' Jacob cares. 'Swear to me the birthright first.' 'So he swore an oath to him, selling his birthright.' That is how laid-back Esau despised his birthright, and how ambitious Jacob seized the opportunity to grab it from him. The same dynamics appear in that story of Jacob's swindling Esau out of their father's blessing, this time without Rebecca's connivance. Jacob's personality emerges as what his name says it is.

Later another funny story takes these issues further.

As a result of swindling Esau out of the blessing, Jacob
has to go off into exile. He journeys to the east, to the
region where his ancestors came from. As well as
finding a safe place to live while the situation cools off
back home, he is also to look for a wife, in the same area
as his father had found one, back where his family had
come from. He arrives at a well, and the macho Jacob
exposes the laziness and feebleness of the local shepherds
who cannot raise enough strength to push the stone
cover off the well in order to water the sheep. He thus
has opportunity to demonstrate his muscles before the
spectacular Rachel who has meanwhile arrived and
whom he rather fancies. Fortuitously it transpires that
she indeed comes from the family of Laban from which
his own mother had originally come, so this is how
Jacob finds someone who seems in every way the right
kind of wife. But there is one major difference in the
story from the account of how Isaac found Rebekah.
There Yahweh kept guiding, and people kept seeking
Yahweh's guidance. Here the story makes no mention
of God. Yahweh is involved through this scene in
Jacob's story, no doubt, but it is noteworthy that there is
no mention of that activity and no mention of people
seeking Yahweh's guidance. Yahweh was working out
a purpose even though people were not seeking
guidance, rather than because they were.

So Jacob finds the girl of his dreams. But he has to
earn her, and then has the same kind of trick played on
him as he had played on Esau. He offers to work for
Laban for seven years if he can marry Rachel. The
couple are thus engaged for seven years, but it seemed
like only a few days to Jacob because he loved Rachel so
much, Genesis touchingly tells us. Jacob the hard man,
the calculator, turns out to be soft-centred, and of
course it will be his downfall. Laban organizes a
wedding reception at which no doubt plenty of wine is
drunk, and as darkness falls Jacob takes his wife off in
her veils to the marriage tent. Then when morning
comes, dawn breaks, and Jacob brings his bride a cup of

tea – it is not Rachel but her big sister Leah, whom Jacob knows very well and knows he did not want to marry.

In any list of scenes in the Bible one would like to have witnessed, that must be near the top, to see the look in Jacob's eyes. Admittedly most people find that the person we marry is in a sense a different person from the one we courted, and in that sense we can identify with Jacob's experience. 'Well,' said Laban, 'I couldn't give you Rachel first, could I? Leah's the eldest, she has to marry first'. Jacob has been caught by his own trick as he once again tries to get the younger ahead of the elder, to make number two number one. 'Of course you can have Rachel as well if you serve another seven years for *her*', says Laban. And Jacob does, without even asking a reduction for quantity.

So Laban cheats the expert cheat of the girl he wanted and gets another seven years of work out of Jacob before he can have the girl he thought he was working the first seven years for. Grabber finds that in personal relationships other people can use the same techniques as he does. He has been concerned to avoid the firstborn having his rights; when he himself wanted the second-born, Rachel, the rights of Leah as the firstborn are asserted over against him by Laban. As a result he finds himself married to two competitive sisters, with an exploitative father, and he is caught between them all. The justice is poetic. Jacob finds that life plays tricks on him, yet that in all this God is at work.

Since the first kick in the womb which Jacob gave to Esau, he has battled to get the rights of the firstborn. And this is a key factor in making his story a story of conflict. The conflicts in the family which now begin are manifold. His sons are born in the context of the envy of these two women for each other, a context of rivalry and argument between Rachel, the woman who is loved but childless, and Leah, the woman who is unloved but fertile. Yet for all this conflict, Jacob is the man who keeps coming out on top, who always falls on his feet. He is in conflict with Esau, but the result of his fleeing into exile is that he gets a wife out of it. He is in conflict with Laban, but it is Jacob who ends up with the best of the flocks. There is conflict in relation to his wives, but he does get the children that God had promised him. Why is that?

The key to the answer to that question may emerge from something which had happened when Esau had been roused by his deceit. Jacob has to flee up into the Judean mountains, flee into country he has heard of but never seen, flee until there is no chance that even the hunter Esau will catch him, flee even though there is no place for him to lay his head. He has not yet reached the country where Laban, Leah, and Rachel live, but he has left the area where Isaac, Rebekah, and Esau live. He is in between, on a journey, on the way, in neither one place nor the other. Moreover he is running away not only from Esau but from the promised land, on his way out of the land that God had given to his father and grandfather and promised to him. He is running away from the place of blessing, the place of the very blessing that he has cheated Esau out of. And in the midst of his running away, in a no-place, neither one thing nor the other, God meets him.

He has stopped, just because darkness has come. Even Jacob cannot run all night; he has to stop to sleep. It would be dangerous, I imagine, but not as dangerous as stopping earlier and taking the slightest risk that Esau will catch up with him. Jacob sleeps, and dreams, and his dreams are the dreams of a man full of conflict, turmoil, fear, guilt and uncertainty. God is miles away. But this is where he meets God – or rather, where God meets him. The story offers no hint that this is a moment when Jacob is seeking God or would have a right to meet with God. But it is the moment when God chooses to meet with Jacob – for whenever God chooses to meet with us, it is of course an outworking of God's grace. It emerges from God's freedom, God's sovereignty, God's love, God's power, and God's control. So this is not a moment when Jacob meets God, but when God meets Jacob. There was nothing in Grabber to make it happen. But God meets him.

Jacob is allowed to see the invisible staircase the angels use on their trips from heaven and back, when they are about fulfilling God's purpose. There is a later occasion in the Old Testament, in a story about Elisha, when a scared young friend of his has his eyes opened to the horses and chariots of fire that are always there to protect Elisha. This is God's world, and there is always more going on than meets the eye. There is always a staircase between earth and heaven for the use of God's aides as they go about their master's business. Usually we cannot see it, but it is always there. Jacob's eyes are opened so that it is visible to him. Note incidentally that it is one of the passages that shows that angels do not have wings, otherwise they would not need a staircase. Angels are like human beings, and they walk between earth and heaven, which helps them to keep fit.

God enables Jacob to see them doing this, and speaks to him. 'I am Yahweh, the God of your father Abraham, the God of Isaac.' Remember my person, remember who I am. Here on the edge of nowhere, where you are not really sure where you are going, certainly not sure what the future will hold, remember who I am and who I have been. And remember my promise. 'I will give you and your descendants the land upon which you are lying'; for though he has travelled several days' journey north from Beersheba towards Haran, he is not yet out of the land of promise. 'Your descendants will be like the dust of the earth. They will spread to west and east, north and south. All the peoples on earth will pray to be blessed in the manner of you and your offspring.' It is a simple reassertion of the promise that God had long been making to Jacob's family. What God does at this point when Jacob is in desperate need is to remind him of that promise, of what God is committed to doing, because it is still true. The promises of God emerge from the grace of God and not from what we deserve, and they therefore can and do still stand when we have got ourselves into a no-place and are on our way into exile because of the mess we make of our lives.

God's words may still seem somewhat irresponsible. We might have expected something along the lines of 'Now Jacob, are you beginning to learn your lesson? Are you on the verge of giving in to me, so that I can start using you?' No, that is not the kind of thing the God of the Bible says. It is too predictable and legalistic. It presupposes that God is one who treats us according to our desert. The God of the Bible takes some pathetic rogue like Jacob or Peter or you or me and undertakes a wild, extravagant commitment to him or her, without regard to desert. This God is very different from the legalistic god we spend most of our time subconsciously believing in.

Further, Jacob is invited to remember God's presence. 'I am with you', says God, or 'I will be with you' (the statement can be read either way and the context has to guide us regarding which way to read it; here the future must surely at least be included). 'I will watch over you wherever you go and will bring you back to this land. I will not leave you until I have done what I promised you.' Much of God's promise to Jacob has repeated statements to people such as Abraham, Hagar, and Isaac, but the close of God's words with its affirmation of God's presence is tailored to Jacob in particular. It is the special aspect of God's promise as it is given to Isaac and his children. It is exactly the undertaking that Jacob needs as he goes off into a foreign land, not sure what he will find; and what he is going to find there will be in some ways very tricky. On the way out of the land of promise Jacob has no reason to think that God is with him. On the verge of this unknown in his life, brought about by his own manipulative stupidity, he is promised God's presence with him.

Having had God meet with him and speak to him, Jacob makes a *form* of commitment to God. 'If God *will*

be with me, and *will* watch over me on this journey that
I am taking, and *will* give me food to eat and clothes to
wear, so that I am able to come back to my father's
house . . . .' It is a marvellous beginning to a sentence:
three clauses about God all beginning with 'if'. In other
words, given that I know which side my bread is
buttered and didn't get where I am today without
having an eye to the main chance – then I had better let
Yahweh be my God. Unsurprisingly, the grabber is as
calculating in his relationship with God as he is in the
rest of his life, with a winsome ingenuousness and
honesty. 'If Yahweh is going to do all that, I had better
let him be my God, and this stone which I have set up
as a pillar can be God's house, and of all that Yahweh
gives me I will give him a tenth'. (Well, that's fair, isn't
it, you give me as much as you like, I'll give you a tenth
back?) Jacob receives a revelation from God, and wants
to turn it into an institution and into a contract. It is not
much of a commitment, but perhaps God took the view
that at least it was something. God always has to start
with us where we are and work out a purpose through
us despite what we are and despite even the severe
limitations of the commitments we are prepared to
make.

The destiny of Jacob

So Jacob had to live with who he was, with his
personality, as well as with his background and
circumstances (and more to the point, perhaps, so did
everyone else). He also had to live with his destiny,
with what God purposed for him. This too was already
announced before his birth. When Esau and Jacob were
already jostling in Rebekah's womb, she not unreason-
ably asked, 'Why is this happening to me?' She asked
the question not merely rhetorically, as we might, but
seriously. And there came a word from God with the
answer. 'There are two nations in your womb. Two

peoples from within you will be separated. One will be stronger than the other, and the older will serve the younger' (Gen 25:23).

There is the outline of Jacob's whole story, of the destiny God set in front of him to be worked out over his life as a whole. Presumably it is possible for God to contemplate the destiny of each of us and it would be possible for each of us to have this destiny revealed at the beginning, though we might prefer this not to happen. It happens to only a handful of people in scripture. A word from God stands at the beginning of Jacob's story, and we see its being put into effect in what follows. The word is one which explicitly speaks of rivalry and of the preferment of the younger over the older. Jacob is someone who is to live a blessed life, a charmed life. In this way God intends to overturn the way the social structure generally worked, with its expectation that the older son would have seniority and privilege. God often disturbs such orderings, not feeling obliged to work the way the world thinks is a good idea. God chooses the foolish things of the world to shame the wise, the weak things to shame the strong, the lowly and despised things, even things that do not exist at all, to nullify the things that do exist, so that no one may boast in the presence of God (1 Cor. 1:27–29).

There was nothing wrong with Esau, except (as it were) that he could have boasted before God. He was the first son, the attractive character, Mr Nice Guy. Jacob was the foolish, the lowly, in order to show that it was God who was at work, and that the way we might expect things to eventuate in this world is not how they necessarily eventuate in practice. There is no other explanation for Yahweh's preferring of Jacob. In a sense there is a randomness about God's choice of us. There is no reason for self-congratulation when we realize that we have come to know Christ, whereas other people have not. It perhaps means that we are people like Jacob, not that we are holy, insightful, wise, or sensible. At least as likely the background is God's extraordinary preference for reaching the world through people who do not look very spectacular. Jacob was the junior, lowly, despised, not very nice; it is purely because of God's word that he lives a blessed life.

Yet it is also because of that word (as the answer to Rebekah's question makes clear) that Jacob lives a troubled life, a life of conflict. To Jacob God brings not peace but a sword. To Jacob God says, 'In the world you will have tribulation'. His story of conflict on all sides is a story that God led him into and one somehow involved in God's fulfilling a purpose for him and through him. God's election is a blessing; it gives us a charmed life. It is also a burden; it gives us a troubled life.

Jacob works for Laban for 14 years, and indeed gets on even better than Laban himself. In due course he becomes the number one sheep-farmer in Haran, which arouses Laban's jealousy and thus Jacob's anxiety. It looks time to run again. Where will you go this time Jacob? On across the northern horizon? Off to the east into the real desert, where you can run and run till no one can find you? Where will you find another fresh start, Jacob? (Jacob always reminds me of Travis striding through the desert with determined directionlessness in the film *Paris, Texas*.)

At this moment Yahweh speaks again, for the first time since the dream at Bethel. 'All right, Jacob, it's time to move, but not time to keep on running. Get back, Jacob, back to the land of your fathers, back to your family.' Back to Esau, does that mean? 'I'll be with you', Yahweh says, the same way as he had said it at Bethel when Jacob was on the way out of the promised land. He had promised that he would go with Jacob through that dangerous exit as he ran away from his responsibilities, his past, his personality, and his destiny, promised that he would be with him as he ran away. He has been with him, protected him, and prospered him (though not changed him, as far as one can tell). So now when God again says 'I will be with you', there is reason to believe it. Maybe Yahweh could take Jacob back to face Esau, back to face his family, his past, and his responsibilities. Maybe we can take the risk of facing such things if God says 'I'll be with you as you do it'.

God's reasserted promise ought to mean that things will turn out all right. But as the story unfolds, things move first one way, then another. Jacob is met by God's angels; but Jacob is scared stiff, sending messengers to meet Esau, and not reassured by the message that comes back from him. Jacob is praying, movingly and sincerely, as far as one can tell, as he casts himself on God; but Jacob is then calculating as ever, dividing his company into two so that if one gets slaughtered he still has the other. There is a winsome ambiguity and ambivalence about him. At one moment he can pray and listen to God speak to him, at the next he is deceiving and calculating.

It is in the context of all this that God once more meets with Jacob as he approaches the River Jabbok. As it was in the context of fear, anxiety, conflict and guilt that God met him fleeing into exile, so it is in that context that God meets him on the way back to the land of promise. One cannot separate the context from the meetings with God. Jacob's story assumes that there are no troubles and no troubled relationships that have to be separated off from the possibility of God's meeting with us, and perhaps that there are no meetings with God except ones which take seriously the realities of troubled human life with its conflicts and struggles.

Once again he shows himself still the same old Jacob, calculating, street-wise. He sends friendly greetings on ahead to Esau, and the messengers return with the news that Esau is coming to meet Jacob personally with 400 men. Which Jacob interprets the obvious way (though it was the wrong way) and infers that high noon is approaching. Jacob panics, though he stays the calculator, dividing his family and flocks into two groups so that if Esau gets one, the other lot may get away, and everything will not be lost. And he prays.

This is the only time in his story that Jacob prays voluntarily, opens a conversation with God, and it is because he is in a panic. It is interesting that the story does not tell whether God was listening.

Whatever Yahweh's response to the prayer was, Jacob carries on assuming he is responsible for his own destiny. He sends 200 female goats, 20 male goats, 200 ewes, 20 rams, 30 female camels and their young, 40 cows, 10 bulls, 20 female donkeys, and 10 male donkeys, herd by herd, to try to buy Esau off. We are invited to imagine Esau's face. He is just looking forward to seeing his long lost brother, but will never be able to get through to him for goats, camels, and donkeys, and all because Jacob, poor little Jacob, wanted to be number one.

I am number one: principal of the college where I teach. I never had any aspirations in that direction and was quite happy as number two, but circumstances happened to work out in an unexpected way and here I am, number one. I could start enjoying it. My wife says I look different when I walk up the path towards college – I look as if I am enjoying myself, as if I own the place. That is the Jacob instinct.

You count if you are number one. The college trains people for ministry, and a tough aspect of that training is that during it people are no longer number one in the sense they may have been before. They were teachers, managers, or social workers and what they said at work decided things. Now they are in the position of students, workers, or clients, and it feels more like being controlled than controlling, more like Jacob than Esau. One of the things that makes college interesting is that different people have so many good ideas for improving college – starting a hang-gliding class or a synchronized swimming team. But one stimulus to people's dreaming up new activities like that is the subconscious desire to make one's mark, to count, to be number one. Clergy, too, like to be number one. That is partly why people offer themselves for the ministry.

They look forward to running their own church. They are Jacob.

Jacob always wanted to be number one. So God rejected him? No! Once again the Bible surprises us. It turns out that this haunted man is the one God chooses. It is not exactly because he always wanted to be number one, though it is not far from that. It is indeed because he was only number two. The pattern that runs through the Old Testament is that God supports the number two: Isaac, not Ishmael; Joseph, not Reuben, Simeon, or any of Jacob's older sons; David, not any of his big brothers. God works through the number two, not the number one, to show that it is God who works, to show his contempt for the way the world arranges things, to show that the things that people call weak and foolish may turn out to be true strength and wisdom. The foolishness of the cross is already advertised in God deciding he will work through feeble Isaac, about whom they could not think of any stories to tell, and through insufferable Joseph with his dreams of his elder brothers bowing down to him, and through driven, obsessed, haunted Jacob, looking for the fool's gold of being number one.

Perhaps the reason why God takes hold of some people and calls them to the ministry is that they wanted to be number one and God can even use someone with that motivation for his purpose. But then when he has them in the ministry and they are preoccupied with running their own church, as they will put it, he will have to make the point again by using ordinary people in the way he does not use them. I should never have been principal, I should only have been number two, but now I am number one, so God will actually use 'ordinary' tutors to show that he is not dependent on the numbers we put on ourselves or on each other. The suburbs are number one and the city is number two, and you can see the people of the city having to be street-wise like Jacob if they are to survive, let alone to catch up, but maybe God will make the city the object of his blessing precisely because it is number two. The Western Church is number one, the elder brother, with the money, the resources, the cathedrals, the tradition, and the power, but perhaps it is already the case that God is therefore making the church in Africa, Asia, and Latin America the object of blessing and the means of blessing the world. It is dangerous to be number one.

Jacob has proved that he can get the best of anybody – Isaac, Esau, Laban, he will be number one. Then he is alone at the River Jabbok when he has a mysterious encounter. A man wrestles with him throughout the night. It is often termed the story of Jacob's wrestling with God, but that is a double misunderstanding – at least partially so. First, the story does does not describe Jacob as taking the initiative in this match. Someone takes Jacob on. If prayer is about wrestling with God, this offers an extraordinary insight into the nature of that struggle. It concerns God taking us on, not us taking God on. Second, while Jacob's assailant is indeed God (so it will become clear in due course), at the beginning it is not clear. Is this other person a man? Is it a demon? Is it Esau himself? Is it a figment of Jacob's imagination? Is it an angel? Is it God? Jacob does not yet know.

It is the match of a lifetime for both parties. Jacob turns out to be not the sort of lonely traveller who will collapse at one blow and beg you to take his credit cards as well as his wallet. He more resembles Crocodile Dundee demolishing the mugger with his boomerang. That is Jacob; except that this is no ordinary mugger. Both participants in this match get more than they bargain for. They fight all night; it is evidently a very even match. Only at the end of the night does the assailant win, by doing something special, almost by cheating; once again Jacob is the recipient as well as the exponent of below-the-belt treatment. Seeing that he was going to win in no other way, his assailant touched the socket of Jacob's hip and strained or dislocated it.

'Let me go, it's daybreak': perhaps that is a hint that this is in some sense God who is wrestling with Jacob, for Jacob must be protected from looking on God as the light dawns, from seeing God's mystery. 'Let me go!' But even now Jacob does not give in. He still holds on. That is what being number one is about. 'I am not going to let you go unless you *bless* me.' You might think that Jacob has done enough to ensure blessing and has known enough blessing in experience. The story is about blessing, yet this exhausted prayer reveals an insecurity in Jacob, always concerned for blessing. It haunts him. He ever seeks it. Perhaps he knows that blessing that is won by cheating and deceit is not really possessed or enjoyed because of the way it is obtained. 'I will not let you go unless you bless me.'

'All right, then. What is your name?' What has that got to do with it? Everything, apparently. Everything hangs on a name, in a culture where names mean something. 'My name's Jacob' – Grabber. Is he having to acknowledge something about himself, to come to terms with who he is? Grabber by name, grabber by nature? 'You're not going to be Grabber any longer', says Jacob's mysterious wrestling partner. The idea does not seem to be that he is suddenly – or even gradually – to become a different personality. There is little evidence that he does, and it would be a strange thing for God to do, to change Jacob's created personality. There was nothing wrong with Jacob's personality, with the drive, the aggression. When God gives a person a new name, as happened when Simon became Peter, it means that God gives them a new destiny. God purposes to do something with them and guarantees it, because their name states their destiny and calling as God promises it will be. God was going to use his personality, not change it.

'Your name will no longer be Jacob, Grabber, but Israel.' 'Israel' means 'God struggles'. And God does: struggles with Jacob, struggles with Israel, struggles with the church, struggles with each of us individually,

winning perhaps half the time, but persevering. But the
Bible likes punning with names, and instead of picking
up the obvious meaning of Jacob's new name it
presupposes a different idea, the idea of Jacob as the
struggler, which he certainly is. 'You have struggled
with God and with human beings and you have won.'
You have beaten Esau and Isaac and Laban and even
God himself. The mysterious wrestler speaks on behalf
of the defeated God who remains God even in defeat.

There is further significance in God's speaking to one
called Israel. This is not merely a name with a meaning
but one with a reference. Everyone who heard this story
in Israel knew at this point that the story had been
about them. If it is about Israel, it is also about us,
because we belong to Israel now. We hear the story of
Jacob the grabber and in it we find ourselves, in it we
hear the story of the church, but in letting us hear it God
says to us 'I know, the church is like that, always
struggling with me, often defeating me, but it's OK, I
can live with that, I don't have to be number one you
see, that's your problem'.

Is it indeed God? Jacob says, 'Please tell me your
name'. 'Why do you ask my name?' To know the name
of God is to know something powerful, something as
powerful and dangerous in its way as seeing God.
Instead of declaring the name, God blessed Jacob,
reverting to his first request. And Jacob called the place
Peni-El, 'Face of God', explaining 'It is because I
saw God face to face, yet my life is spared'. When
mysterious forces have assailed Jacob and all but
defeated him, it turns out that this very process, this
very force, is actually God, assailing Jacob not in order
to destroy but in order to make him. Admittedly when
the sun rose above him as he passed Peni-El, Jacob was
limping because of what his assailant had done to his
hip. And that too is part of the making. Jacob limps off
into history from this point. From now on, Jacob is
someone with a disablement, disabled because of God's
work with him. God is the one who gives him the

blessing, God is the one who gives him the disablement. Somehow these two belong together.

Jacob is turned into Israel, though perhaps not a changed person. Now strikingly, there is indeed an apparently changed person in this story. It is Esau. He behaves differently from the way he did before. It is not so obvious that Jacob is a changed person, any more than Simon was after he became Peter. 'You Israel, you're only grabber Jacob with a new name. But it's OK, I'll be with you, I'll still achieve my purpose, whether through your defeating me or your walking with me. It's all the same to me.'

Jacob does fulfil his destiny, that he should be the ancestor of a nation that would stand for God before other nations. It is less clear whether God's destiny for Jacob as a person is fulfilled, whether God succeeds in shaping Jacob himself. Jacob's story is one of those biblical stories which are left open, not clearly resolved. The result of that in the providence of God in giving scripture to us in this form is that such stories make us ask what is happening in God's purpose for us. We cannot see whether God succeeds with David or Peter or Jacob. The story can be read either way. The question that is thus pressed on us is which way are we going to read it as we look at our own lives in its light. The story resembles *The French Lieutenant's Woman*, which had two endings. You had to choose your ending. You have to do the same with the Jacob story. Is it one in which Jacob is transformed in accordance with God's purpose for him, or one in which he carries on with the same old weaknesses in his character to his dying day? You have to choose your ending in the sense of deciding which one matches you, and which will match you in the future.

EIGHT

Joseph and his Brothers

Like Jacob's story, what we think of as Joseph's story begins in an odd way, with the introduction 'Jacob lived in the country where his father stayed, the country of Canaan. This is the story of Jacob's family' (Gen. 37:1). It will (almost) end that way, too, with the story of Jacob's death, which occupies three whole chapters at the virtual end of the book (47:28–50:21). The story of Joseph and his brothers is the story of Jacob, or the story of Israel, the story of how Jacob becomes Israel. Once again we recall that the people for whom this story was written and by whom it was heard comprised Israel, Jacob. Israel looks back to this story and finds itself, more explicitly than is the case with most other stories. And more tellingly, for it is a story of tension in the family, of family strife.

In romantic theologies of the people of God, their life is characterized by love, understanding, oneness, and mutual support. In real life it is characterized by tension, disagreement, conflict, and rivalry. This was so with Old Testament Israel. It is so with the contemporary Jewish people, divided into orthodox and liberal and messianic. It is so with the State of Israel, divided into hawks and doves, labour and conservative, Ashkenazim and Sephardim, religious and secular. It is so with the church, long divided into denominations many of whom do not recognize the validity of each other's ministries. The denominations are themselves further divided into more conservative or more liberal, favouring or opposed to the ordination of women, accepting homosexuality or opposed to it, and unchurching people who take differing views. All these divisions would be even more depressing if scripture did not reassure us that it has always been so, not only in the New Testament but in the days of Jacob himself.

For Jacob had these twelve sons (and daughters, too). Now a lone child has no one to play with and no one to fight with. Two children lack those problems. Twelve have scope for innumerable combinations of play and conflict, and have the stimulus with regard to the latter, the need to compete for food, attention, and inheritance. Vast is the wisdom needed by the parents of such a family.

Unfortunately parents in Genesis are not wise figures. The world's first parents made the first mistake, Abram, Sarai, and Hagar (we have seen) set up a *ménage à trois* that worked no better than you would expect, while Isaac and Rebekah each favoured one of their twin sons – as the other twin no doubt noticed. And it is one of these two, his mother's boy, rejected by his father, who now has the task of holding together twelve sons. The signs are not good. But the story shows God managing to make it all work out (reasonably well) – and doing so once again by protecting the younger and overturning the seniorities and priorities that human beings set up.

Joseph the dreamer

The story begins with an adolescent boy, one of the youngest in the family (so actually we will not be surprised if he ends up on top, for we have read the preceding stories in Genesis). He is the darling of his father's old age, but also the first son of Jacob's first love, Rachel. He is Jacob's favourite, and everyone knows it; Jacob is as unwise as his father in his favouritism. Joseph's famous coat draws attention to all this. In a sense, then, Joseph is actually number one. He is the spoilt child, and he is a tell-tale. You could hardly blame his brothers for not liking him. Like us, these parents and children live in tangled triangles of loving and being loved, too much and too little (Walter Brueggemann).

Then there were his dreams. Act One of Joseph's story concerns Joseph the dreamer. 'Hey guys, I had this dream of us at harvest, and the sheaf I was tying stood upright and your sheaves gathered round and lay down prostrate before my sheaf. I wonder what that means? And I had this other dream of the sun and the moon and eleven stars prostrating themselves to me. I wonder what that means?' It is one thing to dream barely-concealed allegories of his brothers and his parents bowing down to him. It is another to tell everyone as soon as he wakes up. The brothers can smell the prospect of one person ruling, having domination over others (Gen. 37:8) – the language has not been used since Genesis 3. It designates one effect in the world of people turning away from God. But it is exactly what will happen.

So Joseph's dreams naturally generate resentment, jealousy, and rebuke. Dreams can be divisive. Today in the land of Joseph (and in London and New York) the descendants of Jacob and Esau, two sets of brothers, cousins to each other, with people who believe in Jesus among both groups, live with a terrible wall of hostility between them. This is so because of their dreams, because they have the same dream, because they dream of the land they have and the land they do not have and the land they might lose, the same land, and not least because they dream of a city ('Next year in Jerusalem') they have or half-have or do not have or might lose.

One cannot blame people for their dreams (or can one?

– we hardly need to be Sigmund Freud, one of Jacob's great descendants, dream interpreter *par excellence*, to read suspiciously between the lines of Joseph's dreams). The Bible assumes that dreams can be God's way of revealing the future, and these dreams are exactly that. On the other hand, we are not told that these dreams came from God – the question is left open whether they just came from Joseph's own 'inflated ego' (Gordon Wenham). Paradoxically, it will turn out that the naive unwisdom of Joseph's revealing his dreams sets in motion the process which leads to their fulfilment. Like other words of God, as well as revealing the future, they effect the future.

When people are divided by their dreams, they do not just squabble like children but fight like adults, with knives and rocks and clubs and guns and petrol bombs. Dreams harbinger death. So it was for Joseph.

Jacob and his family live near Hebron, in a mountain valley south of Jerusalem, but they are shepherds rather than farmers, which implies a form of semi-nomadic existence. You have a home, a family base, but the men need to move around with the sheep to keep them sustained, especially during the summer when rain stops falling and grass stops growing. So Jacob (evidently too old for all that) sends Joseph (evidently too young for it or perhaps excluded by those brotherly feuds) to check out how the brothers are getting on as they pasture the sheep further north where there is more rain and thus more pasturage. Literally, he has to check out the *shalom* of his brothers (and their flocks!) (Gen. 37:14). It is an irony, because their father's favouritism made them incapable of speaking *shalom* with him (37:4). It might have taken him a week to get to Shechem (the modern Nablus), where he expected to find them; there he learnt that they had had to carry on even further north, to Dothan (those modern dreams wreak their terrible fruit here too: it would be an unwise descendant of Jacob who today asked the way in Nablus, though one does not stop praying that things may be different tomorrow).

As he wound his way down from the mountain ridge into the green Dothan Valley, the brothers saw Joseph (identifiable by his coat?) coming. They had time to decide that this was the moment to turn resentment and jealousy into action, the moment to kill him and his dreams. But in due course they realize that what they could do is make money on him instead and sell him to some passing Arabs. For us, at least, there is irony there, too. It is a group of Arabs, descendants of Ishmael and Hagar – and Abram – who are the means of Joseph surviving, and they take him to another Arab country, Egypt, and that makes it possible in due course for the whole family to survive. So the Arab camel train makes its way back along that road that Joseph had walked on his own, back along the mountain ridge past Shechem and Bethel and Jerusalem and Hebron. Joseph trudges past the villages where his family live and has no alternative but to continue along the decreasingly familiar road south and west to Egypt, the way Abram and Sarai had once gone, and Hagar.

Meanwhile the brothers tell their father that his favourite son is dead. One can imagine what the family's life is like from now on. Jacob never really recovers from his grief. He refuses to recover, we might say he insists that he will grieve for Joseph until he joins him in death. The brothers watch that process, and could be forgiven for finding that it increases their resentment at Jacob's disproportionate attachment to Joseph and their sense of justification for their hostility towards him. At the same time they live with guilt, and they live with a lie, a lie brought to their attention anew by every manifestation of their father's ongoing wilful grief. In actual fact, in due course Jacob will go down to Egypt to Joseph with his spirit renewed, but in the meantime he can only imagine going down to Sheol to Joseph mourning. And 'if the brothers are to continue in Jacob's family, at least until the reconciliation, they

must do so by maintaining deception as a way of life'
(G. W. Coats).

Joseph the leader-in-waiting

There is Joseph the dreamer. Act Two of the story
concerns Joseph the potential leader, the leader-in-
waiting. When a people like the descendants of Jacob
(or Ishmael or Esau) find themselves under oppression
or in exile, it can seem as if this will be the end of their
story. And such experiences sometimes do bring the
end of a story, in annihilation or assimilation or loss of
the memory that keeps communal self-awareness alive.
But sometimes, on the contrary, such experiences keep
their story alive and take it on, as happened to the
Jewish people in Egypt and in Babylon, and to the
Jewish people again in the 1940s and to the Palestinian
people in the 1970s. When people are put in prison, that
can seem to be the end of their story; what happens
may break them. But it may make them, and it may
prepare them for just the leadership that their jailers
wish to prevent. The great instance in our time is the
decades that Nelson Mandela spent on Robben Island.
Prison can be where a person learns to be a leader.

In exile Joseph first learns to handle responsibility. He
works as a foreign slave in the house of Potiphar, one of
the Pharaoh's ministers of state. Perhaps initially this
was a matter of manual work, but if so, evidently he did
well and earned promotion, so that in due course he was
running the affairs of the house as a whole; presumably
we are to imagine a house such as 11 Downing Street, not
a semi-detached in Luton. Potiphar found this worked
triumphantly well.

But I have missed out a key motif which appears at
this point in the story. This was where God came in. For
so far, God has been unmentioned in Joseph's story.
God was there at the beginning (Gen. 30:22–23),

remembering Rachel, heeding her longing, and opening her womb, so that when Joseph was born she
declared, 'God has taken away my reproach'. Further,
Joseph's very name presupposed a reference to God. It
means 'he adds' – that is, Rachel explained, 'May
Yahweh add to me another son'. It is a parable of the
facts, though, that in this name Yahweh's own name is
presupposed rather than explicitly included. In much of
the story that follows, Yahweh is presupposed but does
not actually appear. In that story of relationships in the
family, of love and hatred and dreams, Yahweh is
unmentioned. In Joseph's search for the brothers, their
plot, their selling him into slavery, and his exile – where
is Yahweh there? Nowhere to be seen, conspicuous by
absence. (Yahweh does appear in the subsequent story
about Judah, but appears killing two of Judah's sons,
not an encouraging exception to the rule.) The narrator
of the story has been telling it the way it appeared, the
way our stories often appear to us, without much by
way of special intervention by God or even crystal-
clearness about what God is doing behind the scenes.
Now the narrator changes tack, behaves as one privy to
special information on what lies behind the surface
events.

'Yahweh was with Joseph'; that was how he became a
successful man. His master could see that 'Yahweh was
with him, and that Yahweh caused all that he did to
prosper in his hands'. I suspect that a person needs (for
instance) certain basic organizational abilities in order to
be a successful administrator. But Potiphar could see
that Joseph's achievements went beyond native wit:
Yahweh blessed Potiphar's house because Joseph was
there. The promise to the ancestors, that the descendants
of Abraham will be a blessing, is coming true again. The
story is not off the rails. It is as well we are reassured of
this, because in a moment matters will look that way
again. But even when the story does introduce the
notion of God being involved behind the scenes, it is
worth noting that at this point this is how God is

involved. Sometimes the people of God experience extraordinary marvels which make them reach out for the language of miracle. When we do not, we are still invited to assume the presence and activity of God with us, in more covert, subtle, behind-the-scenes ways which are visible to the eyes of faith. Further, sometimes God's achievements and human faith or initiative seem interdependent, and God accepts the constraint of being limited by our faith or commitment, not working outside these. Sometimes God smilingly sets about achieving things notwithstanding whether we are characterized by trust or hope or commitment; this is one of those moments.

Meanwhile, however, Potiphar is able entirely to forget the affairs of the house and to take for granted that they will be run well, a great asset to a politician with his mind on other things. Perhaps it would have been better for him to consider the possibility that his wife might have gifts as good as Joseph's, like the capable wife of Proverbs 31, and could partner him in the house-running department. Perhaps it would have been better for him to spend more of his time with her if Joseph could take some of the cares off his shoulders. Perhaps the possibility that his instincts did not seem to lie in that direction is telling, because it rather suggests that things may have gone wrong between the two of them when we discover that she is looking for a relationship with someone. Perhaps the fact that she and Joseph are both involved with the house while her husband is preoccupied elsewhere inevitably threw the two of them together; working together can easily become the development of a relationship. The story does not tell us what sadness lies in Potiphar's wife and leads to her longing to be loved by Joseph; we would be unwise in our ignorance to sit in judgment on her longing. The story is a man's story about how one can go astray. It shows how in Joseph's case exile is the context in which the leader-in-waiting learns to handle sexual temptation.

We know that Joseph is the victim of the sexual conventions of his culture – as we all are. In his case, it meant that his father had four wives. We know that he could not handle his own dreams or his relationships within his family. It would be no surprise, and hardly (again) something to be judgmental about, if he failed to be able to handle relationships with the opposite sex. And it is characteristic of people in power that they are tempted to think that they can ignore the moral and social conventions that society as a whole accepts: we know this in modern Britain and America, and in ancient Israel we can see it particularly clearly in the story of David. Various are the ways in which power corrupts; attitudes to sexual morality is one of them. The story of Potiphar's wife and Joseph is as much about the destructive 'normal' ways of imperial power as it is about the sadness of a lonely woman and the wrong of adultery. All put pressure on Joseph. It is astonishing that he knows how to handle the pressure.

Much good did it do him. Nothing is more hateful than love spurned. Longing turns to wrath and palace turns to prison.

And then God comes in again. There, too, 'Yahweh was with Joseph' and, in addition, 'showed him steadfast love', so that he became as successful in organizing a prison as he had been in organizing a palace. Again, no doubt, innate skills played a part, but there was more to it than that. 'Yahweh was with him, and whatever he did, Yahweh made it prosper.'

In prison, adversity comes to be also where Joseph learns to handle people. There he met the Pharaoh's luckless chief cupbearer and chief baker. The titles are likely honorary ones like British equivalents for the monarch's staff; these two were probably not merely winewaiter and chef. Unfortunately they had somehow displeased the Pharaoh, perhaps as undeservedly as Joseph had displeased Potiphar, and they too had found themselves in prison. They both had dreams, and were troubled by them. They did not assume that the problem arose from what they had eaten the previous evening (last night I went to a loud and beery gig, and afterwards dreamed that there was a border crossing checkpoint on the road just below the college where I teach, like ones in Israel-Palestine). They assumed, like other people in the Middle Eastern world (and other traditional societies), that dreams were significant. They could (for instance) tell you things that were about to happen, if you knew how to decode them. We have already noted that the Bible makes the same assumption, one which Joseph is perhaps living by (one day his dreams will come true, so prison is not the last word). Here the Bible adds the significant qualification which Joseph makes explicit to his two fellow-unfortunates, that 'interpretations belong to God'. The interpretations God gave him were good news for the cupbearer, who would be restored, but unfortunately bad news for the baker, who would be executed. Here handling people involved straightness and courage, though the fact that he got the cupbearer's destiny right did not do Joseph himself any good.

Two years later the Pharaoh had his own significant-looking double dream (three pairs of dreams in one story, each time the significance confirmed by the doubling). In theory he is better placed to get a dream interpreted than are two discredited officials in prison, for he has a corps of experts with a wealth of experience in interpreting dreams and other events. Perhaps there are no precedents for the motifs in the Pharaoh's dream, because the experts are dumbfounded. At the dramatic moment the restored cupbearer, who had no reason but gratitude to remember about Joseph before, now realizes that self-interest gives him another reason to remember his former fellow-prisoner. He could put his boss in touch with someone who could interpret strange dreams. Joseph is hurriedly provided with a change of clothes – a nice touch, that, for his first imprisonment at the hand of his brothers had involved the loss of his coat, and his second imprisonment at the hand of Potiphar's wife had involved the loss of his robe, but his release at the hand of the cupbearer involves a shave and garments fit for an interview with the Pharaoh. It is a hint that the tide has finally turned. If the cupbearer thought he might get the credit for providing the means of interpreting the Pharaoh's dream, however, he miscalculated. As well as confidently telling the Pharaoh what God had been revealing to him, Joseph tells the Pharaoh what to do about it. There will be seven years of good harvest followed by seven poor years. Let him nominate an intelligent and shrewd minister to mastermind a way of exercising state control over the produce of the good years so as to be able to use it during the lean years. A nod is as good as a wink to the Pharaoh, and Joseph gets the job for which he has written the job description.

The story earlier handled two subjects we often avoid, family conflict and sexual temptation. It has now added a third as it has taken up the theme of power. You need to be in a position of power if you are to be the means of implementing a systematic solution to a nationwide problem such as the food shortage that is coming on Egypt (not to say Canaan). The story has become a celebration of power, of what can be achieved by someone in a position to take tough decisions and prepared to face a crisis boldly (Walter Brueggemann).

Joseph the reconciler

So Jacob's family is in Israel and Joseph is in a position of responsibility in Egypt. That could have been the end of the story; many families have lost touch with each other when different members have had to emigrate for one reason or another. But famine takes Jacob's family into Egypt to get grain, and they have to get it from Joseph because he is in charge of grain supplies. So in due course Joseph is saying to his brothers 'I am your brother Joseph whom you sold into Egypt. Is my father still alive?' 'And they were unable to answer him, so dismayed were they at his presence' (Gen. 45:3). I bet they were, given the deed he draws attention to. But he threw his arms round his little brother Benjamin and the two of them cried in each other's embrace, and he did the same with the rest of them. 'And after that his brothers talked with him' (45:15). I bet they did. They had a lot to talk about, not least the vast chunk of the story I have just omitted. And quite a puzzling chunk it is, because this is not the first time they have been down to Egypt and had dealings with Joseph – only on the previous two occasions they did not realize who it was. Joseph knew who they were, but for two years, it seems, he played games with them.

Joseph, remember, is minister of food, and anyone who wants grain has to get it from him. When there is famine in Canaan as in Egypt, Jacob sends ten of his sons to Egypt to buy grain. There they bow prostrate on the ground before Joseph. His first dream is being fulfilled. And he knew it. He knew who they were, but he treated them like any other foreigners, with the brusqueness people often show to foreigners, cross-questioning them in the manner of any decently suspicious immigration officer at an airport. 'You're spies! I shall hold you here until you send for your youngest brother too, to see if your story is true.' And he put them in prison for three days to think about it. They had once put him in prison and deceived their father about what had happened to him. Now he is putting them in prison and deceiving them. And of course he is right that they are liars – so why should they be trusted when they say they are sincere? The scenario is a familiar one, and not least in the contemporary Middle East.

They talk about it together, and the readers of the story are invited to enjoy the unsubtle irony of their reflection. 'We are paying the penalty for what we did to our brother. We saw his anguish when he pleaded with us [actually no such anguish and pleading were mentioned – is this an indication of the way they guiltily reflected on the wrong they had done?]. But we would not listen. That is why this anguish has come upon *us*.' The guilt has been nagging away all those years, and only now does it find expression. It is, of course, remorse rather than repentance, as one can tell from the way it generates argument, rather than resolving a problem and generating peace. 'I told you we shouldn't have done it', says Reuben, whitewashing the extent of his own distancing from the wrongdoing. But no doubt he could never forget the desperation when the brothers were talking about killing Joseph, or forget the sight of Joseph disappearing for ever with the Midianite traders.

Joseph knows exactly what is going on, and is moved to tears, but still leaves them in their remorse and anguish; indeed, he piles it on. He requires Simeon to stay behind while the others fetch Benjamin, and meanwhile has his staff put their grain money in their baggage with their grain and provisions, for them to find the first time they unpack for the night. 'At this they lost heart and turned trembling to one another: "What is this that God has done to us?" ' They wonder whether they are victims of some cosmic cat-and-mouse game. Actually it is an earthly one in which Joseph makes the rules, distributes the pieces, and throws the dice. 'And their father Jacob [no mean deceiver and liar himself in his day, so he hardly has grounds for complaint] said to them, "I am the one you have bereaved of children. Joseph is no more, Simeon is no more, and now you would take Benjamin".' There is another irony: he speaks as if Simeon is dead like Joseph, unaware that Joseph is alive in Egypt like Simeon. 'Why were you so stupid as to tell him about Benjamin?' 'Well, he questioned us so closely – it was almost as if he knew the answers before he asked the questions.' He would have known them, of course, but the brothers are lying again. Joseph did not ask about Jacob and their brother – they innocently volunteered the information. 'OK there is a risk in letting Benjamin go to Egypt. But there is risk in staying here, if we have no food. We are probably going to die one way or the other, so let's get going.' 'All right', eventually says Jacob, 'If I am bereaved of my children, I am bereaved'.

In Egypt, Joseph pretends mystification at the money-in-sacks experience. 'God must have put it there', he says, lying and taking God's name in vain in one go. Next time he plants his best silver as well as their own money in their baggage, then sends his staff to chase them and arrest them. Now they must leave Benjamin behind and fetch Jacob. 'How can we do that?', asks Judah. 'It will kill my father to see us arrive back without Benjamin.' The family is more divided than ever and Jacob is more overwhelmed by grief than ever.

What is going on? Why is Joseph torturing not merely the guilty brothers, but the innocent one, and his father? Is he simply seeking ruthless revenge, heaping coals of fire? He is a hard man, is Joseph, introducing merciless state ownership of food, money, livestock, land, and people (whom 'he made slaves from one end of Egypt to the other') when he had the chance; if the Israelites prophets had been there . . . . Yet the weeping hardly fits the thesis that he is simply a man controlled by ruthlessness. Is he testing them (to destruction!) to see (for instance) whether they really care more about money or people? Is he seeking to draw his brothers to repentance? If so, he fails. All we can say is that the story has the effect of rubbing the brothers' noses in their sin, and our noses too. The storyteller, or Joseph, or God, or all three, think this is a good idea.

Why might they think that? What does rubbing our noses in the brothers' sinfulness do? At least it shows how reconciliation takes place despite what people are, not because they have changed. This might seem odd or discouraging; in fact it is encouraging and challenging. It leaves us without excuse for failing to seek reconcilia-tion now. For in these strange exchanges which combine farce with pathos Joseph is clearly the same man he always was. He is still the dreamer, the boy who wants to be bigger than his big brothers, and therefore now ruthless in his use of power, yet divided in himself: if the question whether his father was still alive was so important to him (Gen. 45:3), why did he make himself wait so long to be in a position to ask it? The brothers are clearly the same people they always were, arguing, lying, blaming. Reconciliation takes place in the end because Joseph knows that God is drawing them all that way despite this. 'I am your brother Joseph whom you sold into Egypt. But now do not be distressed or angry with yourselves because you sold me here. God sent me on ahead of you to preserve life, to preserve a remnant, to keep many survivors alive. It was not you who sent me here but God' (45:4–8).

In what sense had God sent him there? In the introduction I referred to a sermon in which a preacher reflected on the experience of his wife's having a stillborn child. He preached from Matthew 10:29, where Jesus declares that even a single sparrow does not fall to the ground 'without your Father's will': so the NIV. But more literally Jesus simply says 'without your Father': the New Revised Standard Version has 'apart from your Father'. Never a sparrow falls to the ground without your Father knowing or seeing or being there in some sense to catch it. What Jesus implies is not that God wills the sparrow to fall, wills the baby to be stillborn, wills the brothers to sell Joseph to slavery, wills Judas to betray Jesus. It is rather that God puts the arms of the divine love and purpose around such events and makes them part of some pattern, rather than letting them remain as meaningless sufferings. No doubt there are senses in which nothing happens without it being God's will; it is just that this does not seem to be what Jesus is referring to when he speaks of the sparrow. What he does point to – God's capacity to notice, care, take account of, and work with – is a different precious truth.

Jacob's stupidity, Joseph's ambition, and his brothers' resentment do not receive expression 'without their Father'. It is not that their Father notices and disapproves (perhaps their Father does, but that is not the point Genesis makes). It is that their Father has the instinct and the skill to utilize these faults and the pains they bring, so that they become part of a pattern which brings good not only to each of these people but to many others beyond that. To consider only the short-term, they are the means by which the family can survive the imminent five years of further famine. And in due course God speaks for the only time in the Joseph story, speaks to Jacob on his way out of the promised land to the south in flight from famine, as God once had when Jacob was on his way out of the promised land to the north in flight from Esau, reassuring him that it is all right to go down to Egypt, 'because I shall make you into a great nation there. I myself will go down with you, and I will also bring you up again' (Gen. 46:3–4).

So Joseph throws his arms round his little brother and they weep, and he does the same to the other ten, and they talk about some of all the things they have to talk about (45:15). And it sounds like the end of the story. Conflict is resolved, reconciliation is achieved, harmony is reached. But the past is rarely forgotten as easily as that, except by God, who (we noted in reading the Noah story) has better control over memory than we do (Mic. 7:18–19). When Jacob dies, the dynamics of family relations change, as they do when a father dies. 'What if Joseph still bears a grudge against us and pays us back in full for all the wrong that we did to him?' (50:15). 'Not so', says Joseph – but this is the nightmare they live with even after that touching reconciliation scene. 'Not so. Have no fear. Even though you intended to do harm to me, God intended it for good, in order to preserve a numerous people, as he is doing today. So have no fear.'

That is God's dream for the physical and spiritual and

geographical descendants of Jacob: for the Jewish community in its various forms, for communities who believe in Jesus who are divided among themselves in multiform ways, for the two peoples who dream about Jerusalem. In each case reconciliation will come because people are prepared to take risks and to let fear be overcome by the risk of trust, despite the fact that all sides continue to be characterized by weaknesses and wickednesses. That is the way to an eventual embrace in tears, and a life together. Jealousy, deception, hostility, and division can be replaced by harmony, honesty, love, and *shalom* – indeed the story is designed to build up in us the faith that they *will* be replaced by these. But it involves risk.

Ephesians 2 paints a picture of a new humanity in which the division between Jew and Gentile has been abolished and God has made two one through the cross, on whose basis both have access in one Spirit to the Father (2:14–18). It is an implausible picture. As well, then, that Ephesians goes on to remind us that this God is able by the power at work within us to accomplish abundantly far more than all we can ask or imagine (3:20).

NINE

Moses and Israel

'Call nobody happy till they are dead', said the Greek statesman and poet Solon (see Herodotus, *Histories* 1.32). It was not a deeply morose statement about the intrinsic gloominess of human life, but a solemn recognition that for good as well as for ill, nothing is over until it is over. Years of joy and achievement can seem undone by a moment's folly or tragedy. Even apart from such possibilities, it is only at the end of a person's life that its shape can be discerned and an interim judgment on its significance made. The example of Moses well shows how even that is indeed preliminary, because an assessment of the man's achievement has to take into account what he has been to Jewish and Christian history since. But it also shows how the moment of death is a natural moment to consider the significance of the life as a whole. There are biblical characters whom we meet for a moment in the middle of their lives without ever knowing where they came from or how their lives went on. There are people whose birth and/or death is briefly noted, but as no more than episodes in a broader story of which they are a small part. There are one or two people like Moses for whom we get the frame of a life story, and whose death

141

story provides the vantage point from which to look
back over the whole.

When a relationship is established between people,
usually it comes about partly through another person.
Somebody introduces them to each other, acting as
mediator between them. There came to be a special
relationship between Yahweh and Israel – Yahweh is
their God, Israel is Yahweh's people – and they, too,
had someone who acted as their go-between, often
getting caught in the cross-fire between them. We learn
a lot about what went on between Moses and God,
mostly in connection with describing his role in the
joys and the agonies of the relationship between God
and Israel. His spirituality, as we learn of it, is the
spirituality of a mediator.

How the mediator received God's call

So Jacob and his family find their fortune in Egypt. Then
in due course a new government comes to power
and the flourishing of this immigrant community begins
to frighten it. The government seeks to contain it,
but immigrant communities have a way of flourishing
in numbers all the more when you try to put them
down.

First it is compulsion to engage in particular tough
jobs. Next they are confined to hard labour. Neither
works. Then the government determines to restrict
their population growth, requiring the killing of male
babies at birth. It is often the case that women (and
children) pay the consequences for laws made by men.
But more covertly they sometimes hold power, and can
exercise it in a way which subverts male power,
courageously, subtly, and where necessary manipu-
latively. They look weak, but they achieve. The men of
Egypt are motivated by fear of the men of Israel, the
women motivated by fear of God, and they let the
babies live. But that only issues in another edict, that

the babies be subsequently drowned. The story recalls stories from our own age about the oppression of peoples in Latin America, Eastern Europe, and China, peoples who have sometimes found this story a mirror in which to find themselves.

Moses came to be involved with Israel as someone who shared their oppression. He was the baby who should never have lived (Exod. 2:1–10). He was born as an ordinary child of just an ordinary marriage, but in a grievously non-ordinary time. Moses' mother resists the law of infanticide, then in due course turns the baby's basket into a makeshift boat and floats it onto the Nile. We cannot tell whether this is an act of faith ('God will look after him'), of despair ('There's no way he can escape death, but I refuse to do the deed myself'), or of calculation ('I'll leave him where he will get picked up'). The story's implicit interest lies in the way God's providence works via the natural feelings of a mother, the natural curiosity of a child who stays by the river to see what happens to the boat, and the natural compassion of a princess who cannot resist a baby and ends up asking his own mother to look after him for her.

The story thus hints at the characteristically fragile beginning of God's plan to give Israel its freedom and its special relationship with God, like that in Jesus's story where he, too, becomes the sole survivor of a holocaust wrought by an imperious overlord of Israel (Matt. 2) (B. S. Childs). It will not have seemed fair on the children of Israel and their parents in either context, but a positive purpose of God was at work, first to circumvent human evil, then to defeat it. So as a hidden, overruling activity of God on the national scale had ensured that Israel grew rather than perished at an earlier stage of the pogrom (Exod. 1), so now on the personal scale it arranges for Israel's potential liberator to acquire the Egyptian upbringing which will presumably turn out useful when he is called to take on the Egyptian authorities himself. He becomes the person who could be the liberator because on the one hand he was connected with the slaves but on the other had not been brought up with them.

A story from his manhood then tells us that Moses is called as an impetuous activist who knew the positive and the negative side to that (2:11–22). Moses' name was Egyptian (compare names such as Tutmoses; the comment in 2:10 depends on a play on words in Hebrew), his upbringing was Egyptian, and his appearance was Egyptian (2:19). He did not have to see himself as an Israelite (he could be seen as an Egyptian collaborator), but he did. Perhaps the years of courtly upbringing had been years of seething, or perhaps he had never realized how his own people lived until he witnessed the scene which made him burst out into savage action and kill an Egyptian who was beating one of his countrymen, after which he has to flee for his life into the desert. Moses is no haloed saint but a real man, a person in whom courage, compassion, fieriness, enthusiasm, and impetuosity combine in a volatile mixture as he pursues the love-hate relationship with his people and his destiny which this first incident from his manhood prefigures.

It turns him into a refugee miles away in Sinai. If a person tainted by collaboration with the Egyptians is not the obvious person to mediate between God and Israel, neither is a failed activist turned exile. If he spent his youth learning to be somebody, he spent his best adult years as a nobody, a man who was finished. Yet Midian, too, was preparing him for his calling. It will also be useful that he is a man at home in the desert as well as at home at court. It is this period that turns awareness of his brother and sister Israelites' experience of being status-less and home-less into an experience of his own. He marries, and calls his son Gershom, a name which suggests that he still sees himself as 'An-alien-there', in a foreign land: he has learnt a form of contentment and acceptance, though without settling down (or losing the fieriness, as later stages in the story will make clear). Preparation for God's service is likely to involve some form of Egypt and some form of Midian.

When Moses' call came, it was as part of God's response to his people's groaning. The descendants of Abraham have become a despised underclass in Egypt, and in their oppression they cry out to God. God hears their cry, God remembers the covenant promise made to their ancestors, God sees their present situation, and God takes notice (Exod. 2:23–25). And that is how Moses comes to have God appear to him. He finds himself given a ministry, not so that he can find fulfilment or find expression of his gifts or calling. It was not for his sake at all. It was a response to Israel's groaning. It is a groan Moses will hear a lot of.

Moses is an Egyptian – but is not. He is an Israelite – but is not. He is a Midianite – but is not. One day he is out doing his job in the context of his life in a Midianite family. He is not seeking God, but he has ventured near God's mountain. Perhaps it was not so surprising that he found himself meeting God, but if he knew it was God's mountain, to judge from how things work out this does not seem to make him expect to meet God there (it was his father-in-law who was the priest, after all). As with Jacob, there is no suggestion that he was seeking God or took any initiative in relation to God. But in the context of his everyday work experience he had an experience of mystery, of God's nearness. If he had been waiting for 40 years for something to happen, now it happens at an unlikely time, in an unlikely way.

He sees a flame of fire. Fire is a symbol of deity. It suggests light, heat, danger, destruction, cleansing. But it appears in the midst of a desert bush, something lowly and ordinary. A part of God's creation burns with divine flame without being consumed.

But that is to anticipate. Moses just sees a little bush on fire. He might have ignored it. His call, and all that follows, starts with mere curiosity about an odd fire. His curiosity was his main contribution to his call. Without it, nothing else would have followed. I imagine there

was many a moment over the decades that followed
when he wished he had never looked. When his
curiosity is attracted, God immediately seeks to take
him beyond it. On the one hand, God summons him by
name, implicitly drawing him near. On the other, God
warns him to stop, to come no closer. When God really
appears and acts, people feel drawn and at the same
time feel they have to draw back. But God's response to
Moses' fear is to bring good news – not news that
immediately relates to Moses in person but news that
God is coming to deliver Moses' people. God has heard
that cry of anguish and resentment at the way they are
being treated. God is about to take action, to give
evidence that it is indeed possible to mobilize the divine
bias to the poor which we noted God once showed *to* an
Egyptian, Hagar. 'If we pray, the Holy Spirit will come
down', says a Zimbabwean song (born of an oppression
by Britain that will have felt similar to Israel's by Egypt).
It sounds manipulative, but the kind of prayer God
invites us into looks manipulative: 'Come on, mobilize
me!'

If Moses had time, perhaps he wondered why God
was telling *him* about all this. The reason soon appears,
and it seemed less good news. The reason is that God
intends to send Moses to the Pharaoh to bring the
Israelites out of Egypt. It would have been easy for God
to act direct, to do a miracle, to transport the people in
an instant by magic carpet from Nile to Jordan. God
chooses to work less directly, to use human instru-
ments, to act in a way that may astonish but in general
does not actually compel anyone to believe that God
was involved. But in reality in the story of the last third
of Moses' life which is now beginning, God will do
nothing without Moses being involved. The story also
points to the fact that conversely God rarely appears to
anyone without its being in some way an enlistment
into God's service.

So God summons Moses to get involved in politics in
order to bring freedom and justice to his people. One

might have expected the Moses who behaved as he did when he saw his fellow-countryman being beaten to regard this as rather good news, but sometimes people are much less confident or more realistic at 50 than they are at 25, and so it is with Moses. 'How can *I* do that?': it is not the Moses who took decisive action that day long ago. God's response to his hesitation might be a rebuke, but there is no compelling reason to read it that way. 'I will be with you', says God. It is a promise that belongs in moments of great challenge like that one when Jesus is about to make his final disappearance leaving his disciples with the challenge to make disciples of the whole world (when Jesus himself has not even suc-ceeded in connection with Israel after God had been preparing them for a thousand years or so). It is always sobering when God says 'I am with you': it probably means God is about to tell us of some awesome expectation. Mary knew well to be scared when an angel told her that the Lord was with her (Lk. 1:29–30).

The back-up promise that God will be with Moses is given more specific content by the further back-up promise that he will see the people worship God on this very mountain where he and God are now conversing. That will be the sign that he really is the person who will lead the Israelites out of Egypt. But do you call that a sign? I have seen more convincing signs on a French autoroute. A sign is supposed to provide you with grounds for believing that something implausible will actually happen. This is a sign that Moses will see only at the end of the process. In the meantime he still has to live by faith. His sign is no present proof that God really has spoken or really will act. Only later will Moses know in experience. In the meantime he has to walk in moment-by-moment trust.

Moses is therefore pardonably unsatisfied. 'When I go to the Israelites and tell them of this great plan, what do I say if they ask me who this God is?' Again God's answer reveals less than it conceals, though it thereby manages to be the more profound. God is 'I will be':

whatever happens and whatever is needed, God will be there, present, active and involved. That is the kind of God we are talking about when we talk about Yahweh, the God of Israel.

'What if they won't listen?' 'I will give them other signs.' 'But I'm no good at rhetoric, I'm no persuader.' 'I'll tell you what to say.' 'O, couldn't you send someone else?' There are signs as the exchange unfolds that God is getting impatient, and now enough has become enough. God does not exactly give up; Moses will have Aaron's assistance, but Moses will not escape. It is extraordinary that the story of Israel's great leader begins with such a reminder of his feet of clay, which underlines for good and for ill the relative insignificance of Israel's human leadership. God will accept responsibility for Israel's response to Moses, for providing Moses with the words, and for seeing that he has the support he needs for his task.

What the mediator does

A mediator is a go-between or someone who builds bridges. Moses built bridges between Israel and Yahweh.

One aspect of this concerned the gap between the people's weakness and God's strength. After their escape from the Egyptians they found themselves in conflict with the Amalekites. There was to be a high-noon battle for which Moses with Aaron and Hur climbed to the top of a mountain overlooking the battle scene. There, holding Yahweh's staff, Moses stands extending his hand over the battlefield. As long as he does so, Israel does well in battle; when his arm tires, Israel is threatened with defeat. In due course Aaron and Hur have the wit to prop up his ailing arms and keep his hands extended until the battle is over (Exod. 17).

If the story is an example of intercessory prayer, its picture of prayer is rather different from ours. Inter-

cession is distinguishable from action, but it involves
not retreating from the scene of action but remaining
personally identified with it. As is regularly the case in
scripture, Moses prays not hands together, head down,
and eyes shut, but hands upraised, head up, and eyes
alert to see what is happening. In regular prayer in
scripture people's hands are open to receive from God,
but in this instance Moses with God's staff in his hand is
more the general directing the battle from above. He is
directing not merely earthly forces (Joshua is doing that)
but heavenly forces. Israel is weak but in heaven there
are vast resources potentially able to defeat the forces
arrayed against Israel, and Moses builds the bridge
between their weakness and God's strength.

Another aspect of the building of bridges between
people and God involves the gap between their creatureliness and God's awesomeness. In due course the
Israelites reach the mountain where Moses himself had
had his awesome meeting with Yahweh. There Yahweh
appears – or rather mercifully fails to appear, but provides the resonances of the divine presence in thunder,
lightning, smoke, earthquake, and dense cloud which
particularly symbolizes the presence of the hidden God.
Some moral preparation and some symbolic preparation
are appropriate (Exod. 19:3–8,10–15). Hebrews 12 draws
a contrast between this experience of God and the
experience of the Christian community, but it is a
different contrast from the one often inferred. Hebrews
does not comment on how fortunate we are that we no
longer experience God as shaking the earth or consuming with fire. It rather notes how more solemn is our
position in being confronted by a God who shakes not
only earth but heaven and who is still a consuming fire
before whom awed reverence is the appropriate attitude. The awe of Sinai and some more are appropriate.

'You speak to us and we will listen', the people say to
Moses. 'Don't let God speak to us, or we will die.' The
presence of God is too electric for creatureliness to be
able to withstand its voltage. So Moses climbs Sinai to

meet God on the people's behalf. He is no less of a creature, and no less of a sinner, so the risk is as great for him as for them. He climbs Sinai not in order to make his own pilgrimage but to seek God on his people's behalf, to learn so that he could teach. He descends with shining face, for he has met with God. He has not seen God's face, for he could no more stand that experience than Israel could, but the fire of God's face has affected his own. He is willing to be the go-between in relation to their creatureliness and God's awesomeness.

He also builds bridges between their failure and God's rejection of them. There is a tragic and fearful irony about what was happening at the bottom of the mountain while Moses was at the top. God was speaking of the right way of worship, of the shrine with its altar (but no image, for that was forbidden), of the people giving their gold and other precious possessions for it to be made, of burnt offerings and peace offerings being made there. God was promising to come to dwell there and enjoy fellowship with the people, in fulfil-ment of the purpose that lay behind their being delivered from oppression. Precisely while God is speaking of all this, it is being turned upside down at the foot of the mountain (Exod. 32:1–8). Which leads Moses into this further form of bridge-building.

God's inclination is to abandon them and start again with Moses, but Moses does not rejoice in judgment even though he is exempted. His reaction is to seek to act as go-between for the unfaithful people and the offended God. When the boss is about to take decisive action and grasp a nettle, it is sometimes the secretary's task to risk the boss's wrath by saying 'Are you sure that's wise or necessary? Does it really fit in with the policies you've been pursuing? Won't it rebound on you? Does it really fit in with what you have said you would do? Shouldn't you sleep on it?' And sometimes the wise boss takes notice. Indeed, one reason (maybe subconscious) for telling the secretary what was to happen was to try out ideas, to invite a response, to involve this other person in the decision-making. All that is paralleled in God's dealings with Moses and Moses' dealings with God.

Of course one reason why the boss talks things through with the secretary is the conviction that the two of them really do share convictions and aims. As the go-between, Moses is identified with both sides, and in his words to God his identification with God is at least as overt as his identification with Israel. The same is more obviously true about his actions when he reaches the bottom of the mountain, breaking the stones inscribed with the terms of the relationship between Yahweh and Israel which Israel has already broken and inviting Israelites into a sample wreaking of the bloody vengeance from which he had dissuaded Yahweh. Then, remarkably, he returns to the top of the mountain to plead with Yahweh again (32:30–34).

'You have sinned a great sin.' No doubt it was easier at that moment than it often is to recognize that fact and to bring it out into the open. Usually things are more ambiguous and we have more opportunity to avoid doing that. But it was because Moses could not shut his eyes to the people's unfaithfulness and the obstacle this had placed between them and God, that Moses was also in no danger of being unable to see the nature of their need. People's sins need acknowledging so that they can be prayed about – so that we can function as the go-between in prayer. As the go-between, Moses has to be able to understand both sides in the conflict, and this underlies the combination of hesitancy and bravado in his conversation with Yahweh. On one hand, it is 'If you will only forgive their sin . . . ': the sentence runs out like that, unable quite to finish. On the other hand, what happens when it fails to finish is that it somersaults into chutzpah: 'If you are not going to forgive them, you can also blot me out of your book' (the citizen list of Yahweh's people and/or the heavenly corporate plan for the next millennium or so). 'If you won't have them, you cannot have me.' There is a touch of 'Mind your own business about how I run things' in Yahweh's response to Moses, yet also an implicit 'Yes' interwoven with the 'No': Yahweh commissions Moses to lead the people on, which implies an acceptance of his plea for them. They will not be cast off.

The conversation illustrates how God involves us in the process of decision-making. The ultimate objectives in the heavenly corporate plan may not be very negotiable; God's mind is made up about some things (sustaining the world, blessing Israel, building up the church). But the aims and the detailed processes whereby these objectives will be realized are continually up for negotiation (which is why biblical, Jewish, and Christian history is such a winding phenomenon), and prayer is the way in which we engage in discussion with heaven about the specifics of the current situation (of course, heaven is receiving proposals from many subcommittees in this way, and has to make decisions in the light of all these submissions, so that the decisions are bound to disappoint some). Moses invites us as fellow go-betweens into the essential combination of tentativeness and bravado which avoids the demonic alternatives of paralysis and arrogance.

The process continues with Moses' third prayer, which focuses more on his own ministry (Exod. 33:12–23). Able only to have Moses by also having Israel, Yahweh does want Moses to continue to lead the people. Moses wants to know how he is to do that, what support he will have, what evidence he can have that Yahweh loves him and cares about him and will keep faith with him, and he also asks, 'Consider too that this nation is your people'. This looks like re-opening a question Yahweh seems just to have closed. Even when we think we have been allowed to perceive what God is going to do, this does not necessarily mean we have to accept this as God's final word. It implicitly leaves us free to speak again; which Moses does, and finds that Yahweh is flexible and unthreatened enough to do a complete U-turn and say a straight 'Yes'. And that leads to Moses praying another prayer of extraordinary boldness. He wants to see God's glory, the visible shining splendour of God's own personal nature and presence. That will be evidence that he is supported and accompanied in his task. That receives a 'No', but it is a 'No, but . . . .' You would not be able to bear the sight of my splendour. But I will let you see the afterburn. Let that be enough.

In his ministry Moses also builds bridges between faith and obedience and between spirit and institution. It has been suggested that in scripture as a whole and in Christian history there is a line that includes Abraham, Paul, Luther, and Protestantism in general, which puts the emphasis on faith in our relationship with God, and a line that includes Moses, Peter, James, Calvin, and also both Judaism and Catholicism, which puts the emphasis on obedience. Put as starkly as that, the grid may seem rather quaint, but there is something in it. Paul himself is certainly interested in the relationship between Abraham and Moses and emphasizes the fact that Abraham came first, so that the promise to Abraham which depends on grace cannot be made retrospectively conditional on the obligations revealed through Moses. But once that point is made and safeguarded, the question about obedience, response, and covenant obligation can be handled. And that is part of the bridge-building significance of Moses as the figure who comes after Abraham.

The related antithesis is that between spirit and institution. Moses has links with the past, with tradition; Abraham had none. Abraham has his eyes wholly on the future; Moses also has his eyes to the past. For Abraham, God is always on ahead of the people, pursuing a fulfilment of the promise which lies predominantly in the future. For Moses, God is also in the midst of the people; he builds the tabernacle as the place where God will be known in the midst, a place of priesthood and sacrament which mean that, whereas for Abraham, that presence of God is always a matter of promise, for Moses, there is a sense in which it has now become guaranteed (whether or not it was always felt).

The price the mediator pays

Being a go-between involves seeing things from two sides, identifying with both. For Moses, it means standing both on God's side, and on the side of the people. The trouble is, that means that in reality you truly belong to neither side. The story of his journeys up and down the mountain hints at the way in which Moses himself stands on his own.

One of the features of the age in which we live is that leadership can get away with nothing. In state and church there is a widespread disillusion with leadership, and the disillusion is expressed not merely behind closed doors but openly and persistently with a naivety which hides from the fact that replacing the leadership will solve nothing because any new leadership will be just as human and fallible. One is astonished that anyone still wishes to be a politician or a bishop or the minister of a congregation. It is then striking and comforting that Moses had the same experience. As far as we know, the kings and priests of Israel did not have this experience (except behind closed doors, no doubt) – which is one reason why God had to arrange for critique through prophets. They belonged to Israel's Constantinian age, when church, state, and power were nicely one and the wise kept quiet. Moses lived in Israel's pre-Constantinian age and we live in the West's post-Constantinian one; perhaps that explains this link between our age and that of Moses. He had no institutional position; his leadership always depended on consensus.

He knew it would be so from the beginning; the issue underlies those questions he raised with God at Mount

Horeb. It dominates a whole series of stories from after the people's escape from Egypt. The Egyptian army is in hot pursuit and God directs the Israelites into a cul-de-sac. Rather understandably the Israelites turn on their human leadership. 'Was it because there were no graves in Egypt that you have brought us out to die in the desert? We told you it would be like this. It would have been better to be slaves to the Egyptians than corpses in the desert.' 'Do not be afraid, stand firm, and see the deliverance Yahweh will accomplish for you today.' It might have seemed a creditably courageous reply. Yet Yahweh in person intervenes with 'Why are you crying out to me? Tell the Israelites to advance' (Exod. 14:11–15). Yes, Moses stands on his own in a category of one, with the Israelites saying 'Why' on one side, and God saying 'Why' on the other side.

It all works out fine, unless you are an Egyptian. The other side of the Red Sea they set out through the wilderness of Shur and have the first of a series of experiences which will typify life for some years and are presumably given such space there in the story because they continued to typify Israel's life (15:22–27). An experience of triumph and of proving God's power is followed by an apparent let-down: there is no water. The feeling of let-down is compounded when they seem to find the solution and it turns out to be a disappointment: the water they find is polluted. The calling of God's people in this situation is to keep trusting, but the natural reaction is to complain. Often this complaint is expressed as a murmur against their leadership, which is easier than outwardly complaining directly against God. The wise leader knows what to do, to turn not in complaint but in plea to the God who – as Israel has proved already – hears the cry of the needy. God meets the people's need through a typically implausible route, directing Moses to throw a tree branch into the water, which purifies it. The occasion of disappointment and failure thus becomes in God's grace the means of teaching and new revelation, of

Yahweh as healer. Then, the other side of Marah (Bitter) is always an Elim, a place with twelve springs and seventy palms to take shade under.

A whole series of such stories follows in Exodus and Numbers, and in the end in some mysterious way it is these events which issue in the grievous fact that Moses himself never enters the promised land, any more than the rest of the exodus generation does. Yahweh determines that Moses must die within sight of the land, but without setting foot there. Yahweh's explanation speaks of Moses and Aaron themselves having broken faith on one of those occasions when Israel rebelled against its lot. They failed to maintain Yahweh's holiness – failed to let God be God (Deut. 32:48–52). The occasion took place in the Wilderness of Zin, near the end of the people's 40 years in the wilderness. Neither the people's words nor Moses' reaction looks more than marginally different from other occasions, but it seems that both for Moses and for God there was something final about it, and God declares, 'because you did not trust in me, to show my holiness before the eyes of the Israelites, you are not to bring this assembly into the land that I have given them' (Num. 20:12). The way that Moses himself twice expresses it subsequently, he could not lead them into the land because Yahweh was angry with him 'on account of the people' (Deut. 1:37; 3:26). As Psalm 106 puts it, 'They angered Yahweh at the waters of Meribah, and it went ill with Moses on their account, because they made his spirit bitter and he spoke words that were rash'. The people's sin is the cause of Moses' sin, and Moses pays the price for his sin.

So Moses suffers for them, but he is unable to avert tragedy for them. And although he gets them to the edge of the promised land, the price is not entering it himself. He dies before reaching his goal. Someone else takes them there. And that means that Moses' experience points to something less peculiar to him. Moses 'is on the track of Canaan all his life; it is incredible that he should see the land only when on the verge of death. This dying vision of it can only be intended to illustrate how incomplete a moment is human life . . . . Moses fails to enter Canaan not because his life is too short but because it is a human life' (quoted by Gros Louis in *Literary Interpretations of Biblical Narratives*, Vol. 1, p. 129, from Franz Kafka's *Diaries* 1914-1923, pp. 195–96).

Moses stands for the incompleteness of all human achievement, the tragic dimension to human experience, the need to say 'Yes' to God in the most difficult of circumstances. He fails to enter the land precisely because he is Israel's leader. Taking the people to the edge of the land is his superhuman achievement; failing to enter the land is the reminder that he is human like them, and has failed like them (but his symbolic significance means he is not let off as they are). It is he above all who has to embody the fact that the future belongs to others.

Moses is a real human being, a person of huge achievement, huge failure, and huge disappointment. When the moment of death arrives he is at peace because all is within God's purpose and he goes to die with God (and we know, to live with God). And we are at peace as we read the story because we know that Israel's future does not depend on Moses but on God, and that the vital achievements of Moses were to take the people to this point and then to leave them with God, with Joshua, and with the word of God which he spent his last days re-preaching for them (in Deuteronomy) so that it, not he, can be the basis of the life they are to live the other side of the Jordan. It is a shame that Moses cannot enter the land, but it is a wonder that he achieved so much.

So Moses climbs Mount Nebo. He is aware what this moment means: he is going there to die. After that is only the tedium of Sheol – so he thinks. His eyes' last sight is the land of his people's destiny. There is a certain pain in surveying it, as Abraham once had from the mountains the other side (see Gen. 13:14–18); Abraham had had to leave the full possession of it to others, too. Yet there is also certainly a sweetness about doing so: he has seen it with his own eyes.

Thus Moses dies there 'according to Yahweh's word' – another bitter-sweet phrase. They are hard words: could not Yahweh have allowed this so faithful servant to set foot in the land? Was that one slip not forgivable? Yet they are reassuring words. Moses' God is love, and the loving God's will can be accepted. As far as Israel is concerned, Moses simply disappears. They cannot even find his grave. But there is therefore no danger of an excessive reverence being shown to his memory. Let the memorial be not the place where he died but the stature and achievement of the man himself, a man full of years, sight unimpaired, energy unabated, unequaled for his closeness to God and for his signs and wonders and mighty deeds and terrifying displays of power. He was 120 when he died (110 was the traditionally really impressive age, reached by Joseph, so he beat that): 40 years learning to be somebody, 40 years learning to be nobody, 40 years showing what God can do with somebody who has learned to be nobody.

TEN

Joshua and Rahab

So Moses left the people on the bank of a river. Jimmy Cliff once wrote a song called 'Many rivers to cross' in which he described the experience of facing river after river on our life's journey. He sees himself as kept alive only by the will, surviving, but alone, and not sure of ever finding the way to the other side. At different stages of life we stand at the banks of particular rivers – when we leave home, or move house, or go to college, or marry, or divorce, or change careers, or retire, or die. In my work in theological education I am aware that college takes people from one side of a river to the other. It is very obvious that this is the case for people who are going to be ordained. They come to college not because they want to, but because this is a barrier the church makes them cross if they wish to reach the church's ministry. The only way to get to the other side is by wading a river. Joshua and company of course had the benefit of a miracle to take them across, and sometimes we may be inclined to reckon that only a miracle will take *some* people across *their* river. But most people have to wade across for themselves, at a time when it is very obvious to them that the river is in flood. When Israel crossed the Jordan, it was in flood, and one wonders why God took them across at such a silly time of the year, though then wonders whether that is typical of the way God seems to work with us. The water comes right up to your neck one way or the other and threatens completely to overwhelm you, to carry you away. We do survive the swim, and in a strange way we may be quite affectionate about the experience afterwards. It was what took us from being one side to being the other side. We reach the place we wanted to be, the place God had called us to. The swim was worth it, and what we learned in those waters we will never forget.

Living in the light of God's promise and of God's command

When you stand at the bank of the river, to judge from Joshua's experience there are two things that God suggests that you keep in mind. Your crossing and your life the other side involve living in the light of God's promise and living in the light of God's command.

God begins with a command: it is time to get going across this river. But as soon as the command is uttered, like God's original command to Abram it gives way to a series of promises: I am giving you this land, every place your foot treads on will be yours, no one will be able to stop you, I will be with you, I will not fail you or forsake you. Then it is commanded again: be strong, be courageous, be very careful to follow the Torah, meditate on it, do not be frightened or put off by anything that confronts you when you cross the river. And it closes with a promise again: Yahweh your God will be with you wherever you go. God's words raise issues about the nature of life in the light of God's promise and in the light of God's command, and about the relationship between these.

'Every place that the sole of your foot will tread upon I have given you, as I promised Moses.' It is an odd way to put it. You first put your foot down somewhere. There is a vast land that God points to, a land far broader than actually Israel ever controlled. God does not here designate particular places within it or lead you to particular places. *There* is all this land, says God. Now put your feet down somewhere. And when you have done that, say 'God has given us this bit. It is what God promised Moses'. You do not know precisely what lies the other side of the river, precisely what God is calling you to. You do know that God has designated a vast area as the land of promise, and that you explore it as a land God gives you.

'As I was with Moses,' God says, 'so I will be with you'. Admittedly that gives you food for thought. As God was with Moses? So you get given impossible tasks, put under stress, pressured, misunderstood, and rejected by people . . . . 'As I was with Moses, so I will be with you.' We have noted already how it is always worrying when God says, 'I will be with you'. It is a promise that always belongs in the context of some frightening expectation; you have to evangelize the world or you are about to give birth to the Messiah. Mary knew what she was doing when she became so troubled when the angel appeared and said that God was with her. She knew that something horrendous was about to follow. But at least you have that promise. When you are about to cross the river and you have no idea what lies on the other side, God says 'I promise you it will be OK. I myself have been there before, I will give you your inheritance there, I will be with you'. We live in the light of God's promise.

Joshua is also called to live in the light of God's command, in the light of the Torah which Moses gave the people. The English translations use the word 'law' for Torah, but that makes it sound legalistic. Perhaps 'rule of life' gives a better idea of the significance of the Torah for Israel. It is something to guide them, something to measure themselves by. It is a way of life – that is the image that is cashed out here. Sin is a matter

of wandering or waywardness or going astray. There is
a clear path to walk in, says God. So walk in it.

The command seems very general, though it is
probably a little less general than it sounds. When God
refers to the Torah Moses gave Israel, it is a reference
back to Deuteronomy. The Book of Joshua is the
beginning of a vast story which extends through
Judges, Samuel, and Kings and traces (among other
things) how far Israel did or did not order its life by
the expectations laid down in Deuteronomy (it is a
'Deuteronomistic History'). It is striking that the key
concern of Deuteronomy is faithfulness to Yahweh
rather than following other gods. Here is Israel entering
a multi-ethnic, multi-faith context like ours, and it is
warned to keep its rule of life, to keep its commitment
to Yahweh, not to slide away from it under the
pressures of a multi-faith society. It is one of the central
issues for the church in the contemporary world as it
was one of the most important issues for Joshua's
people to get clear on, how to live in a multi-faith
context without wandering from a commitment to the
fact that Yahweh is God, that Jesus is Lord, that there is
only one way.

How *do* you make sure you live in the light of God's
command? 'This book of Torah is not to leave your lips',
says God. That will likely seem rather strange to us.
God is not talking about preaching but about Bible
study, about meditation. You study scripture with the
scriptures on your lips. It is not a head trip but
something that involves the body in the very studying,
– so that it then involves the body in the obeying.
Joshua would approve of the custom encouraged by
Scripture Union and by the lectionary systems of some
churches whereby one reads the scriptures systematically
day by day. He would add an exhortation to let the
scriptures possess the whole person – body as well as
mind.

Live in the light of God's promise and live in the light
of God's command. I am struck by the way those

invitations are interwoven in what God says. The relationship between them is tricky, and maybe people vary about which they most need to hear. I was once in a conversation about preaching. I had said that I thought it was much more important in preaching to talk about the grace of God, or the promise of God to put it in the terms of this passage, than to talk about our obedience to God – I reckoned that if you got grace straight, obedience would follow, and that preachers were too fond of giving congregations a kick in the pants to get them to be more committed, when what they really needed was to believe that God loved them.

The person I was talking with commented that she thought she did believe that God loved her and that she did need a kick in the pants. That made me wonder whether there are two kinds of spirituality, whether some of us are people who are convinced that God loves us and that things are all right, so that what we need is to be goaded into action, and others of us are people who are never sure whether God does love us and are always active because we want to prove ourselves to ourselves or to God (the two are related to the Abraham-Moses polarity noted in the last chapter). And I am the latter kind of person.

That may be partly because I am a man. Certainly it is the case that some feminist writers suggest that the besetting temptation of men as men is always to be active, assertive, aggressive, trying to discover themselves, whereas the besetting temptation of women as women is to be relaxed, content, unassertive, not feeling the need to discover themselves. Like most generalizations it will not always work, but it corresponds to some bits of experience, like the fact that it is often men who dominate discussions and arguments and make it difficult for women to get a word in edgeways. Perhaps one bit of agenda from God for any Christian church or community is to get the relationship right between relaxing in God's promise and actively living by God's command, and helping each other to see

where individually and corporately we need to do
something (or do nothing) about that.

Joshua behaves like a man and is rescued by a woman

'Live in the light of God's promise and live in the light of
God's command', Joshua is told. So what does he do?
He behaves like a man, but fortunately is rescued by a
woman, and learns a spiritual lesson or two from her.
He is encouraged also to live in the light of what God
has done for Israel in the past, and to live in the light of
what God has done for us personally.

Joshua sends two men secretly from where Israel is
encamped at Shittim to take a look at the land, and
particularly at Jericho. Why? Presumably to discover
Jericho's strategic situation, its strengths and weaknesses, so that the Israelites can attack it in due course.
But that is odd, because they are not going to attack
it. They are only going to march round and blow
trumpets. A choir practice would be more logical
preparation. So here is Joshua seeking some reassurance that everything will be OK, which he does get. But
why is he seeking it? Is that not what he has just been
given by God?

Of course I am being hard on Joshua. Yet look where
his initiative leads. He sends the spies *secretly*. But the
King of Jericho evidently has his own intelligence
system, because he finds out about them. Their lives are
in danger. They have gone inside a walled city, night
has fallen, the gates are shut, and they are caught like
mice in a trap.

Then there is the particular place in Jericho where
they were reckoning to stay, the house of a prostitute
called Rahab. Now it may be that Jericho was a little like
the Wild West, where the saloon, the hotel, and the
whorehouse are the same place. Perhaps there is only
this one place for the spies to spend the night. But it is

still a pretty odd place to find two nice Jewish boys.
Their lives were not the only thing they were in danger
of losing.

Yet it would not be the fact of being in a house of ill-
repute that would most trouble an Israelite. The hint of
the real problem lies in the place we have been told they
set out from, Shittim. When the Israelites had arrived
there the men had got involved with the local women
and been invited to their religious festivals (we must be
open to learning from other people's faiths in a multi-
religious, multi-ethnic context, perhaps they thought),
and they had joined in the worship of the Baal of Peor
and antagonized Yahweh. Here they are at the other
end of the time at Shittim walking straight into the same
mistake. There was that one priority in Israel's rule of
life in the promised land, keeping your religion pure,
and it is already imperilled. So God says 'Be bold, be
faithful, and you will begin a long life in the land'. But
they need some evidence if they are to be bold, and they
risk their commitment to Yahweh and imperil their lives
altogether.

Now the story does not labour all that, but simply
hints at it. Once again we discover that the Hebrew
Bible isn't moralistic the way Christianity is. It is capable
of shrugging its shoulders when believers do the wrong
thing; it does not always underline it. This may be
because it believes in God, whereas Christianity is
inclined to put all the burden on us to bring in the
kingdom. The Hebrew Bible reckons that is God's
business, so it can be more relaxed about our failures.
That is why I like living in the Old Testament. This
Joshua makes mistakes. Confronted by the river, knowing the promise of God and the command of God, he
stops trusting, compromises his commitment to God,
and puts everything at risk. It is so encouraging that he
did that, and that because he and we are both
surrounded by Yahweh and the angels, we need not
worry overmuch. In my small way I have to act as a
Christian leader, and one reason I could sometimes

wish it was not so is that I make mistakes. It is wonderful that God is not frustrated by our mistakes.

The result of Joshua's mistake is that these young men are sitting on the sofa with Rahab, wondering what happens next, when there is a commotion in the street, then banging and shouting two doors away. It is a gang of heavies from the palace. 'Any strangers here tonight?' You knew you should not have been here. It was a stupid mission. It was the wrong place to be. And you are going to pay for it with your life. Because obviously Rahab will give you up.

But no! 'Quick, up on the roof', she says. The roof, of course, was a bit like the back garden and the outhouse for us, it was the place you hung the washing and kept things. There was flax for dressmaking laid out to dry in the sun. It was a place they could hide.

Then when the heavies get to the door, there is an amusing conversation. 'Hi, guys, welcome, what can I do for you? How long can you stay? Wouldn't you like to lay down your arms and surrender to mine? O yes, there *were* two foreigners here. No, they didn't say where they came from. They just stayed an hour and left. You'll probably catch them if you move . . . .'

Living in the light of what God has done

The whole story would make a splendid Whitehall farce – the naive young Jews, the blundering soldiers, the prostitute with a heart of gold. I imagine the Israelites laughed every time they told the story, until it got stuck in plate glass in the Bible. But the best funny stories are profound and serious at the same time, and this is one, because from it the Israelites learned how to live in the light of what God had done for Israel in the past, and how to live in the light of what God had done in their own experience.

For why did Rahab change sides? Sociological reasons probably played a part. It is easy for men to fantasize prostitutes and think they must all be nymphomaniacs, sex goddesses. In the city where I live, and in Jericho, a prostitute is more likely to be someone on the margin, someone who could not make ends meet, someone in trouble, someone who had to find a livelihood and for whom this seemed the only way, someone whom the community fails and then uses to provide a facility and then despises and (in our society's case) criminalizes. That is why it was no chance that Jesus made friends with whores and that they responded to his friendship. It gave them a fresh start in a community that did not operate with the values of the old community that had failed them, used them, and despised them.

So it is no coincidence that Rahab is the person who changes sides. She is the person with nothing to lose. It *was* a good idea to stay at the whorehouse. The God of Israel is the kind of God who reaches out to the marginalized, and they can tell that the God of Israel is their kind of God. When Jesus started with whores, he was as usual only doing what he had learned from the Hebrew Bible. Indeed it was in his blood. One of his ancestors had been a prostitute. A scarlet thread links Tamar and Rahab (compare Gen. 38:18,28 with Josh. 2:15,18,21). The whorehouse *was* just the place the spies should have expected to be welcome − not just as customers but as bearers of good news, news that God has exalted the lowly and brought down the mighty.

When people talk about mission, one of the things they sometimes say is that we do not go out into the world as if God is not there, we go in the conviction that God is there and is involved and we go to try to find out where God is involved, to get stuck in alongside and reap the benefits. So sometimes one will speak to someone about Christ and be amazed at the way God has been preparing the way. I recently met a woman from *Peru* who had come to join a team witnessing to *Jewish* people in *Britain* and who got into conversation with an *Italian* with whom she had to speak in *Spanish* (because Italian and Spanish are fairly similar) and who came to know Christ. It is extraordinary how God can make things work.

Two spies went to the wrong place for the wrong reasons and found God was there. There is no hint that they gave their testimony in the brothel. They found the madam giving them hers. There they were hiding among the stalks of flax on the roof, humiliated by the Canaanites, the exact opposite of what was supposed to happen. Rahab comes up to see them as they are getting ready for bed and wants to talk about God. 'I know that Yahweh has given you this land and that we are all scared stiff of you, because we have heard how Yahweh dried up the Red Sea before you when you came out of Egypt, and we have heard what you did to the peoples the other side of the Jordan. We are all petrified of when you cross the Jordan, because Yahweh your God is God in heaven above and here in this world.' That is why Rahab changes sides. There never was any future for her in Jericho. She wants to live in the light of what God has done for Israel.

It is a wonderful irony. If Joshua had been prepared to do that, the spies would never have been hiding on the roof of a brothel in Jericho at all. Not living in the light of what God has done for Israel has got them in a near-terminal mess. But it is all right, because the God who dried up the Red Sea to get the Israelites out of Egypt is not going to be put off by a triviality like that from getting them into Canaan. So Yahweh does something extra for them, scaring the pants off the people of Jericho and providing them with a nice lady to tell them all about it. She thereby shows them that she realizes that she needs to live in the light of what God has done for Israel, and that they ought to be doing so too. And thus in addition she shows them that they can also live in the light of what God has done for them personally, shows them how to link their story onto God's story, shows them that God's acts are not just in the glory days of the past but in the sinful present. They have failed to live in the light of what God has done for

Israel, and as a result they experience God doing something for them.

Back on the roof Rahab has completed her testimony. 'Right, come on you two, no time for sleep now.' 'But we've paid for a bed for the night.' 'Do you want to die or not? Time to move it.'

Now we have noted that it was past nightfall and the gates were shut. There was no way out. But as it happened Rahab's house was set into the city wall and she had a window looking out. She lowered a rope toward the ground outside and hurried the young men down. Jericho has the Judean hills (as they will one day be called) one side and the River Jordan on the other, and Rahab had sent the troops towards the river, in the direction of the Israelite camp. So now she whispers down to the two men as they clamber down the rope, 'Go and hide in the hills till the coast is clear'. 'OK. We'll be back though. Leave the rope hanging out of your window. Then everyone will know it's your house and that you're on our side.'

Thus they made their excuses and left, made their ignominious exit, and hid in the hills till things quietened down. Then they crossed over to the camp and told Joshua all that happened to them – which must have raised some eyebrows. But they were able to say to Joshua, 'The people over there are scared stiff. It really is true that Yahweh has given the land into our power'.

They have learned from God that they are to live in the light of God's promise and to live in the light of God's command. They have learned from Rahab that they are to live in the light of what God has done in the past for Israel, and to live in the light of what God has done for them personally.

All the time we spend wondering whether we can cross the river or are actually wading it, we must keep these things in mind.

ELEVEN

Deborah and Ya'el

How is God's purpose achieved in the world? How is oppression (sometimes) brought under control and justice (sometimes) done? How do men and women play a part in the achieving of such ends? And how are they affected by their involvement in these affairs? The story of Deborah and Ya'el, and of Barak, Sisera, Jabin, and his mother, with its portrayal of motherhood and machismo, suggests perspectives on these questions.

In Israel's world as in ours a significant role was fulfilled by officially-recognized leaders of church and state with their institutional positions, by kings such as David, Solomon, and Josiah. When there were no kings in Israel (and, indeed, sometimes when there were), the role was played by people who had no institutional position, people who were the ancient equivalents to Martin Luther King, Mother Teresa, and Bob Geldof. They are usually referred to as 'judges', though administering the legal system is not prominent in the stories told about them. In the Bible's way of speaking, being a 'judge' is a matter of seeing that God's 'just and gentle government' of the world becomes a reality. That involves bringing people the gift of freedom, so that judging people is not so different from bringing them salvation and they can as easily be called 'saviours' as 'judges'.

By definition the judges were people who had no place in an institutional or constitutional structure. Neither were they people who would have had such a place if there had been such a structure, as is apparent when one considers who they were. The first was Othniel, who brought about a famous victory over an Aramaean king with a name long enough to mirror the threat he signified to Israel; and Othniel was merely Caleb's younger brother. A theme of these stories is announced: we know very well already from Genesis that younger brothers are despised by human reckoning but/and favoured by God. The second judge is a man called Ehud, who indulged in an assassination worthy of a place in a late-night horror movie. He had to do his stabbing with his left hand, because he was disabled (not merely left-handed, as the translations say: literally, he was 'bound as to his right hand'). He was not the sort of person who could have been a king (for kings such as Saul and David are emphatically handsome blue-eyed boys) or a priest (for priests had to be physically without blemish, like the sacrifices they offered). The third judge was an obscure man called Shamgar son of Anat, who killed six hundred Philistines with an ox goad. 'He too delivered Israel', the story comments; but his name marks him as Canaanite (and Anat is the name of a Canaanite goddess) who presumably acted on his own people's behalf and benefited Israel only accidentally.

Later in Judges we will read of the liberating, judging activity of a further line of unlikely heroes, unlikely in their case not because of their position in society but because of their personal and moral qualities. There will be the disbelieving, fearful, sign-seeking, vengeful Gideon, who ends up leading Israel into the idolatry from which the judges were supposed to deliver people. There will be his son Abimelech, who was so

stupid he wanted to be king (a post no one in their
senses ever covets). There will be the outcast Jephthah,
who was willing to kill his daughter rather than
reconsider his relationship with Yahweh. There will be
Samson with his fateful addiction to sex and violence.

Deborah: judge, prophet, leader, poet

Amidst such a line, Deborah has the right to hold her
head rather high, even if it will not be surprising if she
too turns out to have her blind spots. Let it not be said
that a woman cannot hold her head high as a leader.
The encouragement her portrait offers scarcely prepares
us for the horror of the way a woman is treated in the
last story of the Book of Judges, though the violence
even of her story perhaps does.

The stories of younger brother Othniel, handicapped
Ehud, and Canaanite Shamgar have put question marks
by eldest-ism, able-ism, and racism; Deborah's story
will undermine sexism. They have all been marginal
people, such as everyone knows God does not use – the
young, the disabled, and the foreign. Now there
appears a woman. Everyone knows women have no
place in the structure of responsibility and power. Their
job is to follow the men's lead.

When Deborah is introduced, the story places great
emphasis on her being a woman. She is 'Deborah' (a
woman's name, of course), 'a prophetess' (Hebrew has
a feminine noun for that like English), and 'woman' or
'wife' of Lappidot. Even this word *lappidot*, meaning
torches, flames, or flashes, is a feminine word, a strange
usage if it is the name of a man. Perhaps 'woman of
flashes' is a description of Deborah herself, not the
name of her husband. This would then fit with the
fact that her husband is not otherwise mentioned – a
married woman tends to be described as 'the wife of so-
and-so' more often than Deborah is described as
'woman of *lappidot*'. She is not even identified by her

father. She operates as an independent person: she is
just 'Deborah'.

Many of the names in this story do seem to be
significant. Deborah's own name means 'bee'. That
other characterization as 'woman of torches' hints at her
being a woman of fire, a woman who flames and
flashes, as indeed she is. She is a woman with the gift of
prophecy, with a sting in her tail and a flash in her eye.
With the help of Yahweh her story will subvert the
patriarchal presuppositions of Israel's social order (or
ours). She is a woman who takes the lead, and in
national life; there is no hint that a women's role is
confined to the home. The story we are about to
consider begins with the Israelites as thralls and chattels
and ends with them once again free to control their
own destiny; the change comes about because of the
initiative of a woman.

She is almost the first person to be called a prophet in
Israel's story. Abraham was once called a prophet
because he was a person whose prayer God heard (Gen.
20:7). Miriam was called a prophet because she was
someone who led Israelite women in praise (Exod.
15:20). Bee is the first named prophet who brings a
word from God that shapes history in the way the word
of God will do in the Books of Kings. She will not be the
last woman in the prophetic line; it continues in the
persons of figures such as Isaiah's wife and Huldah. It is
perhaps also as a prophet that she leads the singing
preserved in Judges 5, like Miriam after the Israelites'
escape from the Red Sea. To judge from Joel. 2:28–32,
Acts 2, and 1 Corinthians 14, she stands as a promise
regarding the way God can use a woman, a promise
open to being newly fulfilled once the Holy Spirit is at
work in the church of Jesus.

Bee was also active as a judge in Israel. In general,
judgment in the sense of deciding legal cases was the
business of the senior men in the community, who
would gather in the square inside the city gate to decide
on legal matters. But on some occasions of contention

people might have recourse to a person who was known to have special insight and who would be asked to decide between their conflicting claims. In a famous story two mothers went to Solomon to get him to resolve a dispute over who was the true mother of a child, and he has the God-given wisdom to be able to do so in a way which makes absolutely clear which of them is the pretender (1 Ki. 3). Bee was that kind of wise woman. Her wisdom, too, came from God. She sat under a palm tree between Ramah and Bethel, available for consultation in that connection. That in itself hints at God's involvement. This was no ordinary palm tree. Palm trees do not grow on the ridge of the mountains of Ephraim a thousand metres above sea level, and the word the story uses is not the ordinary word for a palm tree but one which is also used for a pole or column, a religious object which reminded people of the presence of God, like the pillar Jacob set up at Bethel. Bee sat there in the presence of God and sought God's wisdom for people. So as well as being Israel's first proper prophet, this woman is Israel's first proper judge (in the sense of someone who sorts out disputes). Her woman's insight is given by God, given back to God, and used by God.

She is 'a mother in Israel' (Jdg. 5:7). The Book of Proverbs shows how parents in Israel shared with each other the responsibility and authority to provide for their children and to teach them the ways of godly wisdom. The story tells us of no family of her own that Bee had, but as a metaphorical mother she exercised a parent's responsibility and authority over Israel. As someone who combined the role of judge, prophet, leader, and poet, there is no doubt that she is the greatest figure in the book. It is certainly striking that the only person in scripture who combines all these roles is a woman, but then it is often the case in modern Western culture, too, that women have to learn to live with a more bewildering and demanding combination of roles than men do!

The situation in which Deborah initiates the action is the one which recurs through the Book of Judges. Israel had turned its back on Yahweh, who had responded by casting it off for a while and allowing it to come under the control of 'King Jabin of Canaan, who reigned in Hazor'. The second phrase helps to make sense of the first. The Canaanites were the indigenous population of Palestine, in possession of the land before the Israelites. They were not one political entity, however, but a series of independent city-states, and in this sense there was no such thing as a king of Canaan as a whole. But Hazor was much the biggest Canaanite city, and we know that its king was viewed as *the* king in Canaan by the far-away power in Iraq.

The city of Hazor stands in a commanding position 15 kilometres north of Lake Galilee, controlling the high-ways north to Lebanon, northeast to Syria and Iraq, south to Palestine and Egypt, west to the Mediterranean. It is an imposing site, a kilometre square, not much by modern standards, but gigantic by those of ancient Palestine; no other city comes near it. The story of Joshua conquering this huge city (without a miracle) in Joshua 11 is a far more astounding one than the story of his conquering little Jericho. But Israelite possession of it evidently did not last, for it is again a centre of Canaanite authority, ruled by a different Jabin (presumably) from the Jabin of Joshua's day. His name may also be significant, in an ironic way. It means 'discerning'.

Jabin's army commander is a man called Sisera. His name is significant for a different reason. It is not an Israelite or Canaanite one; the best guess is that it is Philistine. The Philistines immigrated into Canaan just after the Israelites from the opposite direction, from the Greek islands. It was they who gave the country the name 'Palestine'; we do not know the location of Sisera's city, though it is significant that its name was 'Haroshet of the Gentiles'. The Canaanites, Philistines, and Israelites lived in uneasy coexistence in the country, sometimes two of them in alliance against the third. We have noted the hint that the Israelites could at least recognize Canaanite Shamgar as someone with whom they shared the Philistines as a common enemy. More often, perhaps, it was the Canaanites and Philistines who were in alliance, and this is one of those moments. These two peoples have combined forces and they hold the Israelites in a pincer.

Some awareness of Palestinian geography helps to clarify one way in which they did that. To oversimplify, the main part of the country (west of the Jordan) divides into four blocks. The northernmost is the mountains of Galilee. The southernmost two blocks comprise the mountain ridge north and south of Jerusalem, which among the Israelites was allocated to the tribe of Ephraim and the tribe of Judah. Between these mountain areas is a sizable plain.

Either side of the plain and controlling communications in both directions lie Hazor and a number of other cities such as Bet Shean, Taanach, and Megiddo, which were in Philistine or Canaanite hands. The Israelites live in the mountains either side of this plain and have difficulty reaching each other because of these powers in between, like Palestinians trying to get between different parts of Jordan, Lebanon, the West Bank and Gaza today. Caravans cease and travellers have to avoid the main roads and travel by sidetracks that will bring their own hazards (Jdg. 5:6).

The fact that the Israelites lived in the mountains reflects the fact that they were the technologically less sophisticated people of their day (again, like contemporary Palestinians in the West Bank). Jabin and Sisera had a vast fleet of iron-reinforced chariots, but the iron age has not dawned on the Israelites, who lack even sword or spear (5:8). As ever, the technologically more sophisticated nation can use its expertise to control the destiny of the less sophisticated.

Only when they saw the trouble they were in through turning away from Yahweh did the Israelites turn back and cry for help from Yahweh. Their 'crying for help' deserves noting. It is one of a number of ways in which a story such as this one reminds us of the Israelites' rescue from Egypt and their receiving their new home in Canaan. During their oppression in Egypt and during the generation they spent as nomads in Sinai they had often 'cried out for help' to Yahweh, and received it. Their experience of oppression in Canaan, deprived of true enjoyment of the homeland promised them there, is like a continuation of that earlier experience. After all, the the name of the villain, Jabin, is the same. The technological problem is the same; it was the Canaanites' possession of superior equipment that had hindered the Israelites' making a more complete job of occupying the land in Joshua's day (Jos. 17:16, Jdg. 1:19). The Israelites therefore respond to the crisis in the appropriate way. Their experience in Egypt and in Sinai proved that Yahweh was the kind of God who hears the cry of the oppressed, even when their oppression is their own fault. They know they have to live with the exodus-Sinai God as exodus-Sinai people. They set their hope on the exodus-Sinai God's honouring that.

Barak the reluctant general

Apart from cry out to Yahweh, as far as the story tells us, the Israelites do nothing. Until Bee makes them. She sends for a man called Barak ben Abinoam, Barak son of Abinoam (adding a man's father's name or a woman's husband's name being the equivalent of adding their surname in English). Barak belonged to the tribe of Naphtali and lived in a town in northern Galilee called Kedesh, well beyond Hazor. Bee herself lived near the southern end of the area of the tribe of Ephraim. They come almost from two extremes of the area of the tribes most affected by the constraints imposed by Jabin and

Sisera. The tribes Barak summons are the major
Galilean tribes of Zebulun and Naphtali; the other tribes
who also take part are from the mountains on the south
side of the plain, Ephraim, Benjamin, and Machir
(Manasseh), along with Issachar, who shared the plain
itself (in theory) with Zebulun. Other tribes a little
further away are chided for not taking part; those of the
far south are not mentioned (see Jdg. 5:14–18).

Something else links but distances Deborah and
Barak. Barak's name is again significant. Bee was the
woman of 'flashes'; 'Barak' itself means 'lightning'. They
are very similar people, but very different.

So Bee summons Lightning. 'Yahweh the God of
Israel commands you, "Go, take up position at Mount
Tabor, bringing ten thousand from the tribe of Naphtali
and the tribe of Zebulun. I will draw out Sisera, the
general of Jabin's army, to meet you by the Wadi
Qishon with his chariots and his troops; and I will give
him into your hand" '. Mount Tabor and the River
Qishon stand on the northern and the southern sides of
that plain which the Canaanites and the Philistines
control; the main road which the Israelites cannot use
runs past these places on its way from Damascus and
the east to the sea coast and Egypt.

The pattern of Israel's original victories over the
Jabins of Joshua's day is being repeated: once again
Israel is being challenged to take on the Canaanites
against all the odds. God gives Lightning a command
and a promise. If he will do what God says, he will see
God act. The Israelites will not really have to fight; all
they will have to do is provoke Sisera to action and then
receive the victory Yahweh simply gives them. Yet they
do have to muster, march, and provoke. What God
does could not come about without God acting; but it
could not come about without the human army acting,
too. Victory involves people and commanders offering
themselves willingly and marching down from the
mountains to the plain prepared to do battle, yet even

their self-offering is a reason for praise of God (Jdg. 5:2,9), presumably because even it reflects God's providence or inspiration.

Why summon Lightning in particular? I have this fantasy that this was exactly the question he asked. 'Why me?' Certainly his response is all of a piece with the way people like Moses, Gideon and Jeremiah responded when God summoned them. The last thing Lightning wants to do is take on a Canaanite army with 900 chariots which distinctly tip the balance of forces the Canaanites' way. Lightning does not wish to be cast into the macho role of the great military hero, especially when he can weigh up the odds. 'Why me? Why wasn't I fishing in the River Jordan when Bee's message arrived? Why wasn't the phone off the hook?'

So his fax back to Bee was, 'I'll only go if you come with me. You're the one who's thirsting for a battle, itching to indulge your reckless enthusiasm, at a moment when a bit of rational thought points in a quite different direction. I'm quite willing to keep my head down and wait till the Canaanites go away. I would really rather settle for a quiet life. But if I am to go, you must come too.' Barak wants to hide behind the skirts of the woman through whom God speaks; he is unsure whether God will be there if God's representative is not. God wants him to stand on his own, humanly speaking – to stand on his own with God, in this sense to be a man. Lightning has God's skirt to hide behind; he does not need a woman's, even a woman who is the most remarkable leader/judge/prophet/poet he will ever see.

For of course it was not merely the message of a stinging, flashing woman. It was the message of Yahweh, who was capable of being somewhat macho from time to time, and who proposed to be the military strategist in the planned confrontation between Lightning and Sisera. 'If you will go with me, I will go; but if you will not go with me, I will not go', Lightning had said. Moses had once said something along those lines, but

he had been talking to God, the God who had of course
promised to be with him (Exod. 3:12; 33:1–3,12–16). It is
Yahweh who is summoning Lightning. At least, Bee
claims it is, though it must be said that we are not told
that she was right. We are not told that Yahweh had
spoken to Bee; this might be a macho woman's
manipulating a peaceable man with her theology. If so,
however, God strings along with Bee rather than siding
with peaceable Lightning. Lightning wants to avoid
becoming involved, but Bee will not let him, and God
plays it Bee's way.

'I will certainly go with you', she says. But she also
has another word from Yahweh about the matter. His
response was surely not peaceable but feeble. 'The path
you are treading will not lead to your honour, because
Yahweh is going to sell Sisera into the hands of a
woman.' If Lightning insists on taking Bee with him as
his lucky charm, it will be the lucky charm that gets the
credit. At first sight that is all she seems to be saying.
The reality will be more complicatedly humiliating.

When Barak musters troops at Mount Tabor, Sisera is
drawn by the bait. He and his forces with their 900
chariots gather on the other side of the plain. Bee urges
Lightning to attack, promising that Yahweh has gone
on in advance of Lightning and has, in effect, already
given Sisera into his power. If we are to take Bee's later
poem literally, the way Yahweh does that is through
a tumultuous storm which comes at just the right
moment to even out the odds between the two armies
(see Jdg. 5:19–22).

There is a piece of theological poetic justice about
this. The Philistine gods were gods who manifested
themselves in weather phenomena. Dagon, for instance,
who will explicitly appear in the Samson story and in
the account of the covenant chest's adventures in 1
Samuel 5, was a god of lightning, which adds a further
piquancy to that being the meaning of Lappidot and
Barak. The implication is, the real God of lightning is
Yahweh, who now manifests that by acting through

such natural elements and enabling agents such as
flashing Bee and Lightning himself to represent on earth
the energy to which Dagon and his representatives can
only pretend. The Canaanite goddess Anat was also
associated with the stars and rain (which was believed
to come from the stars); further, she was a warrior
goddess. Yahweh of course was neither male nor
female, but/and had characteristics which other peoples
would ascribe to their gods or goddesses, certainly
including control of stars and rain. Here the power
which the Canaanites attributed to their warrior goddess is attributed to Yahweh and to Yahweh's warrior
prophetess.

Sisera had mustered his forces by the Qishon Wadi. A
wadi is a river which flows only when it has rained,
especially in the desert where it will be just a dry cleft
for most of the year. But when there is a storm (maybe a
distance away in the mountains), for a few hours it can
become a raging torrent. The Qishon does flow all year
round as a harmless brook, but the storm evidently
turned it into a flood. One of its effects was perhaps to
make the Canaanite chariots undriveable. One way or
another the result was not merely to even out the odds
between the two armies but to put them in favour of the
one which was not used to relying on such technology.
The Canaanite chariot forces panicked and took unsuc-
cessful flight for home; Lightning (who was evidently
learning to overcome any reluctance to play the macho
hero) led his forces in slaughtering them.

Ya'el, and the downfall of Sisera and of Barak

The Canaanite commander showed himself made of
wiser stuff than his troops (or so it seemed at first). The
survivor is the person who can keep cool in a crisis and
take rational action. Sisera abandons his chariot, which
no doubt made him conspicuous as well as being no use
when it rained, and disappears on foot in the direction

of Lightning's own town, which was perhaps the last direction they would look for him. Near Kedesh, however, was an industrial estate called Elon-bezaanannim which belonged to a tribe called the Qenites. Their name links them with Cain (Qain, as we might transliterate it), whose family 'made all kinds of bronze and iron' (Gen. 4:22). More recently they had become allies by marriage with the Israelites, through Moses's marriage to a Qenite. But a group such as the Qenites, like the modern Bedouin or Druze, survive by reading the political runes correctly and being on good terms with whoever is the power of the day, and still more recently they have become allies of Jabin. Given their expertise, they would be natural chariot suppliers and maintenance engineers. These technological experts have been the key to Sisera's success but are now in more than one sense the key to his downfall.

Among them is a woman called Ya'el, who in personality has some parallels to Bee and about whose position there are some ambiguities parallel to the ones which attach to Bee. She is 'wife of Heber the Qenite', according to the translations. So where is Heber when Sisera arrives? Perhaps the answer is that he had gone off with Sisera to run the chariot pit-stop services for his army, and is now on the run or dead like everyone else. But 'heber' is most often an ordinary word meaning 'company', and Ya'el may simply be being described as 'the woman who belongs to the Qenite group'. Whether or not she is a married woman, she resembles Bee in that she acts as an independent person.

When Sisera arrives at her home, expecting he is on friendly territory if these Qenites were his boss's chariot engineers (or at least were allies of Jabin), he has fled on foot the best part of fifty miles. Ya'el comes out to meet him and offers him an extraordinarily urbane and smooth welcome, in the circumstances. It is reminiscent of the welcome Abraham offered the three men on their way to Sodom, but that is not all. There is a wicked ambiguity about it. When an apparently unattached, certainly unaccompanied woman takes the initiative and invites a man into her bedroom, in any other context it would be the act of a seductress like the one who appears in Proverbs 7. She, like Ya'el, might well be expected to offer a man refreshment and comfort, invite him to lie down and relax, reassure him that everything will be all right and that she will tell no one of his visit – and then be the death of him, Proverbs says.

There is something else this points to. Ya'el's name, like others in this story, may be more than just a name. It means 'goat'. As well as its advice to avoid other women, elsewhere Proverbs gives a husband some positive hints about how to safeguard his marriage. He is to rejoice in his wife as a lovely deer, a graceful goat (Prov. 5:19). In English comparing your wife to a goat would be an insult, and translations therefore use terms such as 'hind' or 'doe'. So it will give more the right impression if we call Ya'el 'Doe'. The term offers one or two more hints about Ya'el and her place in this story. It implies that she is an attractive woman; that is significant in the way the story unfolds. But further, 'goat' is also a title for another goddess, so in addition Ya'el reminds us of Shamgar ben Anat and his implicitly Canaanite faith.

Ya'el perhaps knows the predicament she is in. Whether she is an independent Qenite woman with all the personal insecurity of that position at a moment like this (women in general, but independent women in particular, are often in personal peril in wartime), or the wife of a Qenite engineer whom the Israelites would have reason to view as a traitor, she belongs to a group who have backed the losing side. At this point (like Rahab in Jericho, as well as like Bee) she at least behaves like an independent woman, takes her destiny into her own hands, and acts in a way that brings Israel's victory to its completion in the death of Israel's enemy commander. Because she was a woman she won Sisera's confidence. He relaxed, and it cost him his life.

For like Lightning, Sisera no longer wants to be involved; he, too, has now had enough of playing the macho hero. He was physically exhausted, but when he lets himself fall very deeply asleep it is as if he also wants to contract out of life for a while, though probably not for as long as he ends up doing. Perhaps he knew that a nomadic group like the Qenites were committed to the practice of hospitality: in the desert a mutual commitment to hospitality can mean the difference between life and death. He thought he knew he could trust Ya'el. But perhaps Ya'el knew what this nomadic commitment to hospitality could mean for a woman (see the unsavoury stories in Gen. 19 and Jdg. 19) and is at this point, too, ready for a little role reversal.

She gets together her woman's weapons – gentleness and considerateness, cooking and hospitality, courage and unscrupulousness, a tent peg and a hammer (it was apparently a woman's job to erect the tent), and drives the tent peg through Sisera's skull as he sleeps. He must have been deeply asleep indeed; she must have used very violent force in an act which matches or even exceeds the grotesqueness of Ehud's (Jdg. 3:20–22). Ya'el the Qenite joins Shamgar the Canaanite (see 5:6) in the roll of honour of those who may have acted for themselves but who consciously or unconsciously also acted to free Israel. She is a deliverer, too.

Sisera's convulsions are barely over when Lightning arrives at the encampment, just too late if he now wants to play the hero and realize his destiny of being another Othniel (3:9–10). Ya'el had had no such hesitations. She struts out boldly to tell Lightning where he can find the object of his search, and conducts him to the tent to behold the great general pathetically impaled. 'The road on which you are going will not lead to your glory,' Bee had said, 'for Yahweh will sell Sisera into the hand of a woman'. It is doubly true, and more literally true than either of them had guessed. Even if there is no suggestion that she consciously acts for Yahweh's sake,

God's work is apparently done through her, and her achievement is to be long celebrated (5:24). Sisera and Lightning have both fallen to a deceptive lone foreign assassin. Sisera's last words were, 'If anyone asks if there is a man here, say "No" '. They were ironic words, with regard to himself and Lightning, who arrives just in time to view the body. Lightning reminds us of Inspector Morse's assistant (or Sherlock Holmes's), only there as foil to the great man (in this case the great woman), or even reminds us of Ehud's pathetic minders (3:24–25). Sisera's death is not Barak's victory but his defeat and humiliation.

Sisera's mother and her homely violence

'May Ya'el's achievement be long celebrated', says Bee. 'So may all your enemies perish, Yahweh' (Jdg. 5:31). Thus, like Sisera, impaled on a tent peg and convulsed? Bee remains macho and bloodthirsty to the end. Alongside the blessing on Ya'el, member of a clan which would have been pulled both ways by this battle because of its association both with Israel and with Jabin, is the terrible curse on Meroz (5:23), apparently a Canaanite village which also had an association with Israel but supported Sisera at the crucial moment.

Did God answer those prayers, and approve them? The text is silent about that, as it was silent about whether the actual battle came about by Bee's initiative or by Yahweh's. Ya'el is in scripture (so the prayer for her to be long celebrated is granted) but her story is not read (so it is not). It is not merely that the church has tended to prefer men's stories in scripture, though that is so. It is that the violence of stories such as Bee's and Ya'el's, or Ehud's and Shamgar's, makes us feel uncomfortable. It faces us with the fact of violence within ourselves, which we prefer to avoid. But it also seems in tension with the sense expressed elsewhere in scripture that the solution to violence issues from letting it be done to oneself, not doing it. Lightning is the sad figure in this story, but also an authentic one.

Perhaps the point is subconsciously made by the little vignette with which Bee's song closes. She imagines the scene back in Sisera's home town, in his villa. It is a garrison town and they are a military family. They know what it is like to psych themselves up for war, to send the men off to battle not sure how many will return or with what horrendous injuries. When they are away, everyone is jumpy and the tension builds as the time passes. No one relaxes.

As a senior military commander Sisera would have a house in a commanding position in Haroset, a position designed to catch the breeze in summer but also thus offering a vantage point over the area around. His mother paces the floor as the time goes on and they ought to be receiving some news. She peers through the wooden lattice which bridges the stone window openings, again designed to get maximum benefit from the breeze without losing privacy, and itself indicating that this is a rather fancy villa in Upper Haroset. Her son seems a long time, he and his men . . . . She and her household staff keep their spirits up by discussing the good reasons that may have delayed the men, but their words do not convince us, and perhaps did not convince them. Her villa is her prison as well as her home; she dare not move away from the telephone lest the call comes. As the iron chariots had stuck in the marsh and become worse than useless to their men, so the summer villa has become a prison on the way to being a backwater to its women.

Lightning has no escape from his man's role, and she has no escape from her woman's role, though like him, in the end she has entered into it enthusiastically. Behind every powerful man is a mother . . . . It involves her in something of a betrayal of her own sex. Why is there no sound of a returning chariot? It must be because they have won such a stupendous battle against those pathetic, primitive Israelites that they are working overtime dividing up the plunder. Like someone looking forward to the return of her son from a business trip abroad, she wonders what he will bring her as a souvenir: some nice native embroidery? But she thinks not just of the materials but of the people and imagines his forces embarrassed by choice among the young Israelite girls. Rape and pillage is what war is about, and she is quite happy about that as long as the Canaanites are winning. Her musings are ironic, of course, and so is the description of her staff, her 'very wise' ladies-in-waiting. They are not wise enough to recognize that the power balance has changed or to guess that womanhood has been Sisera's downfall rather than vice versa. The kind of motherhood that Bee embodies and that Ya'el embodies in active ways is also the kind that Sisera's mother embodies in a more passive way, a violent motherhood that will now grieve at what other mothers have done to her son. The returning army will bring her not embroidery but sackcloth.

Issues concerning oppression and deliverance have been resolved for a while. Questions about community relationships and family happiness remain. Even Jabin is to some degree a victim. It was God who had sold Israel to him in the first place, using him to achieve the divine purpose, and now has overpowered Jabin. Perhaps Jabin now wants to avoid being involved, like Lightning and Sisera; there must have been some reason why he avoided fighting, as Lightning wanted to, and left the task to Sisera who had more taste for such activity. But for a leader in a position like his there is no escape until the Israelites have destroyed him (Jdg. 4:23–24). Like his commander he will find the only escape is death.

Bee's story and Bee's song concern some political, military, and historical questions, and some personal questions about what it means to be a man or a woman. The story began (4:1–3) the way we might expect a story about Israel's adventures in the judges period to begin,

but as it unfolds it changes the agenda and subverts our
expectations of such a story. It comes to be about
Israelite power and Canaanite oppression, but also
about women's power and patriarchal oppression. It is
typical of scripture that it interweaves these concerns:
historical issues are determined through people coming
to terms with who they themselves are, and people
discover who they themselves are through their involvement in historical events. The crucial events are as much
the ones that take place in the privacy of Ya'el's home as
the ones that take place on the battlefield where the
business remains unfinished.

Bee's story and Bee's song affirm the significance of
Israel's activity in history, Yahweh's activity with Israel
which makes their victories possible, and women's
activity in a men's world. But it does that in an
ambiguous and ironic way.

How *is* God's purpose realized in the world? Through
kings like Jabin who are involved in the fulfilment of
God's purpose all unbeknown to themselves, in ways
they enjoy and in ways they wish they could escape.
Through the people of God crying out to God in the
midst of their suffering (even when it is deserved).
Through a woman of insight who becomes a woman of
violence. Through a reluctant soldier who learns the
lesson from her very well. Through a woman on her
own who uses her female wiles to become a traitor and
an assassin. It embraces three assertive women, three
women with violent intent; Deborah and Ya'el succeed
because Yahweh is with them, Sisera's mother is disappointed because Yahweh is not with her. It embraces
three men trying to avoid violence and failing, three
male victims, Jabin because Yahweh's purpose runs a
different way, Barak because Deborah has other ideas,
Sisera because he relaxes in the company of Ya'el. They
all play a part in Yahweh's purpose, and in the
introduction of 40 years' peace in the land, for the sake
of which it might almost seem worthwhile to be a
victim.

TWELVE

Samson and Delilah

Samson is one of the great examples of faith in the New Testament, someone the Bible expects us to learn from. So what sort of man was this hero of faith?

The Israelites had again done wrong in the eyes of Yahweh, who had given them into the power of the Philistines. At a political level it is a period of considerable violence in Israel's national relationships. Arguably international relations are thus in their 'normal' state; strife is more that normal state than is peace. On a gloomy day it can seem that to seek peace is always to work against the grain, that nations are inherently violent – they always have been and they always will be. The individuals who make up nations are likewise innately violent (especially the men, for gender questions do seem to come into play here) – individual and national violence feed each other. The story of Samson in Judges 14–17 is part of the story of violent relationships between the Israelites and the Philistines; Samson was to be the man to give the Philistines something to think about. It is also the story of his personal violence.

Old Testament James Bond, yet tragic hero

Samson was indeed someone God used. He was a man
with a calling. Yet he was a tragic hero. But none of that
is where the story starts. The first fact that becomes
clear in his story is that Samson was the Old Testament
James Bond. He fancied a Philistine girl, and went to
win her. On the way a lion attacked him and he tore the
lion apart the way you kill a goat (which would be more
than enough for most of us), with his bare hands. 'But
he did not tell his father or mother what he had done',
the story says. Well, you wouldn't, would you? When
he got to Timnah, the Philistines swindled him out of 30
lengths of linen and 30 suits (£3000?). So he went on to
the next Philistine town, killed 30 men, and paid his
debt with their clothes.

It seems he was not really satisfied with this revenge.
Eventually he went and caught 300 foxes, tied torches to
their tails, and turned the foxes loose in the Philistine
cornfields and orchards. The Philistines, in their turn,
killed Samson's wife and her father, though Samson got
his own back on them in the end. 'He smote them,
hip and thigh, with great slaughter.' This time the
Philistines invaded Judah, looking for him. Samson's
own people persuaded him to surrender himself, and
the Philistines tied him up, but he broke their ropes as if
these were sticky tape. He looked around and spotted a
dead donkey, grabbed the donkey's jaw and went
flailing at the Philistines, killing another thousand of
them. The interwovenness of personal and national
violence, and the place of God in all this, is noted in the
observation that his parents have to be forgiven their
opposition to Samson's marriage plans because they did
not realize that these were giving Yahweh opportunity
to intervene in politics and take some action to free
Israel from Philistine oppression for a while (Jdg. 14:4).

The way the story has opened has revealed Samson's
other obvious characteristic as well as his violent streak,
his eye for girls. Mieke Bal has noted how the inter-

wovenness of sex and violence is characteristic of the
Book of Judges as a whole, and it is the combination of
sex and violence that invites us to view Samson as an
Old Testament James Bond, though it must be noted
that in due course even James Bond cleaned up his act
somewhat in the light of Aids. Samson is pre-Aids,
more a child of the 1960s. Samson first got into trouble
because he fancied a Philistine girl, and later he was
nearly caught in Gaza when he was spending a night
with a girl there. But then there was Delilah, who was
not just pretty or sexy: he fell for Delilah.

That brings us up short. James Bond does not fall in
love. This is the point at which we move from Samson
the Old Testament James Bond to Samson the tragic
hero. Women and violence are the two themes that link
Samson and James Bond, but the links are superficial.
James Bond is always the successful ladies' man. If a
heart is broken, it will not be his. He rides off into the
sunset with a sequence of attractive girls.

For all the similarities, Samson is not quite the same.
There are four women in Samson's story. There is the
girl he married, the girl he picked up, and the girl he fell
in love with, who occupy Judges 14, 15, and 16. But
before we come to them, we read in chapter 13 about a
very different woman, the one who bore him. She was
like a number of other women in the Old Testament
such as Sarah and Hannah. For years she had not been
able to have children. They had tried and tried and
hoped and prayed, and it had never happened. Then
God promised she would have a son, and they called
him Samson. It is a suggestive name: it means 'Sunshine'. As far as his mother was concerned, the sun
shone out of his eyes. You can almost see her glowing
pride as he grows to be bigger and stronger than
anyone else in the area. That was the first woman in
Samson's life. The picture of her and her husband
contrasts sadly with the story of the woman he married
because he fancied her and the woman he spent the
night with because he felt like it.

Then there was the woman he fell in love with. Here is when Samson becomes a human being, when he softens and becomes vulnerable – though I suspect there would be a feminist/psychoanalytical critique of this so-called falling in love. If he does grow as a person, it is the means of his downfall. The tragedy was that it was a tale of unrequited love. Delilah was able to be the woman who found out the secret of Samson's strength and to tell the Philistines, for 30 pieces of silver. 'And the Philistines seized him and gouged out his eyes, and brought him down to Gaza, and bound him with bronze fetters. And he ground at the mill in the prison.' Delilah is a woman like Ya'el but working for the other side, using her womanliness in that connection as Samson is using his manliness, but also using her intelligence as he is not, because men so easily throw sense to the winds when diverted by what they think is love. In Judges Yahweh's spirit may convey power but it does not necessarily convey insight.

Man with a calling, man God used

What exactly was it that was tragic about Samson? He was a disappointment to his family, he made a mess of his relationships, his manliness and strength were pathetically overcome and made fun of by the Philistines, but what was tragic about Samson was the contrast between what he was and what he was supposed to be before God. Samson was a man with a calling. He was supposed to be God's agent in liberating Israel from the Philistines. What happens, however, is that at the beginning of the story he marries a Philistine, and at the end of the story he dies with the Philistines.

There were other aspects to his calling. To mark him out as Yahweh's servant, he was supposed to be a Nazirite, someone especially devoted to God. A Nazirite was different in three ways from other people. He abstained from alcohol; it was perhaps a symbol of being filled with another Spirit. He avoided eating certain things, keeping a special version of the kosher laws that all Israelites observed. The point was not that there was anything wrong with these foods; they were not a threat to health. Abstaining from them simply marked the Nazirite out. His third distinctive mark was that he kept his hair long. That was another sign of his consecration, and thus another sign of the strength which came from the God he was consecrated to.

Those were Samson's vows. He breaks each one of them. First we see him at the same kind of wedding feast as everyone else, where (no doubt) the wine flowed freely. Then he eats some honey produced by bees who had made their nest in the carcase of that lion he killed, which means that the honey would be unclean. Finally there was his hair. 'How can you say you love me', said Delilah, 'when you keep your secrets from me? What is the secret of your strength?' She nagged him day after day until she wore him down and he told her. 'It's the fact that scissors have never been near my head, not since I was born, because I have been set apart as a Nazirite since birth. If my hair were cut off, my strength would go. I would be as weak as anyone else.' When Delilah saw that he had now told her the truth, she sent word to the Philistine SAS. 'Come back one more time. He has told me'. They came with the eleven hundred shekels they had promised her. She lulled him to sleep on her lap. Perhaps he was tired of fighting, like Sisera, and subconsciously wanted out – in which case he reminds one of the tragic violent heroes of films such as *Once Upon A Time In America* who find they can never get out. As he slept like a baby on its mother's lap, Delilah called a man to cut off his seven plaits of hair, whereupon his strength left him. Then she shouted out, 'Samson, the Philistines are on top of you'. He woke up with a yawn and said to himself, 'Well, I shall soon see them off again', not realizing that Yahweh had left him. It was the contrast between the man he was and the man he was supposed to be that constituted his tragedy.

This might have been the end of the story, but it is not, and that is one good reason why the story appears in the Bible. We do not, of course, need the Bible to tell us James Bond stories. We have Ian Fleming to do that. But part of the reason why this kind of story is there is that inside most of us there is a little James Bond (or a little Delilah). That is partly why so many people like those films. They are fantasies.

The Bible's James Bond, however, lives in the real world, where sex and violence rebound on us. It makes us live in the actual world, not in a celluloid one. Then precisely because many of the instincts of Samson or Delilah are inside us, something of the tragedy of their stories also appears in our lives. We misuse our opportunities, mess up our relationships, and hurt people. We know that we fall short of God's vision and of the commitments we make to God.

The Samson story challenges us to look in the eye what it is that God wants to do with us and to look in the eye the kind of special commitments God asks of us, and to see how we are getting on with them. It presents us with a man who made a mess of his life, his relationships, and his calling. But it then tells us that this is not quite the end of the story, because even in that situation it is still possible to be the person God uses. This does not undo the tragedy, as the end of the story shows, but it takes a little of the edge off it.

The Philistines had captured Samson, gouged out his eyes, and taken him to Gaza. John Milton wrote a poem about Samson, whose blindness he shared. Many painters have painted Samson in his blindness, too. It is this aspect of Samson that has caught their imagination, perhaps because to them sight is so all-important; they recall the sculptor in the play *Whose Life Is It Anyway*, who wishes to commit suicide when paralysis makes him unable to continue the creative activity which defines him as a human being. Milton also wrote a poem in which he overtly reflected on his own blindness.

> God doth not need
> Either man's work or his own gifts: who best
> Bear his mild yoke, they serve him best. His state
> Is kingly: thousands at his bidding speed,
> and post o'er land and ocean without rest;
> They also serve who only stand and wait.

In a terrible sense that will also be true of Samson. Perhaps Yahweh was using Samson's love for Delilah just as had been the case with his attraction for the Philistine woman with whom the story began.

The Philistines had chained him up and set him to grinding corn in the prison. There the hair that had been cut off began to grow again. Then the time came for a festival in honour of their god, Dagon, and they assembled to worship him for delivering their troubler, Samson, into their hands (a woman never gets the credit, even if she does do the work). They fetched Samson from the prison and stood him in the middle of the temple to perform for their entertainment. Samson had to be led by a boy, of course, because he could not see. He asked the boy to put him where he could feel the pillars in the temple. It is helpful to know something about Philistine architecture: temples had two pillars in the middle to support the roof, as is illustrated in examples that have been excavated in Palestine in recent years. Samson began to press with the strength of each arm on the two pillars; and Samson prayed. Samson is praying! 'Yahweh, remember me. Give me strength just once more, Yahweh. Give me one chance to get revenge on the Philistines, at least for blinding me. I will be happy to die with them!' He pushed with all his might, and the temple collapsed on the Philistine rulers and people and on Samson himself. He killed many more when he died than while he lived. The story ends with his family going to get his body, and burying him between Zorah and Eshtaol in the tomb of his father.

It is the end of the story, but Samson is mentioned that once more in scripture, in Hebrews 11. 'What more shall I say? I do not have time to tell about Gideon, Barak, Samson . . . .' Even Samson is in the list of the heroes of faith; even Samson is among the cloud of witnesses. If there is room for Samson, there is room for you and me.

THIRTEEN

Ruth and Naomi

The Book of Ruth is a marvellously rich story. It tells of
how a foreign girl is adopted by the Jewish community,
of how a middle-aged man at last finds the woman of
his dreams, of how the greatest king of Israel found his
grandfather, and it tells of how a Jewish woman loses
everything and then has her life rebuilt. The story
actually begins with this fourth aspect, the experience
of Naomi, and it almost finishes, with her; her angle is a
very important one, and easily missed because we focus
on this as Ruth's story.

Naomi

At the beginning it is the story of Naomi the victim.
These are again the days when the judges ruled, and
not very effectively it must be said, because these were
days when everyone did what was right in their own
eyes, when there tended to be chaos, unfaithfulness to
Yahweh, war, and deprivation. Further, there is a
famine in the country.

In that society (as in most societies, to a great extent),
a man is expected to provide for his family. His wife and

children need food. In a situation like this, what is a
man to do? There was a man called Elimelech who
knew what he had to do. He was married to Naomi,
and they had two sons, Mahlon and Kilion. They lived
in Bethlehem; its name means 'Bread-house', a nasty
irony during a famine. Now from the little town of
Bethlehem in the Judean hills you can look down into
the Jordan Valley and across to the corresponding hills
the other side, in the modern State of Jordan, where
apparently there was food. So Elimelech took his family
to live there.

A Jewish family go to live among the Moabites, who
were almost the first people who had oppressed Israel
in the time of the judges. They cross the Jordan like
Joshua, at the ford just above the Dead Sea, but they are
going in the opposite direction, out of the land of
promise, leaving the land of promise like Abraham
when *he* could not provide for *his* family because of a
famine in this same area. This is not just a tale of a
family moving house. It is stage one in Naomi's life
falling apart.

A Jew goes to live in Moab. Imagine a man who lives
in Bethlehem today, which of course means an Arab,
and imagine he is out of a job, which is not difficult.
Imagine he goes and gets work in Jewish West
Jerusalem (more difficult now than it once was). Or for
that matter imagine a Jew in Afula who loses his job and
goes to live and work in Arab Nazareth. Either gains a
livelihood, makes the survival of his family possible,
but his feelings about it are fairly mixed.

So Elimelech, Naomi, Mahlon, and Kilion move to
Moab and settle down there, and everything seems
fine, until Elimelech takes ill and dies. It is stage two of
Naomi's life falling apart. Now she is a single parent
with two sons to bring up in a foreign country. They
grow up and marry Moabite women: who else could
they marry? But that may have seemed to be stage
three. *Moabites*? Naomi knew who the first Moabite was:
there is an unpleasant story about how he came into the

world in Genesis 19. She knew who were the last Israelite men to get involved with Moabite women, the people in Numbers 25 who ended up worshipping the Moabites' gods and being put to death. Israelites did get involved with Moabite gods in the time of the judges (see Jdg. 10:6). These were not mere stories from the past.

Mahlon and Kilion married, but they never had children. In due course they took ill and died, like their father. It is now a decade since Naomi came to Moab, and it is stage four of her life falling apart. Must she not have wondered whether this was all Yahweh's judgment? They should never have left Bethlehem. But how could they have done anything else? They were caught. That is actually how many people in Bethlehem must feel today: they are caught by circumstances and decisions which they took in the past and which they cannot now undo. But it is also how many people in any part of the world may feel, people who have lost jobs and whose family life has collapsed and who wish they could start all over again, but for whom there seems no way.

So the woman was left without her two sons and her husband. Then she started to return from the country of Moab, because she had heard there that Yahweh had considered his people and given them food (*lehem*: at last Bethlehem was living up to its name again). And Naomi's daughters-in-law were going to return with her to this country where Yahweh had been acting again. So they could not have been stereotypical Moabite women, these two.

The three of them set out, and the long journey gives yet more time to think and talk. On the road between Moab and Judah, one country visible in front, the other behind, Naomi agonizes and wrestles. In due course she comes to a halt as the impossibility of what they are now doing comes home to her. In a number of ways once again they are caught. 'You must go back home. You can't come with me.'

They are caught by ethnic divisions, Israelite and Moabite, Jew and Arab. 'Go back to your mother's house', she bids them. 'We want to go back with you to your people.' 'Go back home, you can't come with me.' One imagines again that Jew from Afula who goes to live in Nazareth; his sons marry Arab girls, then he hears there are jobs in Afula again, and he sets off to go back. He is on the brow of the hill on the way out of Nazareth where you can see both towns, and he suddenly realizes what he is doing. He is taking two Arab girls to a Jewish town. Or one imagines that Arab from Bethlehem, who has gone to live in Jerusalem, where his sons have married Jewish girls. He is on the way from Jerusalem to Bethlehem, taking Jewish girls there. 'We should never have got involved with those Arabs/Jews.'

They are caught by gender divisions, expectations of society regarding the position of women. The very first verse of the book hints at them, like the first verse of the Hagar story: Elimelech and *his* wife and *his* two sons, it says, as if she had no part in them, she is merely one of his possessions. Now all three of these men are dead, fallen to the lonely responsibility of being male (evidently in their society as in ours men have the responsibility and women live longer – apparently in Britain four times as many young men as young women commit suicide). The question is whether the women can survive on their own. The only future for a young woman is marriage: 'Yahweh grant that you may find security in the house of a husband', says Naomi, because that is the only kind of security. 'I can't provide you with that, so there's no point staying with me'.

She embraced them, and they wept, and after a minute they said, 'No, we want to come back with you to your people'. 'No, you must go back. Do I still have sons in my womb to marry you? Why come with me? It has been far more bitter for me than for you. The hand of Yahweh has turned against me. May Yahweh keep his commitment to you,' Naomi prays, 'even though he has turned against me. Go back to your people and to your gods'. They are also caught by religious divisions and by the mystery of the way God deals with us.

Ruth

Orpah sees sense and begins to say goodbye. You cannot blame her, given all those pressures. But Ruth refuses to 'see sense'. 'I won't be put off by society's attitude to relations between the sexes', in effect she says. She 'cleaves' to Naomi, the way a man cleaves to a woman when they get married according to Genesis 2. 'Don't pressure me to leave you or turn back from following you. Where you go, I go. Where you stay, I stay.' Never mind all that talk about marriage. Like David and Jonathan in their commitment to each other, Ruth reckons there are other committed relationships apart from that.

In Western society, it is often said that women come to that kind of committed relationship to each other more easily than men, and men may need to work at its possibilities. Both marriage and same-sex friendship have their risks and their potentials. Marriage has the capacity to image God in the way it combines diversity with lifelong commitment. But it can mean that one partner, probably the wife, has to subordinate her real self, and sometimes that real self can emerge in a same-sex friendship – even if it is also the case that same-sex friendships do not have the particular built-in element of diversity that marriage has. For a woman, especially, reaching full human maturity involves differentiation, reaching out to express herself as a person, refusing merely to be some man's possession, and for Ruth that comes about through a relationship with another woman, a mother-like figure who refuses to bind and can free.

Ruth also refuses to be caught by ethnic divisions. 'Your people shall be my people', she says. 'Where you

die, I will die, and be buried there.' When people died
in Palestine they would be buried in the family grave,
they joined the family. Naomi's family will be the one
Ruth joins.

In Bethlehem I once came across a demonstration by
Palestinian women whose sons or husbands or brothers
or fathers were in jail because of offences related to the
intifada. It was a more effective demonstration than
some, precisely because at one level there was nothing
threatening about it. There were no stones, let alone
guns, only wailing and weeping. In West Jerusalem at
the same time there were parallel demonstrations by
Jewish women dressed in black, mourning the nature of
the occupation of Palestinian territories, women who
found themselves abused by their fellow-countrymen
for the stand they took. Two groups who metaphorically
stood together, unwilling to be constrained by ethnic
and political divisions.

Ruth also refuses to be caught by religious divisions
and by the mystery of Naomi's God. 'Your God will be
my God', she says. Which God is this – the God whose
hand has turned against this faithful but abandoned
Israelite woman? It is that God before whom Ruth now
makes her commitments: 'May Yahweh bring terrible
punishment on me if even death parts me from you',
she says. Naomi's strange arbitrary God is the God Ruth
determines to make her own, because of her attachment
to Naomi herself. Ruth is like Abraham only more so.
She has no word from God, no promise, only whatever
had spoken to her out of Naomi's life, and on its basis
she is prepared to commit herself to Naomi's God.

So Naomi saw Ruth was determined to go with her,
and said no more to her. But what was she thinking? I
wonder if she was less touched by Ruth's moving
speech than we are. 'The silly girl is set on coming with
me so I will just have to put up with it.' Anyway Orpah
disappears from the picture; Ruth and Naomi go on
until they come to Bethlehem. Again, that conceals
more than it reveals. It is not like taking a ten-minute

walk to the shops. It involves going down into the
Jordan valley and across the river itself, which is in
flood at the time (as it was when Joshua crossed)
because it is April (to judge from references in the story
to barley harvest), so one can imagine the scene with
these two women hitching up their long dresses . . . .
One way or another they wade across the river, then
begin the long climb up to Bethlehem, one carrying a
full-grown despair about God and about life, the other
alive with a new commitment to God and to life. Two
friends in a very different position, but together.

When they came to Bethlehem, the news soon got
round the town. 'And the women said, "Is this
Naomi?" She said to them, "Don't call me Naomi any
more".' Naomi means lovely, beautiful, attractive. That
is not how she feels now. 'Do not call me Naomi any
more. Call me Marah.' Marah means bitter, angry, sour.

'Marah' reminds us of another incident from Israel's
past, one we considered in recalling Moses' story. A few
days after escaping from Egypt the Israelites found
themselves running out of water in the wilderness.
Then they came to a place with water, but the water
turned out to be undrinkable, polluted, bitter. Indeed,
the place was called Marah, Bitter. Discovering this the
Israelites, who had been distraught, then hoping, then
disappointed, turned on their leader. 'What are we
supposed to drink, then?' There Moses cried out to
Yahweh, and grabbed a branch from a tree that
happened to be there, and threw it in the water,
whereupon the smell disappeared and the water
became drinkable. What was *marah* became *naom*. Then
Yahweh spoke. 'You see? Now will you just listen to
what I say and shape your life by it, and I'll prove
myself to you as one who heals.' From there they had
moved on and come to Elim, where there were twelve
springs and seventy palm trees, and had camped beside
the water (Exod. 15:22–27).

In Naomi's life, what might be the log that makes the
bitter water fresh and drinkable? What are the standards,

the rule of life, that is key to escaping suffering and finding healing? Naomi walks past Jericho, the city of springs and palm trees, and asks, 'Am I ever going to reach my oasis, my city of springs and palm trees, and camp beside the water there?'

The beginning of an answer was before her eyes, but she could not see it yet. Indeed, there are three pieces towards this jigsaw. First, she has come back to Bethlehem with her daughter-in-law. To say she is empty is rather a slight on her. Second, they arrive at Bethlehem as the barley harvest is beginning. So the famine is over; it is a time of hope. Those comments come at the end of chapter 1. The third comes at the beginning of chapter 2 – it is another of the uninspired chapter divisions in scripture. Among her family back in Bethlehem is a prominent rich relative of Elimelech's called Boaz. Because he is a close member of her family, he has the moral obligation to care for her. Even if she had taken him into account in trying to identify what might be the raw material for turning bitter water into fresh, she would hardly have guessed how well he would do it.

They arrive back in Bethlehem and find somewhere to stay, presumably with relatives. They talk, and rest their feet after the long journey. But they cannot do nothing for ever, and they cannot presume on people's hospitality for ever. So Ruth suggests to Naomi that she should go to the fields and join with the people who are picking up the stray grain that the main harvesters miss as they reap the barley harvest (people who have no land of their own). Here is where Yahweh's words come in. Israel's rule of life included caring for the needy, for people like Naomi and Ruth who were widows. They had the right to join in the reaping in this way as gleaners. The reapers even had to make a point of leaving the corners of the fields for them, rather than reaping right to the edges.

Israel's rule of life also said they had to be considerate to foreigners, to people such as Moabites and Arabs. I once listened to a sermon by the pastor of a messianic congregation (a congregation of Jews who believe in Jesus) in Jerusalem. He was preaching on Jesus' story about the man who gets mugged, and I wondered whether this Jewish preacher would be able to say, 'The Arab is my neighbour'. I was thrilled when he was. Live by my standards of behaviour, live by the rule of life I give you, Yahweh had said at Marah, and you will find healing. It is coming true for Naomi.

Boaz

So Naomi accepts Ruth's idea, though once more we cannot read between the lines. Is she enthusiastic? Or just compliant? Why is she not joining in herself? As it is, however, Ruth goes on her own, and gleans in the field behind the reapers. The fields would be divided into strips, the harvest is very neat and systematic, and it is easy to follow the actual harvesters. There Ruth just happened to be in the part of the field that belonged to Boaz.

The story of Ruth is not as non-theistic as Esther, but it is not far off. God does not keep appearing in this book. God has been spoken of but does not actually do anything at all until the very last scene of the story. As in some other stories we have considered, such as Joseph's, God works behind the scenes of human decision-making and unintended coincidences, as happens in our lives. Ruth happens to glean in the right part of the field, and Boaz happens to come along from the town at the right moment.

He greets the reapers. 'The Lord be with you.' 'And also with you.' He is quickly established as a polite, believing, caring person who knows the liturgy of a church service. Then he sees a woman he does not recognize and he asks the foreman about her. It is a scene from any church or factory or office. A new young woman arrives and the unattached men are asking,

'Who's she, then?' Except that it is even more patriarchal than we are: the question is, 'Who does *she* belong to?' She is a woman, so she is some man's property. That is her identity.

The foreman explains, and that gives Boaz the chance to play the caring macho hero: 'You stay here to reap, young lady, I've told the men not to bother you. If you get thirsty, get yourself a drink over there'. Later on it is 'Would you like a bite to eat? What are you drinking?' Furthermore Boaz is telling the reapers to be even more careless than the teaching of Moses required regarding how much grain they left behind, telling them to exercise some positive discrimination in favour of this new gleaner.

'Why are you bothering with a foreigner like me?' 'Because they've told me about the way you have stuck with Naomi since Elimelech died. They've told me how you left your family and your native land and came to a people you did not know before.' It is not clear whether Boaz realizes, but we realize once again that Ruth is the women's equivalent to Abraham. 'May Yahweh reward you for your deeds, Yahweh the God of Israel under whose wings you have come for refuge.' Boaz's prayer is a significant one; Ruth will remember how he prays.

Ruth gleans all day, beats out the barley she has gathered, and it comes to 20 kilos. That is a significant amount: it is the standard baggage allowance on an airplane. Anyone who has tried to carry it knows that is a lot of baggage, or a lot of barley. Yes, the famine is over. New life is beginning. Ruth nonchalantly shoulders it and carries it back to town to show Naomi. She also tells her about Boaz, and Naomi exclaims, 'He's a relative of ours! In fact he's one of closest relatives, one of the ones who would be committed to looking after us! Blessed be Boaz by Yahweh. Yahweh hasn't given up being committed to us.'

Naomi has come a long way. Sometimes when one has been ministering to a person who has felt everything was dark and hopeless and God was nowhere, after a time a gleam of light begins to return and suddenly that person has said something that suggests a spark of faith. The tree has been thrown into the waters. The bitter water is becoming fresh and drinkable. But what about the twelve springs and the seventy palm trees?

Now Naomi takes the initiative. 'Ruth, it's all very well you coming with me, it's all very well for now, but I need to do something to make sure that you have some security for the future.' Back in chapter 1 Naomi had prayed that Yahweh would enable Ruth and Orpah to find security in the house of a husband (1:8–9). Now she is being the means to her prayer being answered.

She formulates an extremely risky plan. April and harvest time means it is getting to be fine weather. It is quite a way from the fields back to the town, and in any case the barley needs guarding, so Boaz and the others sleep at the threshing floor. Ruth is to dress up, almost like a bride, at least like a woman trying to be as attractive as she knows how. She is to keep an eye on where Boaz goes to sleep. And she is to go and lie down beside him. Imagine Boaz's face when he turns over at midnight and finds Ruth there. Why does an attractive young woman come and lie next to a man like that? It is a risky plan. But maybe something had to be done. Boaz has the moral responsibility to see that Naomi and Ruth are looked after. The way he reacted to Ruth when they first met suggested he was attracted to her. But perhaps he was constrained by similar factors to ones we have thought about already. A respectable middle-aged man, a pillar of the Jewish community in Bethlehem, does not cast his hat at the first young Moabite widow who rides into town (what *did* her first Jewish husband die of, anyway?). He does not marry out. He does not even consciously think about the idea. So nothing will happen unless Naomi and Ruth make it happen. Two women, a Jew and an Arab, take their destiny into their hands in a man's world and a world where ethnic divisions mean everything.

So Boaz wakes up, turns over, and finds Ruth there beside him. There is a splendid film called *The Morning After* which begins with a woman waking up to find an attractive man in bed with her. At least in this story the unexpected body is alive.

When he first met Ruth, Boaz had talked about her coming to Yahweh for refuge, coming under Yahweh's wings, under Yahweh's covering, under Yahweh's cloak. Ruth makes Boaz eat his words. 'I need *you* to cover me', she says. 'I need *you* to put your wings over me, your cloak over me.' It is the same word in Hebrew. 'Yes, I've turned to Yahweh as my refuge. But Yahweh uses human agents. *You* cannot pray that prayer for Yahweh to bless me and just leave it at that. You cannot, especially, because you're our next-of-kin, you're the nearest person in the world to Naomi and me. You've got to help us. I need *you* to cover me.'

I find that a beautiful image. One of the first Bruce Springsteen songs I ever liked was 'Cover me'. 'When life seems hard and I feel afraid and the world seems cold and competitive: cover me.' I feel exposed, I need to hide, I need shelter, protection, cover me. Here each of us is, exposed to the world, vulnerable, cold. I need someone to cover me. God does, but God also uses people. God uses us that way in relation to each other. It is an important aspect of marriage, but it is not limited to that; it must not be. Friends do it for each other. I have mentioned that my wife is disabled. During the weeks I was completing this book, she had a serious relapse of her multiple sclerosis and I had a harrowing few weeks until she recovered. Over those weeks friends overwhelmed me with love, and I especially appreciated three or four occasions when someone hugged me from above (for example, they were standing and I was sitting), so that they were in a position of protectiveness, shielding me from a life which seemed tough, sheltering me. 'Cover me', Ruth asked.

'I want to', says Boaz. I would not have dared offer to. Apart from the social constraints, I thought I was too old. I never thought you would be interested in me. But I want to.

Then comes the complication. There has to be one, in any decent love story. There is another man in the offing who is a closer relative of Naomi than Boaz, so he needs manipulating out of the way, though that may be tricky. After all, to take on Ruth is to take on Naomi, and to take on Naomi is to take on Naomi's inheritance from Elimelech, her land, and that is worth having. This other man has to have first refusal. Once again, like Naomi and Ruth, Boaz is constrained by a patriarchal society, one which can help make sure that people like widows, orphans, and foreigners are looked after, but the other side of the coin is that people and property easily get confused.

The matter cannot be sorted out till morning, so Ruth tiptoes home, if it is possible to tiptoe with another 20 kilos of barley over your shoulder. Ruth must try to be discrete. Now that the relationship is becoming serious, it is important not to give the wrong impression. Gently she lifts the latch on Naomi's door as dawn breaks. But Naomi is wide awake. 'How did you get on?' 'It worked – well, subject to fixing this other man.' 'Don't worry', says Naomi. 'Boaz will sort it out.' Naomi has taken another step forward. From bitterness, to resistance, to silence, to acquiescence, to initiative which actually believes there could be a future, to confidence that there will be.

There is now nothing else Naomi and Ruth can do. Officially it is indeed a man's world. The question on the table is, 'Which man will buy Ruth for the sake of another man who is not even alive (Elimelech)?' Women have ways of getting their way, but these have to be unofficial ways. When it is an institutional matter, as this has now become, it is men's business.

The women watch from a distance as Boaz asks the other man to sort the matter out with the elders, the *men*, at the city gate, where they always gather to resolve community issues. 'You have the right to take Elimelech's place, to acquire his land and take on his family. Are you going to?' 'Yes.' The story threatens to fall apart. What about the love of Boaz and Ruth, and of Ruth and Naomi? Then the complication of Ruth's presence comes out, and the man has second thoughts. He cannot, or will not, take on Elimelech's land and family after all.

The story is odd at this point because it goes into great detail about the transaction but it still does not quite make clear to us what the problem is, so of course that is what all the scholarly ink has been wasted on over the decades, but it does not matter. We can heave a sigh of relief, because the bottom line is that everything is going to work out. *Boaz* is the one who takes on Elimelech's land and family obligations, and those include Ruth. 'Today you are witnesses that I have acquired from the hand of Naomi all that belonged to Elimelech and all that belonged to Kilion and Mahlon. I have also acquired Ruth the Moabite, the wife of Mahlon, to be my wife, to maintain the dead man's name on his inheritance, in order that the name of the dead man may not be cut off from his kindred and from the gate of his native place.' It now seems a terrible thing for a man to have to say, but men have to live with a share in the guilt for being part of a patriarchal society.

So Ruth and Boaz can marry; or rather, Boaz can take Ruth and she comes to belong to him. And they make love, and Yahweh causes her to conceive, and she has a little boy. The child she had never born to Mahlon she bears to Boaz, and thus David acquires his grandfather, who was half-Arab, half-Jew.

For the most part we have been reading this story from Naomi's angle, however, so let us not allow even David to have the last word. When Ruth gives birth to her baby the Bethlehem women said to Naomi, 'Blessed be Yahweh who has not left you this day without next-of-kin; and may his name be renowned in Israel! He shall be to you a restorer of life and a renewer of old age; for your daughter-in-law, who loves you, who is more to you than seven sons, has borne him'. Then Naomi takes the child and sits him on her lap and becomes his nurse. And the women give him his name, Obed, and pronounce, 'A son has been born to Naomi'.

Earlier on in the story that was exactly what Naomi said could never happen. 'Do I still have sons in my womb? The hand of Yahweh has turned against me.' The space in her life that was once occupied by her children, and by God, and by hope and happiness, was all empty. She could not imagine it would ever be filled again. Children can easily become too important, perhaps especially to their mothers, but we cannot blame Naomi, and we may have had experiences of our own that enable us to identify with her. The things that counted most have been taken away and God seems to have turned against me.

The end of the story shows that that experience does not necessarily have the last word. God acts for the only time in the story, not against Naomi, perhaps offended by what she said, but for her. It is God who enables Ruth to conceive, but the child is not so much Ruth's, nor Boaz's, and more importantly not Elimelech's, in the way the women see it. 'A son is born to *Naomi*', they say. The life which seemed empty and hopeless is restored and nourished. The tree has been cast into the bitter waters, Israel's rule of life has been kept, and Ruth, Boaz, and Naomi have reached their Elim, the place with the twelve fresh springs and seventy palm trees for shade, and they can rest by still waters.

FOURTEEN

Hannah and her Sister

I once heard someone comment that all Christians were exhorted to learn from the stories about Abraham in scripture, but only women were exhorted to learn from the stories about Sarah. The story of Hannah is one that captures something of the hurt and the joy there can be in being a woman before God, but also in being a man.

A woman who suffers and who prays

Like the stories of Sarah and Hagar or Naomi and Ruth, Hannah's story is lived the way almost any woman's story has been lived throughout history, in the framework of the story of men. It starts by telling us about a man from Ramathaim, a village in northern Israel that is so obscure that the text gets corrupted in the first verse of 1 Samuel; apparently the copyists did not recognize its name. The man is called Elkanah, and we are told about his father, his grandfather, and so on, so that the story starts just like any man's story; it is a surprise when it turns out to be a woman's story.

This woman asks God for a baby, except that what she asks for is a son, because a daughter will not be the

same. The middle of the story is about an interchange
with another man called Eli, a clergyman who sits in
judgment over Hannah's spirituality without knowing
what he is doing and despite the fact that his own life is
on the way to judgment. The story ends with the birth
of her male child; when that has happened, a mere
woman like Hannah can be allowed to disappear from
the scene. She has fulfilled her function. Hannah's story
is lived in the framework of obscure, inadequate, and
important men, like ours; but in that context she lives
with God, all right.

She is Elkanah's wife, but she cannot have children.
For her, as for other women in the Old Testament story
whom we have considered, that would likely be a
matter of personal pain. The Israelite hearers of her
story (like the modern Christian ones) would no doubt
include other people for whom that is true, so that the
story raises issues which are also painful for them, and
maybe the storyteller prayed that somehow this piece of
scripture could be a blessing rather than a curse for
them. For Hannah, as for those others, the personal
pain would be compounded by the attitude that society
took to it. What use was a wife who could not have
children? Once more patriarchal society takes its toll of
Hannah. Matters are made worse when Elkanah takes a
second wife and she *can* have children. Of course that
can be a man's pain too: a British newspaper once
reported the story of a man who could not beget
children, whose wife committed adultery half-wishing
she would get pregnant, as she did, because she so
wanted a baby.

Perhaps you can live with that hurt much of the time,
in ordinary day-to-day life, but it will come to the
surface of your mind when you are unable to sleep, or
when you come to worship. Our hurt about my wife
Ann's multiple sclerosis lies dormant much of the time,
but one of the occasions when it comes to the surface is
at 'healing services' when you pray for other people to

be healed (and sometimes hear how they are), when you are not.

The pain comes to the surface for Hannah when they go to Shiloh for the New Year Festival. They go to the shrine where the all-powerful redeemer God of Israel dwells, the God who had closed Hannah's womb. They celebrate God's relationship with them with great joy. This all brings the hurt to outward expression. Elkanah loves Hannah, does his best to make up for the pain he knows she bears, and wants her to believe that what they mean to each other ought to make being childless not matter. But what he says is counteracted by the way his other wife provokes Hannah, makes her jealous, keeps drawing attention to the fact that Hannah may have been Elkanah's first love and may have his love now but it is Peninnah who has the children. Yahweh has not closed *her* womb.

Hannah and her sister are thus together in a moment of deep hurt which two women could share as a man and a woman could not. Except that they are not. Perhaps Peninnah did not do any of that provoking deliberately. The provocation may have come from inside Hannah rather than from Peninnah actually taunting her. But the pain natural to a woman who cannot have children and the reinforcement of her sense of failure and inadequacy by a society that (we noted in connection with Sarai's parallel experience) assumes that women should be barefoot, pregnant, and in the kitchen, serves also to divide Hannah and Peninnah so that like Sarai and Hagar they cannot even stand together as sisters.

So it went on, each year they went to Shiloh for this great celebration of the power and love of God the giver, redeemer, and healer of Israel. Occasions like that are very hard work for people whose experience does not match the theology. It all seems to go on at a distance, as if you were watching a film. It is not something you can quite take part in. Elkanah's words are ones Hannah cannot quite hear or respond to. And perhaps to add to her aloneness there is a reproachfulness about Elkanah when he cannot get through to her. She feels rejected and bitter, so he feels rejected and bitter. His loving understanding is now mixed with hurt of his own.

Hannah is a woman who suffers. Yahweh has closed her womb. But Hannah is also a woman who prays. She had nothing to say to Elkanah when he protested his love for her. The person she wants to talk to is this allegedly Almighty Yahweh. The context is a great festival and lots of people are high as kites and drunk as lords, and that may be why Eli is sitting wearily at the door of the shrine to make sure that nothing unseemly happens. Hannah does not care that everyone else is full of joy and celebration. She has another kind of business to do with God. If it is really true that Yahweh is redeemer, healer, and almighty, what about some action more appropriate than womb-sealing? She has no words for Elkanah, but she has pain, bitterness, distress, and tears to bring to God, bitterness and pain reminiscent of Israel's in Egypt.

We should not idealize Hannah. As in the case of Naomi, bitterness is not a pretty sight. There is a song, 'O Lord, your tenderness melting all my bitterness . . . O Lord, your loveliness changing all my ugliness . . . '. Hurt, loss, and pain do not leave you unchanged as a person. They either soften you or harden you. There are signs that they hardened Hannah – only signs, because this story, like others we have considered, only hints at what is going on inside, so that we have to meditate on the hints, and the very fact of our having to do that is part of the way scripture works on us as God's effective word.

The story does not present us with Hannah as a saintly ideal but as a hurt human being like us. She does not come to God on the basis of being a saint, which would be no encouragement to us sinners. All she contributes to what happens in this story is her need, her helplessness, her insistence that God hear her. I have already referred to the page or two in an old book on *Prayer* by Otto Hallesby to which I find myself coming back when I feel that in some way I have reached a cul-de-sac in prayer, when I do not know how to pray and feel spiritually dry and thus helpless. 'As far as I can see,' Hallesby goes on to say there, 'prayer has been ordained only for the helpless. It is the last resort of the helpless. We try everything before we finally resort to prayer. Prayer and helplessness are insepar-able'. Only the person who is helpless can truly pray. If I feel sinful or abandoned, cold or depressed, doubting or dishonest, the feeling of helplessness this awareness induces is not my barrier but my way into prayer. 'Prayer therefore simply consists in telling God day by day in what ways we feel we are helpless.' Hannah knew that was true.

Perhaps she reminds herself of Samson's mother, another of those infertile women in Israel's story, only a few pages earlier in scripture. Perhaps that is why she accompanies her prayer with a promise to give the child back to God as a Nazirite like Samson (not a very good Nazirite, admittedly) if God will only give her a son. Now making promises to God is a standard part of Israelite prayer, as is the awareness that a key thing you have to achieve in prayer is somehow to get Yahweh's attention, to get God to focus on you. Hannah might almost be the woman in Jesus's parable who browbeats the judge till he gives in, to get rid of her. But her prayer does make you wonder whether poor embittered Hannah thinks you can make deals with God, bribe God with the right promise. What kind of God does she think she is praying to?

Eli thinks there is something adrift with her praying, but for a quite different reason. All this emotion in church will not do. She is another drunk. Poor Eli beautifully anticipates Pentecost. He sees what is going on, except that he does not. It is not just his physical eyesight that is failing. But of course we must not sit in judgment on Eli any more than on Hannah, because *we* know he is in the wrong only because of what the story has told us about Hannah. If we had been put into the situation cold, maybe our pastoral judgment would have been no better. It is easy to give in to the temptation to tell someone not to go on at God the way they do.

Hannah stays appropriately deferential to Eli. After all, he is the vicar. 'No sir, I'm not drunk, I'm praying. I'm depressed and hurt and the only person I thought I could really pour out my heart to is Yahweh.' Hannah has seen what prayer is about, that it is indeed ordained for the helpless. The Psalms illustrate the way this is so. Prayer is ordained for people who are paralytic with fear or anxiety or anger or grief. When we are like that we are invited to bring those paralyzing turbulences to God.

We think there is something wrong with fear and anger. Believers do not get angry. The Psalms know that they do, and they invite us to bring our anger, anxiety, pain, and grief to God. They give us the prayers to express such feelings; a story like Hannah's shows us how Israel actually used prayers like the Psalms. One of the reasons we may hide from our anger and our fear is that we are afraid that it may consume us if we let it out, and if we do that on our own perhaps it might, but in Israel you did not pour yourself out to God on your own but in company, perhaps in your home village, perhaps at a shrine. People wept with weepers. Eli will have known that his ministry includes helping people to weep and thus to pray. It is a ministry which needs to be encouraged in the church. It involves learning to weep and to pray oneself, and then learning to help other people to weep and to pray.

I said 'we' hide from our fear and our tears. Again it may be significant that it was a woman who did not. In Western culture, at least, fear and tears are not macho, and we are very macho. The gift of tears may be something else that men need to learn from women.

What can happen instead is that women are also afraid to shed their tears, because they have learned to survive by coping the way that men do. So perhaps together we have to release each other into praying that can incorporate weeping. Hannah is a woman who suffers, and a woman who prays.

A woman who believes and who surrenders

In due course Eli, who has been trying to remember what the principal told them at college about dealing with drunken women on the church doorstep, does get his pastoral act together. 'Go in peace then, and the God of Israel give you what you have asked.' In the Psalms, there is often a change of mood before they come to an end. You began in fear and pain and anxiety, but you end in confidence and praise. How does the change come about? Perhaps sometimes it was simply that passing the problem onto God did the trick. But the transition from lament to praise can be very marked and very sudden, and some Psalms give you a clue to what brought it about. There is a word from God quoted, which took the person who was praying from pain to praise (e.g. Ps. 12). They knew their prayer was answered, because through someone like a priest or a prophet God answered it. They had not *seen* the answer in actual deed yet, but they had been given the assurance that their prayer had been answered.

So the task of a prophet, priest, or Levite was not merely to sit alongside someone to enable them to express their hurt and their anger. It was also to sit alongside God and listen to what God had to say in response. They would not get it right every time, as Eli shows because he is not actually listening to God at all at first, but in the end he gets into prayer-counselling mode. 'Go in peace, and the God of Israel give you what you have asked.' Eli proves able to speak God's word of acceptance and promise.

There is a significant model here for pastoral ministry. It is a ministry which overlaps with counselling, but it has its special privilege and challenge. It starts as a matter of enabling someone to express their grief and their pain. That *is* a privilege in itself. One of the highlight films of recent years for my wife and me was *Truly, Madly, Deeply*, a marvellous portrayal of a woman coping with bereavement when her lover dies (to demythologize it a little). There are some wonderful scenes where she is talking her feelings through with a psychotherapist, and Ann (who worked as a psycho-therapist before her illness prevented that) was very impressed with the way she confined herself to enabling the woman to express her feelings and did not say anything herself. That listening and facilitating of self-expression is really important. In my own talking with a counsellor about the issues Ann's illness raises for me, I find myself sometimes frustrated by his refusal to say anything, but I know that it is this extraordinary self-denying restraint on his part (which I sometimes find it difficult to exercise when the roles are reversed) that enables me to articulate things myself.

But that is not all there is to ministering to someone. There comes a time when they have said what they need to say, and need to hear what God has to say back, need to hear what the gospel is for them. The spiritual gift we have to covet and seek is the one the prophets in the temple had, the grace of being able to hear what God has to say to this person or these people in response to their prayer. Sometimes it will be directly words from scripture, sometimes not. Sometimes it will be confrontational, as Eli was at first by mistake. Perhaps more often it will be a word of grace, love, and forgiveness. Either way, if one thing about prayer that Hannah's story reminds us of is that prayer is ordained for the helpless, another is that prayer is not supposed to be a one-way conversation.

Some years ago we changed the telephone system at our college, and for a while we had a recorded message to tell people about it. I happened to do the recorded message, and one or two of my friends told me how they had rung up, recognized my voice, and started talking to me, but of course got no answer; I simply carried on with the preset words. I think that is often our subconscious image of prayer. All you ever get is a recorded message. This is not so in the Old Testament. There God answers prayer. We listen to the answers for each other. That is what happened in the temple, what happened to Hannah.

And she said, 'May your servant find grace in your eyes'. That would have been quite a prayer a few minutes ago when Eli was dismissing her as a drunk. But now Hannah goes her way, takes part in the festival meal, and her face is no longer sad. What a difference having your prayer answered can make! Not that she has actually seen anything yet, but she has heard the word of God. Faith comes by hearing. She has believed what she heard. She can be with people again. Her very face has changed. What a difference it makes to have someone bring God's word to you. To be able to bring God's word to someone, the word which turns that person from being one who can only look down to one who can lift up eyes to God and life, is surely indeed a spiritual gift worth coveting and worth seeking. Hannah is a woman who suffers, who prays, and who believes.

Next morning they all get up early. We have noted an occasion when Abraham did that; people get up early in scripture when they have something important to do. The family worship for one last precious time here at the shrine. They set off for home. And Elkanah and Hannah make love. I do not know how it felt that time, I dare not even think about it. What the story tells us is that that night Yahweh remembered Hannah. They are the words which were used, for instance, with respect to Noah. It was not exactly that God had forgotten her before. Indeed God had had her well enough in mind to seal her womb. Her infertility was not an oversight. It was deliberate. But why? The narrator apparently did not know why Yahweh had acted that way, only knew why in terms of where the situation was going in due course, knew the special thing God was going to do when Hannah's womb was unsealed.

I have referred more than once to a theologian's sermon on the saying of Jesus about not even a sparrow falling to the ground without your Father's will, a sermon preached only weeks after his wife had had a stillborn child. Hannah's story makes me recall it once again. When the sparrow falls, when the baby is stillborn, when the broken-hearted childless woman pours out her grief to God, it does not happen without your Father remembering, taking notice, paying attention.

Yahweh remembered Hannah. So in due time Hannah conceived and bore a son and called him Samuel, because (she said) 'I asked Yahweh for him'. There is something strange about Hannah's Hebrew at this point. If you wanted to mark the fact that you had asked for your baby from God, the natural name to give him is Saul; Saul means 'asked'. As in English, 'Samuel' is like 'Saul', but not identical. What is going on?

There was a strange sense in which the person Hannah had asked for was indeed Saul. Samuel's birth set under way a sequence of events which would lead to Saul being king. As far as Hannah was concerned, all she wanted was her own baby. What she got was much more. She gave her baby back to God's service, as she said she would, and he turned out to be a prophet, arguably the most important prophet Israel ever had. He was among other things (but most importantly) the one who would anoint Saul as Israel's first king, and de-anoint him.

Perhaps that suggests something else about prayer. When our answers come, often they are given not just for our sake. The design that God is weaving, the purpose God is pursuing through being there when the sparrow falls to the ground or a woman loses her baby or another grieves over never having been able to

conceive one, the purpose is one that extends far
beyond our little lives, even to a purpose for the whole
creation.

Hannah is a woman who suffers, who prays, who
believes, who surrenders. But this is all too human. Let
us end with God. Hannah's God, yours, and mine is
one who closes wombs; that is hard. But Hannah's God
is one who gives when we ask, who remembers us and
acts, who formulates a purpose and even uses womb-
closing to bring it to completion. No wonder Hannah
said 'My heart exults in Yahweh. There is no rock like
our God.'

Postscript:
Some Reflections on Scriptural Interpretation

The world is full of books and articles on the interpretation of scripture; I have made my contribution to the surfeit. One of my realizations is that discussing interpretation by moving from theory to practice is one thing, but doing so by moving from practice to theory is another, and sometimes at least as fruitful. In this postscript I want to try to identify some of the tacit assumptions or implications about interpretation which underlie the chapters above or emerge from them, which I perceive as I look back over the chapters.

The Old Testament and spirituality

One of my concerns has been to look at Old Testament patterns of spirituality, and I begin with two initial issues raised by the attempt to study that. First, spirituality is a vogue word, but a slippery one. In the narrow sense it refers to our individual life of prayer, but in a broader sense it refers to the whole of our lives individually and corporately as lived with God, for God, and before God. Narrower definitions risk individualism and the separation of our life of prayer from the rest of our life of faith and our way of life, and thus risk distortion of both. Broad definitions risk spirituality becoming a waffly subject, difficult to focus. In these studies I compromise over the matter, sometimes looking from one side, sometimes from the other.

The role of the Bible in relation to spirituality is also a slippery matter. On a broader understanding the Bible relates to spirituality as it does to theology and ethics by providing the theological framework within which one's relating to God happens, as when it discusses the nature of God (e.g. God's being a person and thus someone we might be able to relate to) or the basis of the relationship between us and God (e.g. the relationship of faith and works). It also does so in more precise ways by offering actual instructions on how to pray, stories about people praying, and examples of prayer and praise. Again the broad understanding has strengths (it encourages us to base our relating to God on a conscious theological foundation) but risks diffuseness, while the narrow approach may have the virtue of practicality but the vice of offering shallow 'hints and tips'. Here too I have compromised. No doubt from the biblical material it should be possible to construct a systematic 'biblical spirituality', parallel to a 'biblical theology' and a 'biblical ethic', and the study of various models of spirituality which appear in scripture could be a stage on the road of constructing such a biblical spirituality. My aim here has been to look at how the Old Testament portrays life with God actually working.

A common way to relate Old Testament stories to our spirituality is to take them as paradigms which indicate (negatively or positively) what should be our attitudes and behaviour as human beings in relation to God. This move is one presupposed by some New Testament usage of the Old Testament (e.g. in Heb. 11), but its danger is that it can encourage a moralizing approach to narratives – one which presupposes that the decisive factor in our life with God is our own attitude and activity rather than God's grace. My own instinct is nearly always to see Old Testament stories as paradigms of how God relates to us in love as human beings despite, as often as because of, our attitudes and behaviour. Exegetically it generally makes better sense of Old Testament stories to take them in this way, and theologically it is in in better harmony with the fundamental biblical stress on God's promise and God's grace rather than on human achievement. Stories *are* meant to be character-shaping, but generally they fulfil this function indirectly (by thrilling us with who God is and what God has done) rather than by direct assault.

I acknowledge that I could be reading my own spirituality into the narratives when I take them in that way. I have noted the possibility that as human beings we relate to God in one of two ways. Some of us, perhaps people whose identity is secure, find it easy to believe in God's grace and love for us; we thus need God to push us hard about commitment. Others of us are very active in God's name precisely because we are less sure in the depth of our persons about that love and acceptance of God's; we thus need to be told to relax, to be reminded that God loves us anyway. If people *can* be divided into these two types, then I belong to the second, and that might underlie my instinctive approach to Old Testament stories. I see there the message that I need to hear. Thus, while it was partly because I wanted to concentrate on the actual story in Genesis 22 (and in the light of the redactional theory mentioned below) that I stopped my treatment of the chapter at verse 14, it is suspicious that this enabled me to avoid verses 15–18, which make a link between God's promise and Abraham's obedience. It is a fundamental awareness of hermeneutics in its modern sense that who we are shapes what we are open to seeing in scripture, for good and ill. But we need to give stories the chance to

confront the experience of life with God that we already
have as well as to confirm it.

There is another aspect of the treatment of Old
Testament stories as paradigms which needs considering.
Most of the stories we have looked at belong to one of two
macro-narratives (Genesis to Kings and Chronicles-Ezra-
Nehemiah) which tell the once-for-all story of how
Israel came by its special relationship with God and
began its life in the context of that relationship (Ruth is
the exception, though not even that in the reordering of
the English Bible). Their purpose was not to describe
the kind of event which is regularly repeated in Israel's
life with God, but to relate the particular historical
events which lay behind its ongoing life. They are its
aetiologies, its purely once-for-all accounts of how Israel
came to be, which do not necessarily suggest any
repeatable patterns. On what grounds or how far can
we say that the pattern of those events is to be expected
to be repeated in Israel's life – that they are its
paradigms as well as its aetiologies (the distinction
comes from Rudolf Smend)? I suspect it is a question of
balance, but that the aetiological element is more
prominent in the scriptural stories than we instinctively
make it in our application of them. We need to let the
once-for-all events on which faith depends be prominent in the shaping of our life with God in the present.
They have this significance even when they are not the
kind of events which will be repeated in our experience.

It is for the life of *corporate* Israel that they are
aetiologies, and perhaps indirectly paradigms. How far
are we justified in applying them to the lives of individual believers, as is our inclination because of modern
individualism? Perhaps it is again a question of balance.
Abraham, Jacob, and Samson are, after all, individuals.
But we need to remind ourselves to let scripture correct
our individualism, as I was consciously doing towards
the end of the Jacob example, but was perhaps doing
insufficiently overall. We also need to note the political
aspect to life with God as Old Testament stories tell it,

reflected especially in Judges. The Old Testament does not talk about either prayer or politics in isolation from each other.

How historical must interpretation be?

I have noted how James Barr declared, 'When the modern churchgoer is solemnly assured that he is in essentially the same situation as the Prophet Moses . . , he ought to burst out laughing' (*The Bible in the Modern World*, p. 47). We have to handle discontinuities as well as continuities between Old Testament situations and experiences and our own. Samson brings out both very sharply. The prominence of sex and violence in his story makes it thoroughly trans-cultural; those themes recur in all human contexts. Many of the particularities of his story, however, make it quite unlike ours. Further, every retelling of a biblical story is itself contextual. My original version of this chapter was pre-Aids; as I have noted, even James Bond has cleaned up his act now. My study of Genesis 22 formally acknowledges the horrendous particularity of the story, but depends upon taking that particularity (*at God's instruction a man almost kills his son*!!!) as not of the story's essence. The way of applying it to us risks trivializing the original. Similar issues are raised by the fact that the Old Testament's stories are generally not about ordinary people but about characters such as significant ancestors, anointed leaders, and judges. But irrelevance is our Scylla, trivializing is our Charybdis.

My studies presuppose a basic similarity between the life into which Yahweh invited Israelite believers and the life we live in Christ. I do not find myself very often drawing attention to discontinuities between Old Testament and New Testament, and have been chided by students for preaching from the Old Testament without referring to Jesus. There are a number of reasons for this. My livelihood depends on the theological validity of the Old Testament (Marx has taught us that we see what we have an economic interest in seeing). The New Testament assumes the theological validity of the Old Testament, whereas Christianity does not, so there is considerable imbalance the other way to be compensated for. But most of all (I think), it works.

In the Genesis 22 example I utilize the Romans 8 reference to the story because it helps to bring out a point involved in the story itself. But the point I am making is still a Genesis 22 point – I am not treating the story typologically and risking compromising its own point. So also with the allusion to the cross in connection with the Jacob story. I ignore the Hebrew 11 reinterpretation of Genesis 22, presuming that this is to be regarded as itself more like a retelling of the story (like a Chronicles retelling of Samuel-Kings); it is a piece of exposition rather than a piece of exegesis, and as such does not impose an interpretation on the original. I utilize the Hebrews 11 allusion to Samson, but against itself, in a sense, insofar as Hebrews 11 generally uses the Old Testament to illustrate faith at work, and that is not the reading of Samson suggested by much of his story.

Related to this is the conviction (*a posteriori* rather than *a priori*) that the Old Testament *is* about human beings and believers who are actually more like us and are living lives more like ours than we commonly dare admit. Much Christian talk about the nature of the church's life and of individual believers' lives seems to presuppose that those are other than they are. The promise that one day people will no longer need to teach each other about the acknowledgment of God (Jer. 31:31–34) does not yet seem to have been fulfilled, so that the implementation of a new covenant still lies in the future (cf. the reference to this passage in Rom. 11:27, less well-known than that in Heb. 8 and 10). One might compare the Jewish argument that the Messiah cannot have come because the reign of justice, peace, and righteousness is manifestly not yet here. The Old

Testament enables us to be realistic about ourselves before God.

My concern throughout is the stories rather than the historical events to which they refer. Opinions vary as to how much historical material underlies each of these stories. What difference does one's view on the stories' historicity make to the way one sees their impact on our life with God? I am not clear that their message changes at all.

In her very suggestive study of the Book of Judges, *Death and Dissymmetry*, Mieke Bal notes that (male) study of Judges has focused on an attempt to trace the history of the book's composition and to establish the chronology of the period to which it refers. The assumption that this focus will open up the key concerns of the book has tended to make such study ignore another potential 'coherence' of the book. 'The Book of Judges is about death', Bal says in her opening sentence. It focuses on the violence exercised by men on men corporately, by individual men on individual women, and by individual women on individual men. The historical 'reading' of the book has purported to be *the* reading. In truth it is *a* reading, one which emerges from the concerns of the readers with matters such as chronological history and the assumption that this is where the theological significance of the book lies. Bal points us to another approach to the text which may do justice to other aspects of it, aspects of far-reaching significance for a violent world and church.

Bal's reading of Judges is, of course, a feminist reading. Mine, which has profited much from hers, may be a more masculinist one. It is a reading aware that it issues from the interaction of scripture and a man's experience, and wanting to allow each to illumine the other. Perhaps such a reading can access aspects of the richness of this text, which was given by inspiration of God to be profitable for the upbuilding of the man or woman of God, which have been inaccessible to a traditional historical approach. I have made the same assumption in connection with other stories such as those of Hagar and Ruth, though less so (for instance) in connection with the story of Abraham and Sarah – again, not for reasons of principle except the principle of variety affirmed by Hebrews 1:1.

My approach to different passages will have been affected by other aspects of the context for which and in which I was thinking through the significance of individual stories, as well as by my maleness and my awareness of feminist concerns. The study of Genesis 1, for instance, began life as a Bible exposition for a conference on work. I went to Genesis 1 because I believed it had significant insights on that topic. I suspect that coming with that question in my mind enabled me to perceive some aspects of the text's own agenda, but no doubt I missed others. Similarly I read the Joseph, Joshua, and Ruth stories in the context of the work of the Church's Ministry among the Jews, and that angled some things that I saw. At other points the context of my regular ministry in a theological college will be apparent. We always read scripture out of contexts; these enable us to perceive some things, but may mean we miss others.

There are points at which I have provided background information about matters referred to in the text, such as child sacrifice, Nazirites, Philistine temples, and some geographical matters. Narrative interpretation stresses the importance of working with the world of the text, but instances such as these suggest that one does sometimes need to give people information which enables them to hear the story with the same ears as the original audience.

The provision of such information may imply a view on who is the 'implied reader' of the story, though I do not think my reading of the stories usually makes any assumptions about their precise date or about the original situation to which they were addressed. In being part of the macro-work which stretches from Genesis to Kings they belong to a work which in its final form comes from the exile, but that fact does not seem especially illuminating for an understanding of most of the stories; nor do hypotheses about the earlier origin of particular stories seem to lead to illuminating insights on their message. I do not believe that as a matter of principle a historical approach of this kind is irrelevant to seeing the significance of stories for our life with God, but in practice, with many examples at least, it seems irrelevant. The exception is Genesis 1 itself, aspects of which come alive when we recognize that it is a gospel story told for people in exile. So utilization of appeal to a text's historical background is a pragmatic matter; the question is, does it work.

Similarly there are many exegetical points that could be made about the passages I have been concerned with, but I have generally avoided them where I could. The moral for the preacher is, when the translations disagree, slide over the problem rather than having to base what you say on something the experts disagree on. That is one of the advantages of preaching on long texts – there is more you can skip over. The other advantage is that with a long text you do not have to work so hard to find things to say. The Bible does it for you.

Hermeneutically, the assumption that there was a close link between ourselves and the biblical characters in their humanity played a key role in interpreting the stories. I doubt whether one can justify this assumption *a priori*: one can only invite an *a posteriori* recognition that this approach works, giving one entry to the story in a way that other approaches (e.g. one that starts from the story's historical background) does not. Related is the role played by human imagination in recreating a story. In this connection I also note hints of allegorism or midrash in my treatment: e.g. Samson = Sunshine (the religio-historical background is commonly reck-oned to be rather different), 'You wouldn't tell your parents, would you', angels walking to keep fit. I have taken (insubstantial) details in an anachronistic way, to make playful links (in the manner of midrash) between ancient text and modern context.

My examples also assume the conviction that as the 'mere' telling of a story in scripture was effective, so the 'mere' retelling of the scriptural story is effective in reaching our imaginations and enabling us to see how it speaks to us. I have generally tried to let the story be supreme by making it the starting point and ending point. Extensive reflection on my part comes in the midst rather than at these key points. (Though in the context of the current fashionableness of story one also needs to note that story is not the only thing in scripture.)

My direct concern is the 'final form of the text', though not for dogmatic reasons, and not in a dogmatic way. In the Abraham example, on the one hand the point about 'your son, your only son, the one you love, Isaac' depends on an awareness of the detail of the words within the text as its own world. On the other hand, the point about Abraham and the readers not finding the idea of sacrificing one's son inconceivable, as modern readers would, not only depends on a piece of religio-historical awareness external to the text, but also stems from a traditio-historical theory about the story once functioning as an explanation of why Israelites did not sacrifice their sons. I also worked in the light of the assumption that an individual Abraham story such as Genesis 22, which has a coherence of its own, redactionally came to be part of a larger whole in which the promise theme is key. Once again my approach is eclectic and unprincipled except for the principle 'Does it work' – does it generate insight on the content of the text. When appeal to earlier stages in the development of the material seemed fruitful, I used it; when it does not (e.g. the place of the Samson story in the Deuteronomistic history), I ignored it.

I have noted that it is common for Old Testament stories to say less in a direct way about the inner dynamics of its characters than modern Western stories

do. This is well illustrated by the figures of Abraham
and Isaac in Genesis 22, as well as by the those of
Naomi, Ruth, and Boaz. Admittedly it is partly a matter
of technique; motivation and attitude are conveyed by
relating people's actions and words rather than by being
explicit about their inner thoughts (Old Testament
stories thus work more like films than books?) –
Abraham's setting out 'early in the morning' implies the
readiness with which he takes up his task. Nevertheless
the manner of presentation still tends to leave attitudes
and motivation open. R. Alter sees a theological point
here: the stories presuppose the mystery of human
personality in its freedom, which God respects even in
the course of working through it (see *The Art of Biblical
Narrative*, e.g. p. 22). There is also a rhetorical point: by
their unspecificness the stories raise questions about
attitude and motivation which they do not answer. The
answers have to be provided by their hearers, who are
implicitly cross-questioned regarding what their attitudes would be in such circumstances. The silences of
texts need to be noticed, respected (we cannot close
them exegetically, as we are inclined to want to do), and
utilized. (The point should not be universalized, however: characters such as Daniel and Esther are less
complex and rounded, leave less questions open, and
'work' in a different way to characters such as Abraham,
Jacob, and Samson – they are more morally exemplary?)

What are the limits of interpretation?

Finally, particular questions are raised by the treatment
of Genesis 2. If you believe in the divine inspiration and
authority of the scriptures, as I do, that is likely to affect
the way you interpret them; indeed, it would be odd if it
failed to do that. You will come to scripture with
expectations about the worthwhileness of what is to be
discovered there, with a commitment to taking it more
seriously than you take yourself.

To judge from the way biblical interpretation is actually carried on, you will also bring to scripture some unconscious assumptions that may need more questioning. If the Bible is the word of God, in what sorts of ways may God be expected to have spoken? What sorts of words may God be expected to have used? In speaking of God's speaking and of God's word we presuppose that there is some analogy between God's speaking and ours, God's words and ours. Indeed, that needs to be the case if we are to understand God's speaking. How complete is the analogy? What forms of speech can God be expected to use?

As a human being I use various forms of speech. I make factual statements. I express feelings. I announce intentions. I give commands, once in a while. All these God may be expected to do; all these scripture contains. But my more interesting forms of speech, even my more telling ones, may be of quite other kinds. I tell jokes. I ask questions, not knowing the answer. I exaggerate. I wonder out loud. I speak ironically, saying things which I know are not true and which I hope my hearers will recognize not to be true, though I sometimes come unstuck; as we say in our family, I was not wearing my 'Joke' label. I use such forms of speech not just in casual contexts but in the direct course of seeking to fulfil my vocation to be a minister, a theologian, a teacher, and a theological college principal. In other words, these are very serious forms of speech. I use them to seek to be creatively provocative and to encourage people to think, for instance, assuming that I may be most effective when I am not merely providing answers but stimulating questions. I may sometimes know the right answers to questions I raise, but may then nevertheless be less concerned simply to pass on the right answers than to give people the means to discover these right answers. These means may take the form of variegated resources, not all of which I necessarily agree with; indeed they may be contradictory resources, so that I could not agree with them all. If I were a person of more imagination, I might have written short stories or novels, and that might have been a significant way in which I communicated a vision of God and of humanity.

Does God use those forms of speech? One might have thought that by now at least the possibility of God using fiction and short stories was uncontroversial, but this is not so. Interviewed on BBC TV's 'Songs of Praise' on 28 November 1993 about the relationship between being a scientist and a Christian, the Astronomer Royal remarked that of course for him 'the old Adam and Eve story was put on the back burner'. It seemed that only straight factual statement could count as serious speech, as the periodically re-run controversies over David Jenkins also presuppose. Is there, then, after all any analogy between the speech of a minister/ theologian/teacher/principal/novelist and that of God (and I often think that being God must be very like being a principal: it involves having considerable responsibility, and in theory considerable power, but little prospect of achieving much that is worthwhile by the consistent undisguised exercise of this power)? Does God tell stories, seek to provoke, say things that are only half-meant, speak ironically, rejoice to be a little paradoxical and not obviously coherent because people learn better if they figure things out for themselves, provide people with variegated, even contradictory, resources and free them to get on with discerning the truth?

If God does, it would make it easier to understand why the Bible is the kind of volume it is, not only apparently fictional in part, but a book that keeps puzzling us, seems to contradict itself, leaves multiple loose ends untied, and provides us with the raw material for constructing a pattern rather than with the pattern itself. Such features of the Bible have seemed incompatible with its being the word of God, and conservative theologians therefore deny their existence and liberal theologians infer that the Bible is not the word of God. But I usually find it is more fruitful in debates such as this to accept the premises but deny the conclusions. The Bible as the word of God is a piece of effective educational communication, designed to be profitable for reproof, correction, and training in righteousness, to bring men and women of God to maturity in Christ and to equip them for every good work (2 Tim. 3:16–17). Suppose that it fulfils this function by being quite like my words, on one of my better days, in the manner of its working?

I read the Adam and Eve story in the light of that possibility. I am not necessarily attributing to the story's authors such an understanding of God's ways of speaking but seeking to make sense of an enigmatic story and wondering what may have been in God's mind when giving it the imprimatur (this may actually be a more realistic project than seeking to understand the mind of the human author; I suspect that I know more about who God is than I know about who wrote Genesis or what they thought). Genesis 2–3 is full of apparent ambiguity, a feature which we have difficulty in coming to terms with and which we therefore evade. I look at two different forms of that ambiguity, a moral ambiguity about the character of God and an interpretative ambiguity about the human characters in the story.

Offering new interpretations of old texts may suggest the assumption that everyone misunderstood them for two or three millennia (that may seem plausible) until the 1990s when their truly modern meaning could emerge (that may seem implausible). If God meant us to learn from Genesis the lessons I have been suggesting, can we really believe that God not only failed for millennia to get the point home but instead succeeded in providing people with a text capable of being heard with the opposite meaning?

In itself that seems entirely believable. It would be all of a piece with the general failure of God's creative project in the world and with God's success only in providing humanity with opportunities and resources

we misuse. It might be surprising if God's gift of
scripture did not fall into the same pattern. It is certainly
the case that the PhD industry, the need to earn a
living, the demands of being a research-led university
and the instincts of human inventiveness generate
countless articles in theological journals offering 'a new
interpretation' of this text or that as if (someone has
pointed out) some more new interpretations were just
what we needed. In his *A Rabbi's Bible* (p. 7), Jonathan
Magonet has contrasted the instinctive rabbinic
approach to scripture which is worried when drawn to a
novel interpretation, and relieved if one can find it in
the tradition. One usually can. One of my abiding
impressions in writing biblical commentaries is that
there is nothing new under the sun; few modern
discussions add anything that is wholly unanticipated
in the ancient versions or in medieval discussions.

Yet there is also a converse point to be made. Twenty
years ago the scholarly starting point for understanding
Genesis 2–3 was the intention of its author, assumed to
have lived about the time of Solomon. But the idea that
interpreting a story involves asking after the intention
of its author is a distinctly modern one, and the idea
that this story belongs to the time of Solomon is now
seen to have been a conviction without evidence. A
hundred years ago the focus in interpreting the story
concerned its relationship to the scientific account of
human origins, another distinctively modern concern.
Five hundred years ago the story was interpreted as
part of a history written by Moses, who is unmentioned
in any capacity in Genesis. Fifteen hundred years ago it
was the source of the doctrine of Original Sin as well as
that of the Fall, another theme which belongs to its own
day. In other words, Adam and Eve have always been
understood in the light of interpreters' questions and by
the methods of the interpreters' day. The nature of a
story is to leave certain things said but certain things
unsaid, and to leave its hearers constraints (the story
cannot mean anything) and also scope for imagination.

The late twentieth century approach to interpretation
may seem to involve some risk of chaos and arbitrariness. Yet all interpretation involves risk, and the
possibility of chaos and arbitrariness may be allowed
occasionally to override that of predictability and
flatness. Indeed, an opposite response to that fear is
possible. It is the rest of the Hebrew Bible, among other
things, which in retrospect makes the surface reading of
Genesis 2–3 implausible. Conversely, it is also the rest
of the Hebrew Bible (Christians will naturally add the
New Testament) which provides us with a framework
of interpretation for our occasional wild fancies; it is our
safeguard against chaos even though it does risk
predictability.

In discussing the relationship between certainties and
open questions in Christian faith, people sometimes
speak of a firm core and a softer edge (incarnation might
belong to the core, virgin birth to the edge). The
difficulty with the image (which may be a masculine
one) is that sometimes it is things that count as core that
one wants to question: for instance, I sometimes wonder
what we mean when we talk and sing, as we do, about
God's being all-powerful, sovereign, and in control of the
world and the church, and this theme would surely
count as core rather than edge. A colleague suggests the
image of a web, which sounds more feminine and
suggests the possibility of questioning any element,
even something quite 'central' or 'fundamental', because whatever element one questions, the rest of the
web remains intact, supporting the whole, as long as
we are not questioning more than a quarter or so at
once. In connection with hermeneutical adventures, the
web constituted by scripture as a whole provides the
context within which I indulge in hermeneutical adventures over some part. It is this web which suggests what
kind of understanding fits the whole.

It is the text itself which makes clear, furthermore,
that Genesis 2–3 has little to do with the fall and the
invention of sin, because the story is quite explicit that

this comes in chapter 4; it is here that these words first appear. So as I had Eve noting, chapters 1 and 4 form significant brackets offering contexts of interpretation for chapters 2–3, but we ignore them. Chapters 2–3 deconstruct chapter 1 and chapter 4 deconstructs both chapters 2–3 and our interpretation of them. It is Genesis 4 that offers a more straightforward account of the nature of Yahweh.

Of course the idea of deconstruction is not that one version of a story replaces another, that only one is true. It is that reality is complicated and both texts and interpreters tend to simplify it. As Brian Keenan put it in a television interview, once Humpty Dumpty has been broken you cannot put him back together again because there are too many pieces now. We need each of Genesis's sets of perspectives on God, the world, and humanity if we are to see as fully as we may. So the God who was happy to have Genesis in the holy book acts like a teacher who offers pupils a varied selection of reading material and invites them to make sense of reality in the light of the selection. The teacher has not affirmed any of it in isolation, except in the sense of implying that it has the capacity to lead people on. If this story – and some of the others we have considered – is rather ambiguous in its response to questions to which we would like some straight answers, this is because God believed we might he helped by its being like that. As David Jenkins himself once said in the tradition of Lewis Carroll, as a learner I discover what I think only by saying it; and as a teacher I may be more effective in the pork pies that I sell than in the familiar truths that I repeat. Some of this book may even instance this fact.

References and Reading Resources

From time to time I have acknowledged ideas and actual quotations by including an author's name; the reference is to the works listed here. But I originally worked on many of these studies in connection with preaching, and did not note where all my ideas came from. I know I have gained from all the following, and apologize for any further points which should have been individually acknowledged.

R. Alter. *The Art of Biblical Narrative*. New York: Basic/London: Allen and Unwin, 1981.

A. G. Auld. *Joshua, Judges and Ruth*. Edinburgh: St Andrew Press/Philadelphia: Westminster, 1984.

M. Bal. *Death and Dissymmetry*. Chicago/London: University of Chicago, 1988.

M. Bal (ed). *Anti-Covenant*. Sheffield: Almond, 1989.

J. Barr. *The Bible in the Modern World*. London: SCM/New York: Harper, 1973.

R. Bauckham. *The Bible in Politics*. London: SPCK, 1989/ Philadelphia: Westminster, 1990.

A. Bloom. *School For Prayer*. London: DLT, 1970. [USA ed., *Beginning to Pray*. New York: Paulist, 1970.]

W. Brueggemann. *Genesis*. Atlanta: Knox, 1982.

J. Calvin. *Genesis*. Reprinted Grand Rapids: Eerdmans, 1948.

B. S. Childs. *The Book of Exodus*. Philadelphia: Westminster, 1974. = *Exodus*. London: SCM, 1974.

G. W. Coats. *Genesis*. Grand Rapids: Eerdmans, 1983.
'Legendary motifs in the Moses death reports'. *Catholic Biblical Quarterly* 39 (1977) 34–44.

J. C. Exum. 'The centre cannot hold: Thematic and textual instabilities in Judges'. *Catholic Biblical Quarterly* 52 (1990) 410–31.

K. R. R. Gros Louis and others (ed.). *Literary Interpretations of Biblical Narratives*. 2 vols. Nashville: Abingdon, 1974 and 1982.

O. Hallesby. *Prayer*. London: IVF, 1948. [USA ed., Minneapolis: Augsburg, 1959.]

S. Hauerwas. *Suffering Presence*. Notre Dame, IN/London: University of Notre Dame, 1986; Edinburgh: Clark, 1988.

J. Hercus. *God is God*. London: Hodder, 1971.

J. G. Janzen. 'Hagar in Paul's eyes and in the eyes of Yahweh'. *Horizons in Biblical Theology* 13/1 (1991) 1–22.

L. R. Klein. *The Triumph of Irony in the Book of Judges*. Sheffield: Almond, 1989.

I. Kuhn. *In the Arena*. London: OMF, 1960.

F. J. Leenhardt. *Two Biblical Faiths*. London: Lutterworth/ Philadelphia: Westminster, 1964.

M. Luther. *Lectures on Genesis*. Vol. 1. St Louis: Concordia, 1958.

J. Magonet. *A Rabbi's Bible*. London: SCM, 1991.
Bible Lives. London: SCM, 1992.

T. W. Mann. 'Theological reflections on the denial of Moses'. *Journal of Biblical Literature* 98 (1979) 481–94.

J. Moltmann. *God in Creation*. New York: Harper/London: SCM, 1985.

P. Morris and D. Sawyer (ed.). *A Walk in the Garden*. Sheffield: Sheffield Academic Press, 1992.

H. Nouwen. *The Road to Daybreak*. Garden City, NY: Doubleday, 1988/London: DLT, 1989.

J. B. Pritchard (ed.). *Ancient Near Eastern Texts Relating to the Old Testament*. Princeton, NJ: Princeton UP, third ed., 1969.

G. von Rad. *Genesis*. London: SCM/Philadelphia: Westminster, 1961.

Old Testament Theology. 2 vols. Edinburgh: Oliver and Boyd/ New York: Harper, 1962 and 1965.

E. P. Sanders. *Paul and Palestinian Judaism*. London: SCM/ Philadelphia: Fortress, 1977.

J. Schell. *The Fate of the Earth*. London: Pan/New York: Knopf, 1982.

P. Selby. 'Apocalyptic – Christian and nuclear'. *Modern Churchman* 26/2 (1984) 3–10.

R. Smend. 'Tradition and history'. In *Tradition History and the Old Testament* (ed. D. A. Knight) 49–68. Philadelphia: Fortress/London: SPCK, 1977.

M. Sternberg. *The Poetics of Biblical Narrative*. Bloomington, IN: Indiana UP, 1987.

E. Tamez. 'The woman who complicated the history of salvation'. In *New Eyes For Reading* (ed. J. S. Pobee and B. von Wartenberg-Potter) 5–17. Geneva: WCC, 1986/Quezon City, Philippines: Claretian, 1987.

P. Trible. *God and the Rhetoric of Sexuality*. Philadelphia: Fortress, 1978/London: SCM, 1991.
Texts of Terror. Philadelphia: Fortress, 1984/London: SCM, 1992.

B. G. Webb. *The Book of Judges*. Sheffield: JSOT, 1987.

G. J. Wenham. *Genesis* 1–15. Waco, TX: Word, 1987.
Genesis 16–50. Dallas: Word, 1994.

J. White. *People in Prayer*. Downers Grove, IL: IVP, 1977/ Leicester: IVP, 1978.

J. G. Williams. *Women Recounted*. Sheffield: Almond, 1982.